HARNESSED
TO THE POLE

HARNESSED TO THE POLE

Sledge Dogs in Service to American Explorers of the Arctic

1853–1909

Sheila Nickerson

University of Alaska Press
Fairbanks

University of Alaska Press
P.O. Box 756240
Fairbanks, AK 99775-6240

Library of Congress Cataloging-in-Publication Data

Nickerson, Sheila B.
Harnessed to the Pole : sledge dogs in service to American explorers of the
Arctic, 1853–1909 / by Sheila Nickerson.
pages cm
Includes bibliographical references and index.
ISBN 978-1-60223-223-5 (paper : acid-free paper)—
ISBN 978-1-60223-224-2 (electronic)
1. Sled dogs—Arctic regions—History. 2. Sled dogs—Arctic
regions—Biography. 3. Sled dogs—United States—Biography.
4. Dogsledding—Arctic regions—History. 5. Arctic regions—
Discovery and exploration—American. 6. Explorers—Arctic
regions—History. 7. Explorers—United States—History. I. Title.
SF428.7.N53 2014
636.73—dc23
2013024460

Cover design by Kristina Kachele
Donald Baxter MacMillan's cover photo courtesy of
The Peary-MacMillan Arctic Museum

This publication was printed on acid-free paper that meets the minimum
requirements for ANSI / NISO Z39.48–1992 (R2002) (Permanence of Paper for
Printed Library Materials).

Printed in the United States

Contents

The Expeditions

Elisha Kent Kane
   The Second Grinnell Expedition in Search of Sir John Franklin, 1853–1855

Isaac I. Hayes
   A Voyage of Discovery Toward the North Pole, 1860–1861

Charles Francis Hall
   First Expedition in Search of Sir John Franklin, 1860–1862
   Second Arctic Expedition, 1864–1869
   North Polar (*Polaris*) Expedition, 1871–1873

Frederick Schwatka
   Seeking the Records of the Lost Franklin Expedition, 1878–1880

George Washington De Long
   The Polar Expedition, 1879–1881

Adolphus Washington Greely
   The Lady Franklin Bay Expedition, 1881–1884

Frederick A. Cook
   The Expedition That First Reached the Boreal Center, 1907–1909

Robert E. Peary
   The North Pole Expedition, 1908–1909

You become responsible, forever,
for what you have tamed.

—Antoine de Saint-Exupéry

1

Jules Verne

How Fiction Transported
the First Dogs to the North Pole

The North Pole. That unhinged, landless place where all compass points, lines of longitude, and time zones merge. The spot where past and future become now. The center of the northern ice where the material and spiritual worlds intersect and magic is born. A possible Eden with a warm open sea. A place where, if you have not been there, anything is possible—even the presence of dogs, the first visitors.

And so, Mary Shelley set her *Frankenstein* there, with the monster first appearing by dog sledge and finally disappearing by ice raft, "borne away by the waves, and lost in darkness and distance." That was 1818. At the time, young John Franklin, second in command on David Buchan's expedition to the North Pole, was trapped in ice near Spitsbergen, while Shelley's Captain Walton, narrator of the cautionary tale of the new Prometheus, was having greater success.

In 1848, thirty years after Shelley's monster disappeared "in darkness and distance," an epic search was on for Franklin, now lost somewhere in the vast stretches of the eastern Arctic. In the attempt to penetrate the mystery, the search would map and name the arctic reaches, leaving little room for romantic tales or imaginary escapades.

By 1864, after the search for Franklin and the Northwest Passage had waned, Jules Verne set his visionary sights on the North Pole with publication of *The Voyages and Adventures of Captain Hatteras*, containing two volumes: *The English at the North Pole* and *The Desert of Ice*. The novel, set in 1860–1861, was based on geographical and scientific information known at the time and influenced by Edgar Allan Poe, whom Verne admired, and various theories of open polar seas and a hollow earth. With realistic reference to arctic explorers and their discoveries—especially those of American explorer Elisha Kent Kane and his "American Route" toward the Pole (up the west coast of Greenland, across Smith Sound, and up along the east coast of Ellesmere Island)—it tells the fabulous story of the indomitable English Captain John Hatteras, who is obsessed with getting to the top of the earth. In order to succeed, Hatteras survives mutiny, loss of his ship, and overwintering in arctic ice (as did Kane). What he finds when he reaches his goal is an open sea with a fiery volcano at its heart. Unable to listen to reason, he scrambles to the lip of the crater, peers in, falls, and is rescued. (Kane, too, stumbled into a volcano, Taal Volcano near Manila, and had to be rescued.) One of Captain Hatteras's rescuers is his devoted Great Dane, Duke, who, with his master, has endured all of the challenges of the expedition. The captain survives physically but loses his mind, becoming unable to speak another word. Returned to England, he is committed to an insane asylum, where he lives out his days with his beloved Duke at his side. Having obstinately reached the point "where all meridians meet," Hatteras, a victim of "polar madness," could now walk in only one direction—north, pacing backwards when he reached the end of his northward path, only to start over.

Particularly in the first volume, Duke takes on supernatural powers—powers that, perhaps, explain the expedition's eventual success. Hatteras, the mysterious captain of the *Forward* (Kane's ship was the *Advance*), does not appear or name himself while his ship is constructed, outfitted, and crewed. He communicates entirely by letter with Shandon, the man he has chosen to be his second-in-command. At one point he writes:

> On the 15th of February next you will receive a large Danish dog, with hanging lips, and tawny coat with black stripes. You will take it on board and have it fed with oaten bread, mixed with tallow grease.

When the dog arrives, he "seemed surly, peevish, and even sinister, with quite a singular look in his eyes." A kennel is constructed for him under the window of the locked cabin of the missing captain, but the dog prefers to wander about the ship, untamed and howling, raising superstitious fears among the crew, who come to fear him as a diabolical being. Even the ship's kindly doctor cannot win his good graces:

> The animal did not answer to any name ever written in the dog calendar, and the crew ended by calling him Captain, for he appeared perfectly conversant with ship customs; it was evident that it was not his first trip.... More than one repeated jokingly that he expected one day to see the dog take human shape and command the manoeuvres with a resounding voice.

As the ship prepares to sail at the appointed date and no captain has yet appeared—and no orders—the dog suddenly breaks through the crowd of spectators with a letter that he drops at the feet of Commander Shandon. The letter orders him to proceed to Greenland. As the newly launched ship follows the orders northward, the dog paces the decks, watches the sails, walks the ice at night, howling, and appears to eat no food. Then, off Holsteinborg, Greenland, a second letter appears for Shandon, ordering him to proceed to Melville Bay and into Smith's Straits—the route followed by Kane in 1853. The crew is now convinced that the missing captain's "spirit or his shadow" is on board.

At Upernavik, the northernmost Danish settlement along the coast, Shandon pays four pounds for a sledge and six dogs. Still, there is no captain, but Duke the dog-captain accepts the wild and uncouth canine newcomers. Conditions worsen and the ice begins to close in. Certain members of the crew become more convinced than ever that the dog-captain is the cause of all their problems and must be done away with. They seize him while he sleeps, tie him up, throw him down a seal hole in the ice, and cover up the hole. Before long, however, the dog-captain is back, looming up in refracted form as a huge beast, terrifying the guilty crewmen and bringing the expedition to a breaking point: The sailors refuse to go on.

Here, the supernatural gives way to the realistic. As ice presses in upon the *Forward* and the situation seems hopeless, the absent captain suddenly appears, in the person of one of the sailors whose persona he had borrowed for a disguise. He whistles and calls to Duke by name, and the dog lies down at his feet, verifying his identity. Captain Hatteras, now duly recognized by the crew, takes command to lead his expedition north. He explains that no one would have offered to sign on for the expedition if they had known who the captain was—and what his goal—for he was known to be obsessed with reaching the Pole at any cost. With the mystery solved, Duke fades. Having become more sociable in the company of his master, he now has a much lesser role to play—until the dramatic rescue from the crater of the volcano.

Also on board the *Forward* are the six Greenland or "Esquimaux" dogs, of which we hear almost nothing. None is mentioned by name. Toward the end of the first volume, Duke helps them pull a sledge during a search for coal. Two of the Greenland dogs die during this effort. Five dogs and four men continue north, driven on by the obsession of Captain Hatteras. By the middle of the second volume, the five dogs have become friends: "After all, these Greenland dogs are kind beasts. Their wildness was partly gone; they had lost their likeness to the wolf, and had become more like Duke, the finished model of the canine race,—in a word, they were becoming civilized." Duke, who had not fraternized with them before because they had not been introduced, now taught them manners. Civilized behavior is not enough, however. The Greenland dogs are eaten on the return trip. Only the noble, aristocratic Duke gets to enter the fiery heart of the Pole and then make it safely home.

2

Sir John Franklin

How, in Reality, a Lost Explorer Needed Dogs

If Sir John Franklin had made use of indigenous dogs and their drivers, nineteenth-century arctic history might have taken a different and a happier course. But the Royal British Navy, ignoring local custom, put men, not dogs, in harness, and Franklin was the consummate naval officer: It was appropriate for men, not dogs, to haul.

Though most particulars of the loss of the Franklin expedition of 1845–1847 will never be known, evidence indicates that its 129 members suffered protracted, horrible deaths, many while dragging themselves and their cargo across ice in a futile attempt to reach safety. Their cargo consisted of heavy whaleboats loaded on heavy sledges and containing clothes, boots, books, guns, monogrammed silver plate, silk handkerchiefs, tea and chocolate, and tools for carpenters, sailmakers, and shoemakers.

The Franklin expedition with its two ships, *Terror* and *Erebus*, had set forth from England on May 19, 1845, and was last seen by a whaler in Lancaster Sound on July 26. Its mission was to find and traverse the Northwest Passage, but only silence followed in its wake. In 1848, the British government posted a 20,000-pound reward and the search began, a

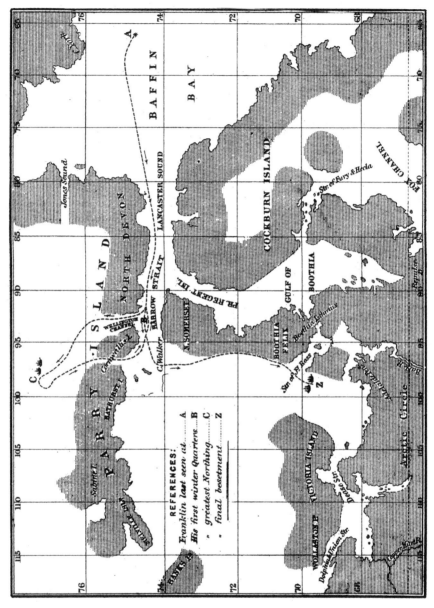

Sketch map of the Arctic regions, at the time of Franklin's last expedition & of his supposed track. (From Admiral McClintock's Fate of Franklin.*)*

J. E. Nourse, editor, *Narrative of the Second Arctic Expedition Made by Charles Francis Hall . . .*, facing p. xxxii.

search that would involve fifty parties over the next twelve years and that would never truly end.

It was this search, bringing back occasional news and artifacts, that enabled the mapping of much of the arctic coastline and the convoluted course of the Northwest Passage.

In 1850, Parliament posted a further reward of 10,000 pounds for evidence revealing the fate of Franklin and his party. This prize eventually went to Dr. John Rae of the Hudson's Bay Company after he returned to England in 1854 from a coastal survey for his company in the vicinity of King William Land (King William Island, just north of Adelaide Peninsula, Nunavut, Canada). Along the way, Rae had collected credible oral history from Inuit hunters, as well as numerous relics including a small plate engraved "Sir John Franklin, K.C.B." The Admiralty closed the case. But the tireless Lady Jane Franklin, the lost explorer's widow, pushed on. She would not give up hope nor would she—any more than the British public—accept the reports of cannibalism Dr. Rae brought home. Leading a campaign against him, Lady Franklin made sure that the messenger's reputation and place in history would suffer—and it did. Rae, who had mapped the area of the Northwest Passage more thoroughly than anyone else, was denigrated and eclipsed, never receiving the recognition or the knighthood he deserved.

In 1857, Lady Franklin launched the expedition of the yacht *Fox* under Lieutenant Francis Leopold McClintock. During his two-year search, it was McClintock who succeeded in finding the most conclusive evidence and the most poignant relics, including the abandoned twenty-eight-foot boat mounted on a sledge—a combined weight of 1,400 pounds—which contained two skeletons and a bewildering assortment of personal articles and equipment, everything from *The Vicar of Wakefield* to glass beads. Most importantly, he found the only Franklin document so far discovered, last dated April 25, 1848, telling of the fate of many of the party. Sir John Franklin, it noted, had died June 11, 1847. The ships, McClintock asserted, had achieved "virtual completion of the Northwest Passage." From then on, members of the lost expedition were hailed as "martyrs" of the quest.

Significantly, the two most successful British searchers had adopted native ways. Dr. Rae, reviled for his reports of cannibalism, was an accomplished snowshoer and dog sledge-driver. McClintock, too, embraced and mastered sledging with dogs. Without "our native auxiliaries," he said of the animals when starting out, "we cannot hope to explore all the lands which it is the object of our voyage to search."

The Royal British Navy began to change its view, now recognizing the benefits of sledging by dog instead of by man. According to historian William Barr, in his assiduous study of the subject, twenty-eight percent of the travel in search of Franklin was made by dog sledge. Much of that was in short-haul visits between overwintering ships locked in the ice.

Dogs were also used for longer runs, with the size of teams varying, as Barr notes, from two for Rae in one instance to twelve for McClintock. Dogs were also used to transport heavy loads, such as gravel from shore to ship for ballast; to supply hunting parties; and to find and warn of polar bears. There was something else, too, as Barr concludes: "The importance of the boost to the men's morale provided by the presence and behaviour of the dogs should not be underestimated."

The British were not the only ones beginning to experience and acknowledge the benefits of indigenous customs. A number of Scandinavian explorers excelled at sledging, chief among them Fridtjof Nansen, famous for his voyage of the ice-locked *Fram* and a fifteen-month trek across the polar north; Roald Amundsen, who attained both poles and traversed the Northwest Passage; and Vilhjalmur Stefansson, leader of the disastrous *Karluk* and Wrangel Island expeditions. Remarkable as they are, these are other stories for another time.

It was the Americans, coming into the Franklin search late and increasingly intent on claiming the geographic North Pole, who made consistent use of dogs and began to write of them as the British had not. Their record, spanning the years 1853 to 1909, shows not only dependence on dogs but interest in them as fellow creatures struggling to survive in one of the world's wildest and most hostile environments. Although we could follow many adventurers laying sledge tracks across the Arctic, we will follow in chronological order eight Americans on a complementary trajectory: Elisha Kent Kane, Isaac I. Hayes, Charles Francis Hall, Frederick Schwatka, George Washington De Long, Adolphus Washington Greely, Frederick A. Cook, and Robert E. Peary.

What they tell us about their dogs often reveals more about themselves than the animals. There is no particular pattern here, no graph revealing an upward movement of consciousness and compassion toward the dogs. Instead, we find an uneven account of roles and relationships. In some cases the explorers elevate their dogs to the status of companions, recognizing them with gratitude and warmth for the invaluable and faithful service they provide. In other cases, they mention them mechanically, underscoring their value as beasts of burden and meat on the paw. There are scenes of affection and scenes of harshness, moments of heartbreak and humor, outbursts of gratitude and exasperation, occasions when loneliness cracks open the well of disciplined emotions and man and animal merge. Sometimes the touch or the gaze of a dog was just enough to push back the polar night, a moment of respite from overwhelming stress. A discussion of dogs over a pipe while waiting for dinner might provide an essential distraction. Watching puppies at play could bring a rare smile. Sometimes a dog was all that stood between madness and death, and neither species was exempt from terror.

Individual writing styles and editorial oversight play roles, as do mores and perceptions of the time. The attitude toward dogs was far different then from what it is now, a universe away from discussion of animal rights. Victorian explorers were not likely to emote nor, in retrospect as they wrote their accounts for publication, to be effusive. Man was man and dog was dog. The Arctic, too, was a harsh place to form bonds; the solace of friendship was tenuous, moments of tenderness few. Life expectancy was short and danger a close companion.

Hall is a prime example of the hazards of posthumous publication. When, after his death, a Navy editor took over his notes to turn them into a book, the dogs Hall so appreciated almost disappeared from the text—an absence he would have regretted.

The track is indeed faint, and these eight American explorers might not have said—and done—all that we would have liked, but what they left in their writings is a delicately drawn canine trail to follow, with certain dogs allowed to live on: Here are the Sherpas of the Arctic, who made discovery possible. Here is a team pulling a sledge overladen with hope and ego, each dog named and known to its driver, each a distinct personality, all hauling toward an uncertain and often fatal destination.

Without their extraordinary energy and dedication to work (not to mention their capacity to withstand hardship), little progress toward the Pole would have been achieved until more advanced technology had become available. In spite of their critical role, however, the record has largely ignored these faithful assistants and failed to recognize their contributions. Now, as arctic ice vanishes, so does their story. It is time to pick up their trail before it is swept away and to follow as best we can before it is lost in "darkness and distance."

And so, we go on a search for Toodla and Whitey, Oosisoak and Arkadik, Barbekark, Wolf, Smarty, Bear, Shoemaker, Tiger, Spike, Toekelegeto, Ublubliaq, Miqijuk, Kasmatka, Snoozer, Bingo, Snuffy, Tom, Jack, Wolf, Gypsy, Old Sneak, Ritenbenk, Disco King, Nalegaksoah, and all their brother- and sister-teammates to salute them and give them a word of praise. Once harnessed to the Pole, let them now be harnessed to history and remembered for the part they played—a part silent but essential.

3

What Was the Greenland Dog?

Not every dog in the American expeditions came from Greenland—
Elisha Kent Kane and Charles Francis Hall had some from Newfoundland and George Washington De Long had some from Alaska—but
most did. As the exploratory ships (some no bigger than yachts) moved up
the western coast of Greenland, they stopped along the way to pick up
dogs, equipment, and local hunters and drivers. They paid little for the dogs
but often had to struggle to gain adequate numbers. Disease sometimes
had decimated populations, and, in some cases, starvation had forced the
local inhabitants to eat their most prized possessions. Sometimes only a
few dogs could be found at a port, and sometimes the local officials put
pressure on their owners to relinquish them. In many cases, the explorers bartered for dogs as they traveled, sometimes covering great distances in the hope of acquiring additional animals. (Hall once made a rigorous
trip of fifty-two days to acquire dogs.) They paid a pittance—fishhooks,
needles, thimbles. A common price was a knife or two and some pieces of
wood for a couple of dogs. A broken oar could make or break a deal in this
treeless land.

Eskimo dog (from a photograph of Captain Chapel's).
Nourse, p. 185

Sometimes, if the dogs survived the expedition, they were returned to their original owners. Some dogs, as with Kane, Hall, and Robert E. Peary, returned with the explorers to the United States, where they quickly fade from the record. Forced into exhibitionism, they had little tolerance for the weather or showmanship.

The dog that carries this story had to be heavy, powerful, thick coated, and able to endure extraordinary hardships of cold, storm, starvation, immersion in freezing water, fighting, predation by wolf or bear, and disease. There was, of course, no veterinary care and a diet that was irregular at best and fatal at worst (as with the salted pork still so popular on nineteenth-century ships). No matter what the conditions, the dog had to be able to pull heavy loads over difficult terrain—and with speed. As a crucially needed working dog, its performance was much more important than its temperament. It was judged by endurance and stamina, not gentleness. Either male or female could be the critically needed—and treasured—lead dog. None was kept as a pet. An old or feeble animal was killed (bullets were spared whenever possible) and fed to its mates. Puppies were cherished and gently raised, but if they came at the wrong season, were defective, or too many were born to a litter, they were killed, just as sometimes the Inuit killed infant girls, who were considered a burden because they could not grow up to be hunters. The team had to be able to move on. The human band for which it worked must be able to get to the seasonal game, the next cache, or the closest group of fellow hunters who might be able to help out in times of hunger; otherwise all would die. In dire times, and only as a last resort, the dogs would be eaten; that was the point, at the threshold of cannibalism, when hope itself died.

This, the hunter's most valuable asset, was the Greenland Dog, an ancient breed tracing back to the original Inuit dog from Siberia. (Remains have been found in the New Siberian Islands carbon dated to about 7000 BC) According to anthropologists Darcy Morey and Kim Aaris-Sorensen writing in *Arctic*, dogs crossed into the eastern Arctic and Greenland with human populations 4,500 years ago but have been prevalent, along with the use of a sled, only for the past thousand years.

Looking today much as it did in the nineteenth century, the male Greenland Dog (also known as the Esquimaux Dog and the Greenland Husky) stands twenty-three to twenty-seven inches at the withers, the female twenty to twenty-four; they weigh up to seventy pounds. Members of the breed belong to the Spitz family. They have a broad head; small, erect, triangular ears well protected against frostbite; thick, coarse outer coats with dense wool-like undercoats; large, bushy tails that they can curl over their face when sleeping; large feet; and powerful jaws. Their color and markings differ, though they carry a triangular mark on their shoulders known as an *úlo* (Inuktitut word for "woman's knife"), which distinguishes them from other breeds.

Eivind Astrup accompanied Peary on two of his earlier expeditions in Greenland (1891–1892 and 1893–1895). In his account, *With Peary Near the Pole*, he devoted a number of pages to the subject of dogs and sledging that provide a univcrsal portrait:

> But if it may be said of the North Greenland Esquimaux that hardiness and toughness are their characteristics, the same remark applies in even a higher degree to their faithful dogs. The fatigue

and privation that they can endure really borders upon the incredible. Their appearance reminds one not a little of the Norwegian Finn dog, though their hair is longer, their build more elastic, and their general appearance handsomer. So great is their strength that a man on level ground has the utmost difficulty in holding in check two or three dogs, if they take it into their heads to be obstreperous—provided, of course, he has no whip to cow them with. North Greenland dogs vary in colour, the commonest being grey, white-spotted, and black. There is usually a round, light patch over the eyebrows. . . .

It is true that the Esquimau dog, as a rule, carries his bushy tail curled neatly over his back, but there are some which, like the wolf, affect a sombre droop. Indeed, there can be scarcely any doubt that the breed of dog we speak of, when still running wild in the northernmost woods that creep into the Arctic zone, was absolutely identical with the large species of wolves of the present day; while it is almost certain that since domestication they have not been crossed with other varieties.

Astrup remarked on their varied diet, fed to them on average three times a week, and how the only water available to them is found in summer, and how they live entirely out of doors. In spite of such hardship, he pointed out, the Greenland Dog has developed "affection, obedience, and faithfulness towards its master." That devotion, he said, is returned by the master—but not in ways we might expect. It is returned by the whip, a tool as necessary in driving dogs as whip, spurs, and reins are in controlling a horse.

Devotion and whip, harshness and affection: How could such contradictory strands forge a bond between man and dog? Survival was certainly part of it. Dog looked to man for protection and food. Man looked to dog for protection and help in securing food. Long ago, the Greenland Dog and the Greenland Inuit had entered into what animal behaviorist Desmond Morris would have called a contract, an agreement establishing a partnership. But there had to be something more,

Dog-skin mittens.
Nourse, p. 107

something that transcended a partnership of survival. Perhaps it comes in the restrained words of Fridtjof Nansen on board the ice-locked *Fram*, describing the domestic scene of his bitch Kvik and her eight puppies: "It is a picture of home and peace here near the Pole which one could watch by the hour." (Five of the litter, considered an excess, had been killed, and later Kvik herself would be killed for meat.) Nansen couldn't say it, but it might be a need for companionship—an emotional connection—that tied people and dogs together in the prison of a frozen world.

Astrup maintained that the dogs howl at night for "joy and gladness," expressing pleasure with food or sleep. Perhaps—and he would never have written this—they howled with happy sensations after a day of pulling sledges, soft snow under their swift paws, an aurora borealis cracking like a whip over their backs, the scent of home blossoming in their nostrils.

Standing dog nursing four pups.
Donald Baxter MacMillan. The Peary-MacMillan Arctic Museum and Arctic Studies Center, Bowdoin College, Brunswick, Maine (img#1994.5.1448)

Dogs close up.
Donald Baxter MacMillan. The Peary-MacMillan Arctic Museum (img#3000.32.1046)

King Eskimo dog.
Robert E. Peary, *The North Pole, Its Discovery in 1909 under the Auspices of the Peary Arctic Club*...p. 71.

4

Sledge or *Sled*?

*S*ledge is the traditional term for a sled that hauls heavy loads or freight. *Sled* is the modern term, connoting a design built for lighter use. To maintain consistency with texts, and where it is relevant, the term *sledge* is used throughout.

Inuit sledge designs were varied, and white explorers took great pains to refine them for their particular needs and to extol their qualities. Elisha Kent Kane, Charles Francis Hall, and Adolphus Washington Greely, among others, named theirs, referred to them by name, and used considerable effort to describe them and their specific attributes and improvements over earlier models.

According to anthropologist Franz Boas, writing in *The Central Eskimo* in 1888, the best sledges were made by the tribes of Hudson Strait and Davis Strait, because they had access to driftwood from which they could make long runners—from five to fifteen feet long and twenty inches to two and a half feet apart:

> They are connected by cross bars of wood or bone and the back is
> formed by deer's antlers with the skull attached. The bottom of the

Ano *or dog harness.*
Franz Boas, *The Central Eskimo*, p. 532

Qamuting *or sledge.*
Franz Boas, *The Central Eskimo*, p. 529

runners is curved at the head and cut off at right angles behind. It is shod with whalebone, ivory, or the jawbones of a whale. In long sledges the shoeing is broadest near the head and narrowest behind. The shoe is either tied or riveted to the runner. . . . The right and left sides of a whale's jaw are frequently used for shoes, as they are of the proper size and permit the shoe to be of a single piece. . . . Sometimes whalebone is used for the shoes.

Hall, who gave great attention to detail, described the sledge he had built in Cincinnati and took with him on his first expedition. It was designed after Kane's favorite sledge, "Faith":

The only difference between his and my sledge was as follows:— Dr. Kane's was 3 feet 8 inches wide, while mine was only 2 feet 6 inches. The shoeing of Dr. Kane's was three-sixteenths-inch steel, while the shoeing of mine, on arriving at the North, was slabs of the jawbone of the whale (the article used by the natives), 1 inch thick and 3 ½ inches wide.

Hall described a sledge used during his second expedition in October 1864 down Roes Welcome Sound, just north of Hudson Bay, with a team of fifteen dogs:

The runners of this sled, made of 2-inch plank, were 16 feet long, each being shod with bone from the jaw of a whale. Its 15 crossbars made of staves, each 3 feet 3 inches long and 5 inches wide, were lashed to the top of the runners by strong strips of walrus-hide. This play of the runners makes the Eskimo sled superior to all others in its flexibility over hummocky ice. Their depth was 9 inches, and the width of the sled outside of them, 3 feet.

Regardless of the design or size of the sledge, in winter the shoes of the runners needed to be iced. According to Boas, if the shoes were made of "good" bone, ivory, or whalebone, the icing would need water only, water that came from the mouth of the driver; but if the runners were made of skin or the shoes were of poor quality,

they are first covered with a mixture of moss and water or clay and water. This being frozen, the whole is iced . . . Instead of pure water, a mixture of blood and water or of urine and water is frequently used, as this sticks better to the bone shoe than the former.

In case additional liquid was needed, the driver carried a bag of water against his skin to keep it from freezing.

The design, construction, and maintenance of the sledge and the icing of the shoes of the runners when necessary were all of utmost importance, but the sledge would not move without an effective harness attaching it to the dogs.

The style of harness used in the nineteenth-century eastern Arctic, constructed of seal skin or bear skin, was the "fantail," or "fan hitch," allowing the dogs to fan out in front of the sledge in a semicircular fashion, not the two-by-two tandem, or "gangline," method more commonly known today. The fan hitch system, attaching each dog to the sledge by a separate tugline, enables the dogs more room to maneuver around obstacles such as upheavals of rough ice and is used in open, treeless areas. It allows each dog to shift position but also leads to "braiding," or tangling, of the traces. The gangline system, by comparison, provides a single line to which each dog is attached, usually in pairs. This method, keeping the dogs in tight formation, is used on narrow trails or in forested areas, as seen in present-day races such as Alaska's Iditarod.

Isaac I. Hayes, who followed Kane, described the fan hitch:

The harness on them was no less simple than the cargo they had to draw. It consisted of two doubled strips of bear-skin, one of which was placed on either side of the body of the animal, the two being fastened together on the top of the neck and at the breast, thus forming a collar. Thence they passed inside of the dog's fore-legs, and up along the sides to the rump, where the four ends meeting together were fastened to a trace eighteen feet in length. This was connected with the sledge by a line four feet long, the ends of which were attached one to each runner. To the middle of this line was tied a strong string which was run through bone rings at the ends of the traces and secured by a slipknot, easily untied.

As Boas noted:

The strongest and most spirited dog has the longest trace and is allowed to run a few feet in advance of the rest as a leader; its sex is indifferent, the choice being made chiefly with regard to strength. Next to the leader follow two or three strong dogs with traces of equal length, and the weaker and less manageable the dogs the nearer they run to the sledge.

The team, of course, must know the leader or they will not run for him or her. Some dogs, newly placed in a strange team, would lie down and howl and refuse to move.

Then it was time for the whip, the third vital tool in successful sledging. According to Kane:

> The whip is six yards long, and the handle but sixteen inches,—a short lever, of course, to throw out such a length of seal-hide. Learn to do it, however, with a masterly sweep, or else make up your mind to forego driving sledge; for the dogs are guided solely by the lash, and you must be able not only to hit any particular dog out of a team of twelve, but to accompany the feat also with a resounding crack. After this, you find that to get your lash back involves another difficulty; for it is apt to entangle itself among the dogs and lines, or to fasten itself cunningly round bits of ice, so as to drag you head over heels into the snow.

This task takes so much energy, Kane asserted, that the "Esquimaux travel in couples, one sledge after the other. The hinder dogs follow mechanically, and thus require no whip; and the drivers change about so as to rest each other."

One more piece of equipment was at times necessary: During spring conditions when sharp needles of ice protruded from the melting snow, shoes consisting of pieces of skin with holes for their nails would be placed on the dogs' paws and tied to their legs.

Dog, sledge, harness, whip: Every element was as important as every other, but none so important as the skill of the driver, the ultimate synthesizer. While arguments persisted as to who was better equipped, Eskimo or foreigner, each man new to the Arctic would have to learn humbling lessons for himself. Even Nansen, who became highly accomplished, described a humiliating first experience after his runaway team caused a spill:

> I lost the board I should have sat on, then the whip, then my gloves, then my cap—these losses not improving my temper. Once or twice I ran round in front of the dogs, and tried to force them to turn by lashing at them with the whip. They jumped to both sides and only tore on the faster; the reins got twisted round my ankles, and I was thrown flat on the sledge, and they went on more wildly than ever.

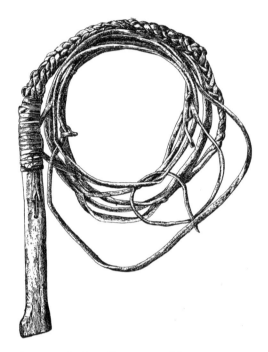

Whip. Length of handle, 28 cm.; of thong, 600 cm.
Franz Boas, *Bulletin of the American Museum of Natural History*, p. 89

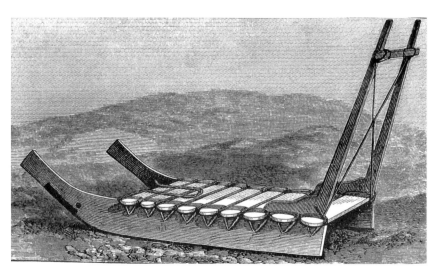

Greenland dog sledge.
Greely, p. 156

Eskimo sledge.
Nourse, p. 221

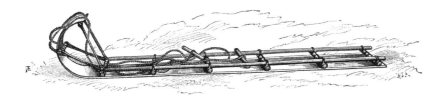

Hudson Bay sledge pattern.
Adolphus W. Greely, *Three Years of Arctic Service: An Account of the Lady Franklin Bay Expedition of 1881–84 and the Attainment of the Farthest North*, p. 152

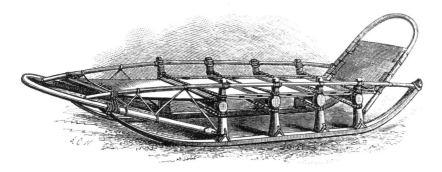

Hunt's St. Michael sledge.
Greely, p. 155

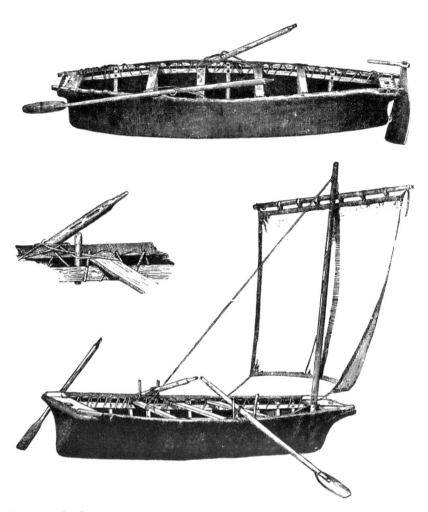

Umiaq *or skin boat.*
Franz Boas, *The Central Eskimo*, p. 528

5

Toodla and Whitey

The First Famous Sledge Dogs

Traveling with Elisha Kent Kane on the Second Grinnell Expedition in Search of Sir John Franklin, 1853–1855

Elisha Kent Kane (1820–1857) was an unlikely candidate for an arctic hero but, as a successful explorer, he became one of the most popular figures of his day. Born of a distinguished Philadelphia family, he suffered rheumatic fever during his second year at the University of Virginia—a disease that, before antibiotics, exacted a life sentence of pain and disability; his doctors held out little hope. In defiance, Kane chose a life of adventure. After graduating from medical school at the University of Pennsylvania, he joined the U.S. Navy as assistant surgeon and traveled widely—China, the Philippines, Egypt, Africa—suffering a number of fevers along the way, fevers that would flare up throughout his life but never keep him from meeting challenges. He descended into and explored the crater of Taal Volcano near Manila (providing Jules Verne with his climactic scene of Captain Hatteras in the volcano of the North Pole). He was wounded in the Mexican-American War. Seeking yet more adventure, he signed on as ship's doctor to the First Grinnell Expedition in Search of Sir John Franklin, 1850–1851, under the command of Lieutenant Edwin J. De Haven. Upon his return, after a successful book and lecture tour (and a much publicized liaison with spiritualist Maggie Fox), he managed to launch a second expedition backed again by whaling magnate Henry Grinnell.

Now in command of the Second Grinnell Expedition in Search of Sir John Franklin, he traveled once more on the brig *Advance*, under orders from the U.S. Navy. He was accompanied by two colleagues from the earlier voyage—Henry Brooks, first officer, and his steward William Morton—along with fifteen others. His ship's surgeon was just-graduated Isaac I. Hayes, who would go on to his own arctic explorations, publications, and fame.

Even before he set out on his second arctic adventure, Kane was concerned with dogs. He wanted a Newfoundland for his beloved, the spiritualist Maggie Fox, whom he was leaving behind to be educated (perhaps so that she would be fit to become his wife): "I have also written for a fine Newfoundland dog—a big, brave, steadfast friend—who will keep love of me alive *in you*." In the great rush to get launched, however, Kane was unable to provide the dog; Fox had to be content with her cantankerous poodle, Tommy. (According to Fox's memoirs, Tommy was a "favorite and ill-tempered poodle, with blue eyes; brought over from England by Miss Charlotte Cushman, the tragedienne.")

Soon after arriving at St. John's, Newfoundland, in mid-June 1853, Kane had on board a "noble team of Newfoundland dogs"—ten of them—a gift of Governor Hamilton, a brother of the Secretary of the Admiralty.

At Fiskernaes, the first port in Greenland, he added to the crew nineteen-year-old Hans Christian (generally known as Hans Hendrik), who would make repeated appearances in exploration of the Arctic and become one of the best-known Inuit hunters of his time. Another Greenlander he added was Carl Petersen, a master sledge-driver and interpreter who had already worked for the accomplished Scottish whaling captain William Penny. There were now twenty men including Kane.

As he continued north up the coast, Kane added local dogs until his "camels of the north" totaled sixty-two: a resource he came increasingly to appreciate. Each had a name and he would often write of them, not infrequently with respect and sometimes with affection—as well as with exasperation. Two would survive the entire ordeal, and he would protect them to the end: Toodla-mik (Toodla) and Whitey.

Whitey was a Newfoundlander, one of the original team of ten. Toodla, a Greenland Dog, came aboard at Upernavik, one of the last stops along the Greenland coast. Though unrelated, they would become joined in exploit and fame.

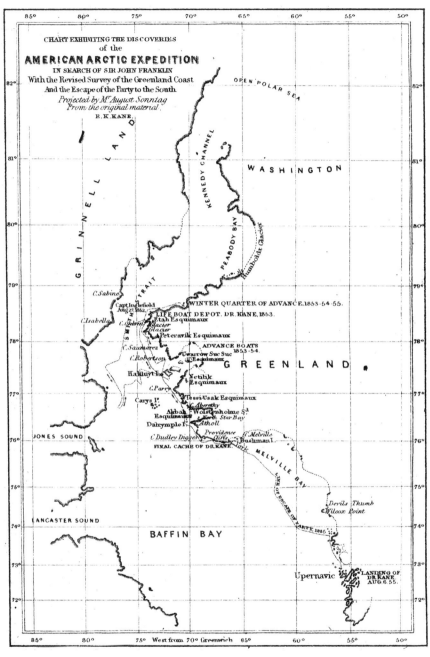

Chart exhibiting the discoveries of the American Arctic expedition in search of Sir John Franklin...

Projected by August Sonntag. *Elisha Kent Kane, Arctic Explorations in the Years 1853, '54, '55..., Vol. II,* facing p. 8

Years later, while writing his account of the adventure, Dr. Isaac I. Hayes, ship's surgeon, paid homage to the remarkable lead dog, Toodla:

> He differed from his kind in having a more compact head, a less pointed nose, an eye denoting affection and reliance, and an erect, bold, fearless carriage. I must express a doubt, however, as to his purity of blood. From the beginning to the end of the cruise, he was master of all the dogs that were brought to the ship....
>
> ...He was a tyrant of no mean pretension. He seemed to consider it his especial duty to trounce every dog, great or small, that was added to our pack.... It was sometimes quite amusing to see him leave the ship's side, in pursuit of a strange dog, his head erect, his tail gracefully curled over his back, going slowly and deliberately at his mark, with the confident, defiant air of one who feels his power and the importance of his office. There were often combinations against him, no doubt induced by the very desperate nature of the circumstances; but he always succeeded in breaking the cabal; not, however, I am bound to say, always without assistance; for the sailors, who were very fond of him, sometimes took his part, when he was unusually hard pressed. A brave dog was Toodla!

Toodla—and his comrades—needed to be brave. They were setting out on an extraordinarily demanding expedition, one that would test man and dog beyond imagining.

Almost as soon as the *Advance* left the coastal settlements behind and reached the south entrance of famously dangerous Melville Bay on July 27, trouble began with ice fogs and icebergs—a new world of navigation for the untried crew. After beating north through the bay and into solid ice, the *Advance* anchored in a cove named Refuge Harbor.

Kane took time to assess his situation, particularly in regard to the dogs. The majority of them were, he noted, "ravening wolves." Already they were starving. There had been no success in hunting except for two polar bears, and these "lasted the cormorants but eight days; and to feed them upon the meagre allowance of two pounds of raw flesh every other day is an almost impossible necessity." Kane would not give them pemmican—canned meat mixed with lard—and they refused the cornmeal and beans that the celebrated Scottish whaling captain William Penny had fed to his dogs. Salted meat, Kane knew, would kill them—though later, in times of exigency, he would break his rule and give it to them.

It was the start of the ceaseless, cyclical crisis of hunger: Dogs were needed for hunting and transport, but dogs also had to be fed. Kane attempted to shoot walrus, abundant in the area at that time, but failed to penetrate their hides; bullets bounced off the animals like "cork pellets from a pop-gun target." Only the discovery of a narwhal carcass—600 pounds of fetid flesh—saved the dogs at that early point.

Kane kept trying to move the *Advance* north, sometimes having the men pull, or "warp," it up the coast. Once, out exploring in a boat, he came across a ledge with a stone hut surrounded by animal bones and a dead dog. Mostly what he saw was ice and more ice, and, as the ice pulled tighter and thicker around him, his patience thinned. On August 16, he took his frustration out on the dogs, recording:

> More bother with these wretched dogs! Worse than a street of Constantinople emptied upon our decks; the unruly, thieving, wild-beast pack! Not a bear's paw, or an Esquimaux cranium, or basket of mosses, or any specimen whatever, can leave your hands for a moment without their making a rush at it, and, after a yelping scramble, swallowing it at a gulp. I have seen them attempt a whole feather bed; and here, this very morning, one of my Karsuk brutes has eaten up two entire birds'-nests which I had just before gathered from the rocks; feathers, filth, pebbles, and moss,—a peckful at the least. One was a perfect specimen of the nest of the tridactyl, the other of the big burgomaster.

Worse, during a stop at Fog Inlet, two of the largest dogs escaped. A boat party had to be sent off to round them up. After rowing through icy water for eight miles, the crew found them—feasting on a narwhal carcass—and managed to capture one, while "the other suicidal scamp had to be left to his fate."

After this first loss, the expedition pushed on, ever slowly, sometimes agonizingly so. A gale blew; the ice careened wildly. On August 22, the crew, harnessed like mules in their "rue-raddies," or shoulder belts, dragged the *Advance* to 78° 41', the farthest north of any predecessor except Sir William Edward Parry in his attempt at the North Pole in 1827.

In order to see what lay farther to the north, they struggled on in a whaleboat named *Forlorn Hope* that had been covered with tin as protection against the ice, and when the *Hope* could go no farther, the party pushed on by sledge. When no site appeared that would serve the *Advance* better for a winter anchorage than where it now rested, Kane turned back south and named the spot Rensselaer Harbor, in honor of his family home outside Philadelphia.

By early September, the brig was surrounded by solid ice and winter preparations were in full swing. Nearby Butler Island became home to the storehouse and kennels, but, as Kane noted, the dogs were not satisfied:

We have made a comfortable dog-house on Butler Island; but though
our Esquimaux *canaille* are within scent of our cheeses there, one
of which they ate yesterday for lunch, they cannot be persuaded to
sleep away from the vessel. They prefer the bare snow, where they
can couch within the sound of our voices, to a warm kennel upon
the rocks. Strange that this dog-distinguishing trait of affection for
man should show itself in an animal so imperfectly reclaimed from a
savage state that he can hardly be caught when wanted!

Kane, more than any other American explorer, acknowledged and
honored the emotional lives of the animals usually looked upon only as
beasts of burden or sources of emergency food. He also applied good sense
in assessing their role. He knew the success of his expedition depended
upon setting up a trail of caches in advance, and that this line of support
could be effected only by dogs:

These noble animals formed the basis of my future plans: the only
drawback to their efficiency as a means of travel was their inability
to carry the heavy loads of provender essential for their support. A
badly-fed or heavily-loaded dog is useless for a long journey; but with
relays of provisions I could start empty, and fill up at our final station.

Kane was especially proud of his ten Newfoundland dogs and personally concerned with their training. They were to be "carefully broken, to
travel by voice without the whip, and were expected to be very useful for
heavy draught, as their tractability would allow the driver to regulate their
pace." He trained them in a light sledge and a special harness running two
abreast, an exception to the more usual fan hitch. The sledge he specifically
designed for them he found to be "beautiful, efficient, and enduring." He
named it the "Little Willie," after his beloved deceased younger brother.

Four of the Newfoundlanders could carry him and his instruments on
short journeys, while six could make a "powerful" team for long-distance
travel. They were to be used to establish the depots within sixty miles
of the brig.

On the other hand, the local, or "Esquimaux," dogs had a role of their
own. They were to be used, Kane noted:

[F]or the great tug of the actual journeys of search. They were now
in the semi-savage condition which marks their close approach to
the wolf; and according to Mr. Petersen, under whose care they were
placed, were totally useless for journeys over such ice as was now
before us. A hard experience had not then opened my eyes to the
inestimable value of these dogs; I had yet to learn their power and

speed, their patient, enduring fortitude, their sagacity in tracking these icy morasses, among which they had been born and bred.

Dog. Sledge. Harness. Whip. Kane was practicing, preparing, and planning, but unaware of what was looming. Unexpectedly, on October 5, he experienced the dread of contagion: a disease that appeared to be rabies.

A number of puppies had been born. Four promising ones were saved, six drowned, two turned into a pair of mittens for Kane, and seven eaten by their mothers. In the midst of all this fecund activity, the mother of one litter showed symptoms of the disease that had not been previously known north of 70°. For some days she had avoided water or had drunk with evident aversion. She started staggering as she walked, her head down and her mouth foaming. Finally, she snapped at Petersen and fell biting at his feet, then snapped at Hans. Kane shot her before she could reach the Newfoundland dogs.

The Newfoundlanders, saved, were called into action for the first time on October 10, when Kane and an assistant harnessed four of the best to go in search of a sledge party twenty days out and now overdue. It wasn't long, however, before the dogs, running on the moving pack ice parallel with the jagged shore ice at low tide, began to tire and needed to be pressed on. The men, running alongside the sledge, were almost as tired, but with the fissures increasing, speed was vital. Three times in less than three hours a man or dog went into the water. Then, when the dogs failed to leap an opening in the ice, the team and sledge all catapulted into the water. Kane instantly cut the lines and the men managed to haul the dogs out. They were able to save the sledge, Kane said, because of the "admirable docility and perseverance" of the team, which managed finally to pull it back onto the ice. The journey continued, conditions wet and freezing. That night, the dogs slept in the tent with the men, "giving it warmth as well as fragrance." Of this experience, Kane noted: "What perfumes of nature are lost at home upon our ungrateful senses! How we relished the companionship!"

The missing sledge party was found, in fairly good shape, though frostbite had left its mark. The conjoined parties returned to the brig with few problems, the Newfoundlanders leaping the ice cracks "in almost every instance." At one point, a slightly injured man riding in the sledge was thrown out during one of the leaps across open water but caught the sledge runner as he fell and managed to be hauled out.

Back at the brig *Advance*, winter preparations continued as the dark and cold pulled tighter around the ice-locked community. Except upon the island of Spitsbergen, Kane noted, "no Christians have wintered in so high a latitude as this." The temperature on November 9 was 33° below zero. (All temperatures are given in Fahrenheit.) Kane's rheumatism worsened and Hans, lovesick, wished he could return to a young woman in Fiskernaes. It was time for arctic entertainment—a fancy ball, a newspaper titled *The Ice-Blink*, and races on the ice—any positive engagement Kane could come up with to keep the men from depression.

But structured entertainment, as practiced by nearly all imprisoned expeditions, could not temper the facts. The *Advance* was trapped with ever-diminishing supplies. Already, though Kane did not tell us how, his lead Newfoundlander, Cerberus, had died. On the night of the solstice, Kane reported Old Grim missing. Having taken over the leadership position among the Newfoundlanders, Old Grim was a favorite. He knew the wiles of tail-wagging and secured everyone's good graces, if not respect. Here, Kane gave an unusually well-limned portrait:

> Grim was an ancient dog: his teeth indicated many winters, and his limbs, once splendid tractors for the sledge, were now covered with warts and ringbones. Somehow or other, when the dogs were harnessing for a journey, "Old Grim" was sure not to be found; and upon one occasion, when he was detected hiding away in a cast-off barrel, he incontinently became lame. Strange to say, he has been lame ever since except when the team is away without him.
>
> Cold disagrees with Grim; but by a system of patient watchings at the door of our deck-house, accompanied by a discriminating use of his tail, he became at last the one privileged intruder. My seal-skin coat has been his favorite bed for weeks together. Whatever love for an individual Grim expressed by his tail, he could never be induced to follow him on the ice after the cold darkness of the winter set in; yet the dear good old sinner would wriggle after you to the very threshold of the gangway, and bid you good-bye with a deprecatory wag of the tail which disarmed resentment.
>
> His appearance was quite characteristic:—his muzzle roofed like the old-fashioned gable of a Dutch garret-window; his forehead indicating the most meagre capacity of brains that could consist with his sanity as a dog; his eyes small; his mouth curtained by long black dewlaps; and his hide a mangy-russet studded with chestnut-burrs: if he has gone indeed, we "ne're shall look upon his like again." So much for old Grim!

Kane admitted he had forced Grim to go to work. Thinking the exercise would be good for him, he had had a rope fastened around him—he could be obstinate and "even ferocious"—and fastened to the sledge. At a stop-

ping place, Grim jerked his line free and started off through the darkness
back toward the ship. Parties with lanterns went out searching for him,
but his tracks stopped at the shore. The temperature was 44° below zero.

The year was now 1854, and the tedious work of winter confinement
continued. The light was beginning, faintly, to return, but the darkness
had taken a terrible toll. Even the dogs, Kane noted, were unable to tolerate the darkness. Most of them died, he said, from "an anomalous form of
disease, to which, I am satisfied, the absence of light contributed as much
as the extreme cold." On January 20, he wrote:

> [T]his morning at five o'clock—for I am so afflicted with the insom-
> nium of this eternal night, that I rise any time between midnight
> and noon—I went up on deck. It was absolutely dark; the cold not
> permitting a swinging lamp. . . . While I was feeling my way . . . two of
> my Newfoundland dogs put their cold noses against my hand, and in-
> stantly commenced the most exuberant antics of satisfaction. It then
> occurred to me how very dreary and forlorn must these poor ani-
> mals be, at atmospheres of +10° in-doors and –50° without,—living
> in darkness, howling at an accidental light, as if it reminded them of
> the moon,—and with nothing, of either instinct or sensation, to tell
> them of the passing hours, or to explain the long-lost daylight. They
> shall see the lanterns more frequently.

Five days later, Kane reported more vividly on the pernicious effects
of darkness. His dogs seemed to be dying of it. For weeks he had been
nursing his "mouse-colored" dogs. They were below decks, carefully fed,
caressed, and doctored, but there seemed no remedy for their mental collapse. Although their physical functions continued, a "true lunacy" manifested itself. They barked at nothing, paced, fawned and pushed against
their caregivers, but with no sense of relief. Sometimes they clawed at their
keepers without reason; sometimes they lingered in moody silence:

> So it is with poor Flora, our "wise dog." She was seized with the en-
> demic spasms, and, after a few wild violent paroxysms, lapsed into
> a lethargic condition, eating voraciously, but gaining no strength.
> This passing off, the same crazy wildness took possession of her, and
> she died of brain disease (*arachnoidal effusion*) in about six weeks.
> Generally, they perish with symptoms resembling locked-jaw in less
> than thirty-six hours after the first attack.

Afterwards, Flora became a pair of socks looking, her former master
commented, "almost as pretty as when she was heading the team." At least
Flora had known another way of life before the *Advance*. Numerous sledge

Elisha Kent Kane, portrait with dog.
Naval Historical Foundation

dogs were born and died with their expeditions, never experiencing any-thing beyond the reach of their ship.

It is not surprising that absence of light is referred to over and over in the ice journals as a debilitating force more powerful than any other. Darkness was the heart of madness. The condition, as it affected people as well as dogs, would come to be known as *piblokto* (*pibloktoq*) or "Arctic hysteria."

By March, disaster and failure loomed. Kane was determined to get farther north, but his dog team was decimated. Of the ten "splendid" Newfoundlanders and more than fifty "Esquimaux" dogs he started out with, all had perished but six, and one of these was unfit for work. Still, the survivors—including the indomitable Toodla and Whitey—gave hope, and he gave himself over to training them to run together. The carpenter was given orders to create a small sledge that would be suitable to such a small team. As part of the daily routine, Kane would harness and work the dogs, as much to keep his rheumatic limbs supple as to prepare the dogs for what lay ahead.

The last day of March brought an almost fatal test: Kane was pushing the team to jump a four-foot crevasse between the sea ice and the shore ice—"Now, Stumpy! Now, Whitey! Good dogs! Tu-lee-ee-ee! Tuh!"—when suddenly the whole team was in a roiling mass sixteen feet below him, their howls indistinguishable from the roaring of the tide. It took Kane time to find an opening in the ice, but he managed to climb down to them, cut them free, and save them and the sledge.

Far worse was to come. On April 8, the first man died—of lockjaw (tetanus)—soon to be followed by a second. But as Jefferson Baker, a child-hood friend of Kane's, lay dying, a group of visitors arrived at the ship.

These people, Polar Inuit, the first Kane had encountered, came from the village of Etah, eighty miles to the south. They brought with them fifty-six "fine" dogs and their sledges. For decades from this moment, Etah and its people would hold enormous importance for American explorers trying to reach the highest latitudes. It can easily be said that they saved many lives, not only by providing meat at critical times but also by serving as teachers and mentors.

The relationship did not start smoothly, however. After a chaotic visit during which the newcomers removed various items from the ship, Kane made a treaty with them. He also bought from them all the walrus meat they had to spare as well as four of their dogs. He paid them with "needles and beads and a treasure of old cask-staves." Delighted, the visitors prom-ised to return with more meat and to allow the use of their teams and sledges for explorations north. The strangers harnessed their dogs in less than two minutes, mounted their sledges, and made off at a rate of seven knots an hour.

The treaty and promises did not work out as Kane had envisioned. An uneasy and complicated association developed with these men of Etah. Since each party had what the other needed, a certain détente was established. Kindness and strict enforcement were equally needed, Kane maintained. Alhough shaky at the start, the relationship deepened into mutual dependence not untouched by fondness and respect—one that would prove of enormous value to subsequent explorers.

Kane was pleased with his new dogs. The reinforcement, he said, "makes a noble team for me." It was now a team of seven—the four he had just bought and three from his previous stock. The two groups melded. After five days, he reported: "The Society for Preventing Cruelty to Animals would have put me in custody, if they had been near enough; but, thanks to a merciless whip freely administered, I have been dashing along twelve miles in the last hour, and am back again; harness, sledge, and bones all unbroken. I am ready for another journey."

The expedition plan called for Kane to go with seven men north up the coast (where he would find and name his major discovery, the Humboldt Glacier), then north and west into unknown areas, crossing the ice of Smith Sound to the "American" side. Execution of the plan did not materialize, however. Soon after starting, the party was weakened by scurvy and progress was slowed by deep and heavy snow. The men sank to their waists and the dogs, floundering and partially buried, could not haul. Snow blindness and various other physical ills absorbed more energy. Bears had destroyed caches. While taking an observation, Kane was seized with sudden pain and fainted, his limbs becoming rigid. He had to be strapped to the sledge. Before long he was delirious and totally debilitated. The party turned back. At the brig, Dr. Hayes diagnosed scurvy complicated by typhoid fever, one of the numerous fevers Kane had picked up in his earlier travels and carried with him.

The work had to go on. Kane, barely able to move, now stayed at the brig to take care of those in worse shape than himself, and Dr. Hayes continued the explorations. Kane, having made up his mind to trust almost entirely to the dogs for future travel, now handed the team to Hayes, with the troublesome William Godfrey, a last-minute recruit to the expedition, as driver.

As Hayes and Godfrey set out,

The dogs were in excellent condition too, no longer foot-sore, but well rested and completely broken, including the four from the

Esquimaux, animals of great power and size. Two of these, the stylish leaders of the team, a span of thoroughly wolfish iron-grays, have the most powerful and wild-beast-like bound that I have seen in animals of their kind.

But when Hayes and Godfrey returned on June 1, both men were completely snow-blind and two of the dogs, especially "poor little Jenny," were totally exhausted and in need of attentive care.

Hayes testified that often they could move forward only because of the dogs. They had covered 270 miles of tortuous ice and had experienced excruciating problems with tangled and broken lines. At one point, Hayes had even had to donate part of his seal-skin pants to patch up some mutilated dog lines. But Hayes and Godfrey got farther than the three parties traveling by foot who had tried before: 79° 45' N.

Now Kane, still disabled, had to press farther. He organized a dog-team venture with William Morton and Hans, which was to push past the Humboldt Glacier over the bay and advance along the distant coast. Three weeks later, they were back, exhausted: "Hans and Morton staggered beside the limping dogs, and poor Jenny was riding as a passenger upon the sledge."

Eventually, the weary travelers told their story. They had fought their way through crowds of icebergs and forded many fissures. At one point, slogging through rotten ice, the dogs began to tremble, then lay down and refused to proceed, trembling ever more violently. The only way to induce the "terrified, obstinate brutes" to move on was for Hans to find a white-looking spot where the ice was thicker and then call to them by name; they crawled to him on their bellies. The retreat to firmer ice required half a mile of this patient coaxing. Once on shore, they found the ice ledge so narrow they had to unharness the dogs and drive them forward.

One day, they tied the dogs up—securely, they thought—and went on by foot. Nine miles away they encountered a polar bear sow with cub. Within an hour Toodla, the invincible leader, and four cohorts mysteriously appeared, as if answering a summons, and made an attack on the bear possible.

The sow, pushing her cub in front of her, headed inland up a stony valley. When the dogs came at her, she would sit on her haunches with the cub between her hind legs, fighting off the dogs with her paws, while roaring. She would snap at the nearest dog while whirling her paws like a windmill. The dogs were tormenting her like flies. When the men came up, it was hard for them to take a shot without hitting a dog, but Hans succeeded. As the dogs sprang toward the sow, the cub jumped on her body and reared up, growling. While tearing mouthfuls of hair from the dead mother, the dogs would jump aside as soon as the cub turned toward them. The men drove the dogs off for a time, then shot the cub, as she would not leave the body. A bullet to the head failed to kill her. She still climbed on her mother's body and tried to defend it, "her mouth bleeding like a gutter-spout." Finally, they killed her with stones. Once skinned, the mother's body was given to the dogs to feed on while the cub was cached for the return trip. With difficulty, the dogs were pulled away and the trip continued.

Farther to the north, Morton reached an area of rotting ice. The frightened dogs refused to move forward. Then, as Morton continued to contemplate the view to the north, he came to the conclusion that what he was looking at was the Open Polar Sea—Kane's doomed obsession. (Kane and Hayes were the last notable explorers to cling to the concept of open water surrounding the North Pole—the concept Jules Verne appropriated for the adventures of Captain Hatteras.)

When Morton and Hans returned, the summer was wearing on, but still the ice did not loosen its hold on the *Advance*. There was discussion of abandoning the vessel, but not for long: There were too many sick and recently amputated men. And, there was still a chance, Kane maintained, of saving the brig. He would go, instead, to Beechey Island, to the south, where he hoped to find help from the British. First, he and Hans would reconnoiter. They would "fit out our poor travel-worn dogs with canvas shoes, and cross the floes to the true water-edge, or at least be satisfied that it is impossible." It was. They were back after sixty miles. The straits to the south were tight with ice. Kane then decided he would take a whaleboat to the south and west.

The vessel was to be, again, *Forlorn Hope*, this time mounted on the sledge "Faith," and it did manage to get hauled across twenty miles of ice to the open water. But gales, illness, lack of food, and, especially, impassable pack ice defeated the goal. It was impossible for Kane to get south.

Only the south-bound birds had no trouble, and their departure signaled the coming of another winter. By the end of August, the young ice could bear the weight of a man and the daily prayer changed from "Lord, accept our gratitude and bless our undertaking" to "Lord, accept our gratitude and restore us to our homes."

On August 28, nine of the eighteen survivors left the brig to find their way to rescue. One returned within a few days. Kane had given them written permission to go—and to return—along with two boats (including the *Forlorn Hope*) and all the supplies he could spare. He referred to them not as mutineers or secessionists but as the "Withdrawing Party." Among this party were Dr. Hayes and the astronomer August Sonntag.

On board the *Advance*, a reduced number of men, almost all disabled in one way or another, some seriously so, now contemplated a second winter of diminished resources and ever greater isolation. Kane knew their lives depended on adapting more fully to a native way of life. The brig became an igloo. The dogs pulled the sledge to wherever moss and turf could be found and hauled it back for chinking. Snow was banked against the sides of the ship.

In the meantime, Kane and Hans drove the dogs—there were now five from the disabled pack who could work—to where they expected to find open water and seals, but solid ice was all they encountered. Another route was tried, and there, within view of seals, came the single most dramatic event of Kane's three-year adventure.

The dogs were running over new ice that rolled beneath them. The men, trying to get to a solid floe they had spied, urged on the dogs with whip and voice, but fear itself drove the dogs and the men's voices fell away to silence. If they did not make the floe, men, dogs, and sledge would be lost, along with the last hopes of the *Advance*. Suddenly everything— *everything*—depended on the dogs. Then it happened: Within fifty paces of the floe, the terrified dogs paused. The left-hand runner went through the soft ice. Toodla followed, and in a second the entire left side of the sledge was submerged. Kane tried to cut Toodla's traces and found himself swimming alongside him in a circle of pasty ice and water. Hans drew near. Kane ordered him to throw himself on his belly and make for the floe by pulling himself forward with his knife. In the meantime Kane was now swimming with the whole sledge and team, with all their confused lines. Toodla, who had been trying to cling to Kane, was now cut free and managed to scramble onto solid ice. Kane kept swimming around the circle, the ice breaking with every effort to grab it, and he was growing weaker with every increase in the size of the hole. Hans reached firm ice and reached out in prayer to his leader. Kane's chances were fast diminishing:

> I was nearly gone. My knife had been lost in cutting out the dogs; and a spare one which I carried in my trousers-pocket was so enveloped in the wet skins that I could not reach it. I owed my extrication at last to a newly-broken team-dog, who was still fast to the sledge and in struggling carried one of the runners chock against the edge of the circle. All my previous attempts to use the sledge as a bridge had failed, for it broke through, to the much greater injury of the ice. I felt that it was a last chance. I threw myself on my back, so as to lessen as

much as possible my weight, and placed the nape of my neck against the rim or edge of the ice; then with caution slowly bent my leg, and, placing the ball of my moccasined foot against the sledge, I pressed steadily against the runner, listening to the half-yielding crunch of the ice beneath.

Kane succeeded in getting up on the solid ice. All the dogs were saved, but the sledge, kayak, tent, guns, snowshoes, and all other equipment had to be abandoned. A twelve-mile trot back to the brig warmed everyone up but not as much as the welcome that greeted them.

The next crisis was the loss of another dog, Tiger, "our best remaining dog, the partner of poor Bruiser." Tiger was seized with a fit resembling what had befallen the dogs during the previous winter. In the delirium that followed his seizure, he ran into the water and drowned himself, "like a sailor with the horrors."

The next canine loss was Nannook, Kane's "best dog." Visitors from Etah stole him as well as the lamp, boiler, and cooking pot Kane had provided for them for their use on board the brig. If the rest of the team had not been so worn down from overwork, the visitors would have taken them, too, Kane asserted. It was discovered later that they had also stolen a cache of buffalo robes and India-rubber cloth hidden some miles from the ship.

Kane sent Morton and another man after the thieves; they found one of them, stripped and tied up the two women with him, packed up the stolen goods on them, along with walrus meat from their own supplies, and marched them back to the brig—thirty miles away. The henchman was then taken to the chief of the Etah village, who traveled to the ship to return a sledge load of stolen goods. During formal proceedings, an intricate peace treaty was effected.

Among the promises extracted from the thieving villagers was one of particular importance—that they would sell or lend dogs to Kane. The *Kablunah*, or white men, promised in turn that they would not visit the Etah people with death or sorcery, "nor do you any hurt or mischief whatsoever." According to Kane, the treaty was never broken, and the two communities went back and forth thereafter with courtesy and mutual aid, though always with a nervous edge. The dogs, he said, became in one sense "common property; and often they have robbed themselves to offer supplies of food to our starving teams."

Soon after the treaty was set, Kane went out on a walrus hunt along with Morton, Hans, and several Etah men. His team consisted of five of his available dogs and two belonging to the native people. That night, while running alongside the dogs, the men took a wrong turn and traveled out toward the open water. It was only the alarm of the dogs that alerted them to the danger: "The instinct of a sledge-dog makes him perfectly aware of unsafe ice, and I know nothing more subduing to a man than the warnings of an unseen peril conveyed by the instinctive fears of the lower animals."

Because of a gale, they had to keep going, feeling their way with the tent poles. Suddenly, Kane heard waves. "Turn the dogs!" he shouted, but there could be no easy retreat as the ice broke up in the storm. He led the party south, the surf chasing them, the ice undulating beneath their feet. The dogs, no longer having to pull the weight of the men, moved with more energy but needed to be urged forward as the men clambered through the tumultuous wall of ice at the shore. Miraculously, the piece of beach where they landed was 400 yards from Anoatok, "the wind-loved spot." This uninhabited camp, consisting of several rough huts always in need of repair, was approximately halfway between the brig and the village of Etah and often, during Kane's travels, provided refuge, as it would to later visitors in need, especially Frederick Cook.

Early in October, back at the brig, the dogs engaged a bear in a furious fight. Again, it was a sow with a four-month-old cub, an icon of maternal ferocity. She had come to the vessel out of hunger and proved a furious combatant. While the dogs hung on her long fur, she would pick one out at a time, snatch him up by the nape of the neck, and fling him a matter of yards. By the time Kane got to the scene, Toodla had already been tossed twice, and as he arrived, Jenny was somersaulting through the air, to land senseless. Whitey, who had been the first to attack, was yelping helplessly on the snow.

With her tormentors vanquished, the bear turned toward her task of raiding the barrels of beef. When Kane put a "pistol-ball" in the side of the cub, she rushed to defend it, putting it between her hind legs. Though hit by a bullet herself, she continued to tear at the frozen barrels while pushing her cub along in front of her. Kane, "going up within half-pistol range, . . . gave her six buckshot." She dropped and rose, pushing her cub in front of her. She would have escaped, Kane said, if not for the newly acquired dogs from Etah:

> The dogs of Smith's Sound are educated more thoroughly than any of their more southern brethren. Next to the walrus, the bear is the staple of diet to the north, and, except the fox, supplies the most important element of the wardrobe. Unlike the dogs we had brought with us from Baffin's Bay, these were trained not to attack, but to embarrass. They ran in circles round the bear, and when pursued would keep ahead with regulated gait, their comrades effecting a diversion

at the critical moment by a nip at her hind-quarters. This was done so systematically and with so little seeming excitement as to strike every one on board. I have seen bear-dogs elsewhere that had been drilled to relieve each other in the *melée* and avoid the direct assault; but here, two dogs without even a demonstration of attack would put themselves before the path of the animal, and, retreating right and left, lead him into a profitless pursuit that checked his advance completely.

Nine rifle bullets finally brought the bear down, while the injured cub, after springing on her mother's body, was muzzled and brought to the brig and chained alongside.

Of the eight dogs who had participated in the battle, only Whitey was badly injured. Two escaped untouched. The others, though they had been flung vigorously, suffered no lasting injury. They knew how to play "possum," Kane noted. One of the Smith Sound dogs, Jack, he explained, made no struggle when he was seized but relaxed all his muscles. No matter how far the bear threw him, he was instantly back up to renew his attack.

Bears were not the only adversary. For the men of the *Advance*, rats became—after cold, dark, and scurvy—the biggest problem. They had exploded through the ice-locked ship. At one point, Kane put his hand into a bearskin mitten that had become the home for a rat family. The mother bit him and carried off the mitten.

Desperate, the commander sent a dog to solve the problem. He chose Rhina, calling her the "most intelligent dog of our whole pack." She had also distinguished herself in bear hunts, but now she was up against a new kind of foe. He sent her to live in the forward area, where the rodents were thickest. She made a bed for herself on top of some iron spikes and managed to sleep for a couple of hours. But the rats would not leave her paws alone and gnawed her feet and nails so ferociously that she had to be saved from them, yelping and vanquished.

Kane ate the rats, delighted that the luxury of "such small deer" protected him from scurvy. As much as he claimed to relish them in a soup, however, he never pressured his men to partake of the concoction. (He probably was not aware of the ancient Romans' appetite for dormice dipped in honey and sesame seeds.) He tried various methods of control. A fox was caught and domesticated, taking on the role of terrier. He had only one fault as a ratcatcher, Kane noted: He would never catch a second rat until he had eaten the first.

Outside, arctic hares were abundant and large, weighing on average seven and one-half pounds, according to Kane; the largest they saw, he claimed, weighed nine pounds. (In 1882, Adolphus Washington Greely

Bear hunt.
Kane, *Vol. I*, p. 387

commented on hares his hunters shot weighing eleven pounds gross, six pounds dressed.) They would have added greatly to the men's diet but were favored by the dogs.

It was mid-October 1854, and the need for fresh meat was becoming ever more acute. Kane wanted to find the Etah hunters, who were out on the ice at an unknown location. He had Morton and Hans take a sledge to Anoatok. After leaving the "old dogs of our team" there, they were to take two of the dogs recently acquired from the villagers, release one, and hold on to the other with a leash. The free dog, it was hoped, would lead them to the hunters' camping ground. The tactic was not necessary, however. They found Myouk, a young hunter from Etah, along with his family, residing in a settlement beyond Anoatok. Myouk and his father permitted Morton and Hans to go with them on a walrus hunt, and the hunt was successful.

While they were gone, thinking it was a wolf at the meat storage house, Kane accidentally shot a dog, "a truant from Morton's team." Fortunately, the dog suffered only a flesh wound. Kane would have been loathe to lose him. Later, another dog, the black Erebus, also broke away from Morton and returned to the ship.

There was much similarity, Kane noted, between the arctic dogs and wolves: "I have a slut, one of the tamest and most affectionate of the whole of them, who has the long legs, and compact body, and drooping tail and wild, scared expression of the eye, which some naturalists have supposed to characterize the wolf alone." If domesticated early, Kane stated, the wolf follows and loves you "like a dog." The wolflike desire to run away means nothing, he added. The dogs might disappear for weeks but, when they came back, they did not want to live alone in the kennel built for them a hundred yards off: "They crouch around for the companionship of men."

The howling and the footprints were the same as those of their wild cousins—and the level of strength and ferocity; the dogs of Smith Sound could vanquish a wolf. And, while wolves were accused (with no proof, Kane said) of carrying off dogs, dogs were culpable of the ultimate rapacity:

> It is not quite a month ago since I found five of our dogs gluttonizing on the carcasses of their dead companions who had been thrown out on a rubbish-heap; and I have seen pups only two months old risk an indigestion by overfeeding on their twin brethren who had preceded them in a like imprudence.

On December 7, five Inuit sledges with teams of six dogs each arrived at the brig, returning two members of the "Withdrawing Party." The others, it was learned, were 200 miles away, starving and in desperate need. Kane immediately set about their rescue. First, he sent the Inuit drivers, whom he did not know, to the starving men with all the supplies he could spare—350 pounds of pork and bread; he was doubtful his wishes would be carried out by these strangers, but, with his scurvy-ravaged crew to care for, he could not leave the brig and figured he had no options.

Five days later, with the temperature at 50° below zero, the rest of the wanderers arrived at the brig in a state of collapse. They had not received the supplies sent on by Kane but had been helped by a number of people they had met along the way, including some friends who had driven them back to the ship. By the time the entourage reached the brig, the escort numbered six men and forty-two dogs. To thank the drivers, and to compensate for *his* men's having helped themselves to Inuit goods, Kane gave each visitor five needles, a file, and a stick of wood. To the two leaders he gave knives and "other extras." And he returned all "borrowed" items.

The crowded igloo-ship was now packed with patients and an overload of danger. An accidental fire in the cooking room that burned through the moss-packed walls could easily have been the final crisis. In fighting the fire, Kane was burned and overcome by smoke. Unconscious, he was carried up to the deck. The temperature, outside the burning interior, was 46° below zero.

No matter how many crises erupted, hunger and scurvy remained constant. Right after Christmas 1854, Kane decided he had to make a trip to where the people of Etah were hunting walrus—100 miles away—though there was no assurance he would find them or have success in hunting. But he had to get fresh meat to keep his men alive. Whether he could accomplish his goal was problematic, he knew:

> My misgivings are mostly on account of the dogs; for it is a rugged, hummocked drive of twenty-two hours, even with strong teams and Esquimaux drivers. We have been feeding them on salt meat, for we have had nothing else to give them; and they are out of health; and there are hardly enough of them at best to carry our lightest load. If one of these tetanoids [infectious, often fatal diseases like tetanus] should attack them on the road, it may be *game up* for all of us.

But he prepared to set out, with Petersen as his one helper, at 54° below zero. Kane's diet would consist of meat-biscuit and rats, "chopped up and frozen into the tallow-balls," though he would make no effort to make his assistant eat the rodents.

On December 28 he wrote:

I have fed the dogs the last two days on their dead brethren. Spite of all proverbs, *dog will eat dog*, if properly cooked. I have been saving up some who died of fits, intending to use their skins, and these have come in very opportunely. I boil them into a sort of bloody soup, and deal them out twice a week in chunks and solid jelly; for of course they are frozen like quartz rock. These salt meats [such as referred to earlier] are absolutely poisonous to the Northern Esquimaux dog. We have now lost fifty odd, and one died yesterday in the very act of eating his reformed diet.

It took only a short time on the trail before Kane's fears were realized and the dogs began to show signs of what he called "that accursed tetanoid spasm." Soon, six out of eight were nearly useless. The temperature was 40° below zero. Petersen wanted to turn back, but Kane pressed on to Anoatok—another thirty miles' march—to the lonely huts that had provided salvation in the past. By the time they arrived, they had traveled forty-five miles in eleven hours. They repaired the best of the huts and moved in with their dogs.

The next morning, the dogs could barely stand. A gale forced Kane and Petersen back inside where, after repairing the walls, they got the temperature up to 30° below zero, made coffee, and fed the dogs. As the storm raged, the men fell asleep. Then, the "Esquimaux lamp" went out, leaving them with no source of heat or light. The men struggled to obtain fire from a pistol when suddenly a burst of phosphorescence came to their aid and Kane was able to charge his pistol and fire it over a cone of paper filled with moss. As the flame burned and relit the lamp, the phosphorescence faded. When the wind abated, the men tried the dogs once more, but they were too broken down to surmount the hummocks of ice along the shore. As a matter of life and death, Kane and Petersen had to return to the brig on foot, driving the dogs before them. They made the walk of forty-four miles in sixteen hours.

The old year had slowly and with much suffering given way to the new year of 1855. The dogs remained a major concern. Still, there was no meat for them except the carcasses of their late companions. If these were boiled properly, Kane maintained, they could provide nourishment.

Kane reported on a starving dog, formerly a child's pet among the Etah people. One night he found her nearly dead at the mouth of the tunnel-like entrance to the brig, wistfully looking at what light leaked through. Immobile, she licked Kane's hand—the first time he had ever had such a greeting from a local dog. Kane picked her up, carried her inside, and cooked her a "dead-puppy soup," which revived her.

He needed every dog for another attempt to reach the Inuit settlements and get help. He would make the next try with Hans; Petersen, he complained, was not reliable.

There were five serviceable dogs among the six that remained: Toodla, Jenny, who had puppies, and Rhina—the "relics of my South Greenland teams"; little Whitey, the "solitary Newfoundlander"; and one big yellow and one "feeble" little black, obtained from the local Inuit people.

With such weakened resources, Kane knew there could be no riding but only running alongside the sledge, and the thought of such a "dog-trot" of 100 miles with the dogs likely to give out at any moment was fearsome. At 50° below zero, the dogs were the only protection. No matter what difficulties they caused, they were essential:

> At home one would fear to encounter such hoop-spined, spitting, snarling beasts as the Esquimaux dogs of Peabody Bay. But, wolves as they are, they are far from dangerous: the slightest appearance of a missile or cudgel subdues them at once. Indispensable to the very life of their masters, they are treated, of course, with studied care and kindness; but they are taught from the earliest days of puppy-life a savory fear that makes them altogether safe companions even for the children. But they are absolutely ravenous of every thing below the human grade. Old Yellow, who goes about with arched back, gliding through the darkness more like a hyena than a dog, made a pounce the other day as I was feeding Jenny, and, almost before I could turn, had gobbled down one of her pups. As none of the litter will ever be of sledging use, I have taken the hint, and refreshed Old Yellow with a daily morning puppy. The two last of the family, who will then, I hope, be tolerably milk-fed, I shall reserve for my own eating.

Discovery of a frozen bear's head saved as a specimen gave temporary relief to the starving and scurvy-wracked prisoners, but the lack of meat would soon be fatal. Rations consisted of four ounces of chips of raw frozen meat per man per day. The dogs were not so fortunate.

Kane had to make his trip to the hunting camps to find what help he could. He and Hans would press on with the dogs as far as they could go, then continue on by themselves. He was loathe to sacrifice the dogs, but necessity drove him; in desperate situations, dogs could stave off hunger for a number of hours or days—and they could be stabbed to death to save ammunition.

While waiting for strong winds to subside and the moon to return, Kane prepared his outfit and itinerary for the trip of ninety-one miles. He would carry only what was absolutely essential. Such a cargo, he noted, eight powerful wolflike dogs could carry "like the wind." But he had "four wretched animals, who can hardly drag themselves."

As Kane had feared, the dogs soon broke down. Toodla and Big Yellow were the first to collapse, Big Yellow with convulsions. The moon had gone down and there was nothing to do but grope along the jagged shore ice in the dark. After fourteen hours, they made the hut at Anoatok and had barely secured themselves and the dogs inside when a storm broke. The men slept, cooked and drank coffee, slept, and drank again until they figured twelve hours had passed and they allowed themselves the luxury of a meal—bites from the raw hind leg of a fox along with biscuits spread with frozen tallow.

The temperature, extraordinarily, went up above freezing, and the hut began to melt. After two days, Kane and Hans pushed on, but heavy snow swallowed up the dogs, sledge, and drivers. They returned to the hut. The temperature dropped, melted snow turned to ice, and the provisions, paltry as they were, ran even shorter. There were still forty-six miles to cover.

On another attempt, by another route, Hans began to cry as the dogs floundered and stuck fast. Although the men finally found a clear channel of ice, the moonlight was waning and the dogs were disabled. Once more, they had to return to the hut. Kane was confident that they could reach the brig, refresh themselves, and succeed at last in reaching the Inuit settlements.

Back at the *Advance*, conditions had only worsened, with the meat giving out and the scurvy biting deeper. Hemorrhages had become common. Kane, needed for doctoring the sick, sent Petersen and Hans out on the next trip. But three days later, they were back. Petersen had broken down and Hans could not carry on alone.

The days, now with lengthening light, dragged by with worsening medical reports and relentless searches for game. They were also filled with plans to repair the whaleboats and sledges and float them over the 1,300 miles that separated the ice prisoners from rescue to the south.

On February 23, Rhina, the "least barbarous of our sledge-dogs," assisted Hans in tracking and finding a caribou that had been wounded earlier (caribou are often referred to as reindeer, a similar but smaller species, or simply "deer"). It was a challenge for the dogs to haul the carcass to the ship and for those men who were well enough to get it up on board. The nicety of skinning was abandoned; the feast began immediately.

Hunger, however, quickly returned. On March 6, with the crew ever closer to death, Kane sent Hans, alone, to find the hunters of Etah. There were two dogs left. Hans took them and the lightest sledge. On March 10, he and the young Etah hunter Myouk, along with the two dogs, were back—with tales of famine at Etah. Starving, the villagers had killed and eaten all but four of their thirty dogs. But Hans and one of the Etah men had managed to secure a walrus and provide a feast. Best of all, Hans was able to bring fresh meat to the dying men of the *Advance*.

A week later, Hans and Myouk drove out to search for walrus or bear. They had four dogs. Young Whitey, exhausted, had been left at Etah. Two days later the would-be hunters were back. They had found nothing but solid ice. They had seen bear tracks and tried to follow, but the dogs were weak and the cold excessive; they decided to return to the brig.

On March 19, Hans set off for Etah armed with Kane's Marston rifle. Simultaneously, Kane was fending off a mutiny. Two men, John Blake and William Godfrey, were plotting to steal the dogs and escape to settlements south of Etah. The plot was discovered and broken, but Godfrey made his escape. Kane feared the runaway would catch up with Hans at Etah, seize the dogs, and head south. "Should he succeed," Kane noted, "the result will be a heavy loss to us. The dogs are indispensable in the hunt and in transporting us to Anoatok." (Anoatok was to be their first step in the long trip down the coast to rescue, a vital staging area where the disabled men could be tended.) A few days later, he reiterated his fears: "nearly all my hopes of lifting the sick, and therefore of escaping in boats to the south, rest upon these dogs. By them only can we hunt bear and early seal. . . . I am entirely without a remedy."

The scurvy-breeding days dragged by with the occasional victory of a ptarmigan or two. On April 2, Godfrey was apprehended near the brig. He had returned, with the team—and walrus meat—from Etah, where he said Hans was lying sick. Then the mutineer escaped, again.

On April 10, Kane set out with five dogs and the lightest possible load to travel to Etah to discover the fate of Hans. The dogs, he said, were in "excellent condition," and luckily for them all, the ice was good for traveling. In spite of low feeding, they carried him sixty-four miles in eleven hours. On the way, he discovered Hans—"Faithful Hans! Dear good follower and friend!"—out on the ice seal hunting. Hans reported that he had been truly ill after walrus hunting and was still a "little veek." He had also been cared for solicitously by a young woman, the daughter of Shanghu (or Shunghu) of Peteravik, with whom he had clearly fallen in love, replacing the romance of Fiskernaes. Peteravik was one of a group of small settlements to the south of Etah.

Now there was new hope. Hans had cached meat for the men of the *Advance*. Furthermore, Kalutunah, the leader of the southern settlement of

Netelik and the most successful hunter of that area, had managed to save seven dogs. Kane authorized Hans to negotiate for four of them, even as a loan—and with the promise of the return of the whole team when Kane reached the open water on his way south.

On April 13, Hans was back with the brig's dogs and a life-giving load of rabbit and walrus. Hans also brought Metek, the chief of Etah, and a young nephew of Metek's called Paulik. They brought distressing news of the Netelik settlement on Northumberland Island to the south, a place that had always been a hunting stronghold: There was now a general north-ward migration. So desperate was their situation, the people had killed their dogs.

By Kane's estimate, the entire Inuit population of the area he knew could now have no more than twenty dogs. "What can they hope for with-out them?" Kane asked.

Kane counted eight settlements with a total human population of about 140. Because of the number of deaths he knew recently to have oc-curred, he figured that the people of the area were close to extinction.

Because Hans had failed in his negotiations to acquire more dogs and because Kane had to apprehend Godfrey, the deserter, and make an exam-ple of him, the commander made the arduous 200-mile round trip to Etah. He was accompanied by Metek. Pretending to be Metek's nephew Paulik, Kane was able quickly to make a prisoner of Godfrey, who was forced to walk and run before the sledge on the way back to the brig.

On a subsequent trip to Etah Bay to hunt walrus, Kane was summoned back to the brig by news of the rapidly declining health of one of his men. His four tired dogs brought him back, as well as a load of walrus meat, with him running alongside them and sometimes riding on the sledge. He covered fifty miles in seven hours.

Kane was determined to make one more exploration north before attempting escape to the south. Kalutunah offered to help, and his help would be essential; Kalutunah had sixteen of the extant local dogs—and they were at that moment chained around the brig. Only Kalutunah's dogs could secure Kane's "closing expedition," a local exploration to bring to an end the once-ambitious search for Franklin.

The party soon set off with Kalutunah, Shanghu, his principal asso-ciate, and their companion Tatterat, with their three sledges, along with Kane and Hans and their sledge. Hans carried the Marston rifle, the Inuit hunters their long knives and their lances made from narwhal ivory.

Soon bear tracks became evident. Before long, the dogs were in wild chase. When the bear was brought down, both drivers and dogs gorged themselves to the point that they could not pursue a second bear; distended, they had to rest. The next day, Kane could not steer the hunters north. They argued—rightly, he noted—that bear meat was essential for their families. Kane gave up on his projected survey of the northern coast.

Now he wanted to get back to the brig and negotiate with Metek for the purchase or loan of *his* dogs as his last chance. But Kane was not allowed to return quickly, not while hunting was possible. Kalutunah's dogs as well as the hunters had energy and purpose enough to make a huge sweep of icy territory before coming to rest. At one point, exhausted, Kane, Hans, and one of the hunters with his dogs crawled into a makeshift snow hut and, providing warmth to one another, fell asleep. The outside temperature was 12° below zero, and during the night the dome of the hut fell in on them but did not wake them.

The careening series of bear hunts finally came to an end and Kane and the hunters returned to the brig. Kalutunah promised to find Metek and make available his four dogs. He and Shanghu, in the meantime, also promised to lend Kane one dog from each of their teams. And they did, indeed, each leave one dog behind, only begging Kane to watch the dogs' feet; each animal had become precious.

Metek, however, did not bring his dogs, and Kane's own were exhausted with runs back and forth to Etah, bringing meat from the village to the ship. The commander knew what had to be done. The time to abandon the *Advance* had come; the expedition was now one of retreat and escape.

At this critical juncture, Hans was gone. After the last hunt, he had asked permission to return to Peteravik to get some walrus hide for his boots. Kane consented. Hans never returned. He had found his love and though lost to Kane, he would rise with her in subsequent chapters of arctic exploration.

For one last time, Kane headed north to explore as far as he could. He took Morton, a light sledge, and the two dogs borrowed from Kalutunah and Shanghu, as well as his own. But conditions proved impossible, Morton broke down, and Kane's energy had ebbed. Unable to keep up his diary, Kane tersely summarized: "The operations of the search were closed."

All effort now was on the escape south. Three small boats (the smallest one to be used, if needed, for firewood) were to be mounted on sledges, along with supplies, to be pulled by men and dogs over the ice to open water. The departure date of May 17 was chosen.

On that day, after prayers, Kane took down the portrait of Sir John Franklin while others dismantled "Augusta," the figurehead, and packed it on a sledge.

The march south began—an agonizingly slow process of round trips between the officially abandoned brig and the hut at Anoatok that Kane had prepared as a field hospital. First, the invalids were carried there by dog sledge, one or two at a time, while hundreds of pounds of supplies were also transported. Second, the boats mounted on sledges had to be hauled there, by the men who were capable of the work; and only then, after staging at Anoatok, did the real journey begin. As the camp at Anoatok became established, Kane then started moving goods south to Etah.

The effort, Kane noted, would have been impossible if not for the "little Esquimaux team," consisting of his four dogs and the two borrowed dogs. These six dogs, he said, "well worn by previous travel, carried me with a fully-burdened sledge between seven and eight hundred miles during the first fortnight after leaving the brig,—a mean travel of fifty-seven miles a day."

Traveling by night, to avoid the glare of the sun, at temperatures still below zero, the party was moving the boats about a mile a day.

At one point, the dogs did collapse and Kane was forced to stop and camp out with them on the ice but was able to continue on his way the next morning. Another time, Kane sent Godfrey with the sledge to Etah to obtain fresh meat.

As the ice over which they were traveling began to melt, Kane feared the loss of supplies being cached along the slow way south. He determined to ask the residents of Etah for two of the four dogs that were still there in order to move provisions to safety. On his way to the settlement, he met a group out auk hunting who welcomed him into their midst. As he left, they not only exchanged their team for his worn-out one but also filled his sledge with the life-giving walrus meat his scurvied crew desperately needed.

Trips back and forth and among the sick-station at Anoatok, Etah, and the brig followed, as the boats were tortuously moved south toward open water. With the ice softening, the dogs moved sluggishly. Gales and deep snow further delayed progress.

One extraordinarily fierce gale ripped the harness off the dogs and the fur jumpers (jackets) off the men's backs. The men threw themselves on their faces until a lull, when they called the terrified dogs around them and made for the rocks of a nearby island. Clinging to the rocks, they could see neither one another nor the dogs. But they had to cross what was left of the ice and get to solid ground. They succeeded and there burrowed into a huge mound of snow. They called the place Cape Misery.

Pulling the sledge and the dogs in with them, Kane and Petersen cowered among them. The snow piled up over them until they were buried, hardly able to hear the storm still raging around them. Soon the respiration of animals and men caused drenching conditions.

Toodla was seized with a fit and, as was their custom, the other dogs charged into a fight that could be ended only by the sacrifice of Petersen's "pantaloons and drawers."

Toodla recovered and Kane sent Morton with the team on to Etah while he helped pull the boats on their sledges. With every hour, the ice was softening and every effort to move through it was becoming more dangerous.

In the meantime, Morton returned from the village with meat, blubber, and "every sound dog" that belonged to the residents, providing Kane a "serviceable" team: "The comfort and security of such a possession to men in our critical position can hardly be realized. It was more than an addition of ten strong men to our party."

With the new and more energetic team, Kane raced back to the brig to strip it of whatever food was left and then on to Anoatok to move the invalids south before the loss of ice made the task impossible. Partway to the ship, landslides almost ended the journey of terrified dog and man.

While Kane was pursuing his mission, the men hauling the boats were encountering horrific challenges of their own. At one point, the boat *Forlorn Hope* was almost lost when one of the runners of the sledge it was traveling on broke through the soft ice into the water, carrying six men with it: "Her stern went down, and she was extricated with great difficulty." Making heroic efforts to save it, Christian Ohlsen, the carpenter, was badly injured. (Petersen states he "burst his bladder.")

As the party, sometimes using sails to speed their progress, got closer to Etah, two residents came out with the good news that Kane's original team was refreshed and nearly able to travel again. And one of the Etah hunters agreed to make the trip to Anoatok to pick up the last two invalids. Hope grew, except for the fate of Ohlsen, whose condition rapidly worsened. Within several days, he was dead, the third crew member lost of the original twenty who set sail from Upernavik for Melville Bay with such promise in the summer of 1853.

Kane sent the Inuit hunters with his dogs off to obtain birds and held a hurried, secret funeral for Ohlsen in a rocky trench on a cape. Even at this stage, Kane feared any show of weakness to the Inuit people. For that reason he had not told them the truth of his extraordinary travel plans, though, as he got ever closer to open water, increasing numbers of local people came to his assistance. They helped pull. They provided food. They fed Kane's party and his dogs at the rate of 8,000 little auks a week, all of them caught in delicate hand nets.

On June 15, 1855, the party reached open water. The local people—twenty-two of them—crowded around as Kane and his men prepared the small and unseaworthy boats for launch. Only two women and an old blind man remained at the settlement, and Kane went to visit them before leaving. Impressing them with his magic powers one last time, he made a lens of ice and "drew down the sun" to light the moss under it.

In a final scene before the assembled villagers, Kane gave out gifts. The amputating knives, given to hunters Metek and Nessark, were considered the greatest gift, "but every one had something as his special prize."

The dogs went to the community at large, as tenants in common, except Toodla and Whitey: "I could not part with them, the leaders of my team: I have them still," Kane wrote as he was finishing his book in Philadelphia in the summer of 1856.

In a parting address, Kane told the people of Etah of the settlements to the south and how, someday, they might get there, to enjoy a milder climate.

On June 19—two years after the expedition sailed out of New York—the men of the *Advance* and the two dogs set out for those same settlements with their three small and fragile craft leaking and constantly threatened. Storm, starvation, sickness, and terror accompanied them. By the end of July, they were in desperate shape when, miraculously, they were able to shoot and secure a seal—and save the lives of the dogs:

> The dogs I have said little about, for none of us liked to think of them. The poor creatures Toodla and Whitey had been taken with us as last resources against starvation. They were, as McGary worded it, "meat on the hoof," and "able to carry their own fat over the floes." Once, near Weary Man's Rest, I had been on the point of killing them; but they had been the leaders of our winter's team, and we could not bear the sacrifice.

More seals sustained the sailors until they reached land.

On August 6, the remaining crew of the *Advance* came ashore at the settlement of Upernavik, where Toodla had come aboard the northbound brig on a promising July day in 1853. The sixteen survivors (Hans had since departed for Peteravik and his beloved) had been in the open air for eighty-four days—days and nights when it was never possible to get dry. On September 6, all but Petersen, whose home was here, left the village on the Danish supply ship *Mariane*. Five days later they met up with the American rescue ship *Release* in Godhavn. Toodla and Whitey were included and returned with Kane to his home in Philadelphia. The only remaining artifacts of the expedition were the whaleboat *Faith*, the figurehead, the furs the men wore, and the documents they could save.

More important were the accomplishments achieved: The expedition had explored and mapped the stretch of water between Greenland on the east and Ellesmere Island on the west—Smith Sound and Kane Basin—reaching the farthest north in Kennedy Channel at approximately 80°58'. They found and named the immense Humboldt Glacier and established the cartographic foundation of the "American Route to the Pole," which would be followed by Hayes, Hall, Greely, and Peary. What they failed to find was the elusive Open Polar Sea.

In the tumult that followed, it is hard to track the course of Toodla and Whitey. Kane returned to an enormous welcome and the tangled affair of his relationship with spiritualist Maggie Fox. When newspapers reported how Kane had broken off the engagement, scandal ensued. Both public scrutiny and family pressure increased. Newspapers took sides and gossip flowed. Sick and exhausted, Kane had his book, *Arctic Explorations*, to write and edit and important people to communicate with, including the famously persuasive Lady Franklin exhorting him to lead the next search for her husband.

In spite of all the demands on his time and health, Kane stayed physically active. According to the sanguine biography by William Elder—endorsed by the Kane family—he would restore himself after grueling periods of work with fast gallops on his horse and vigorous practice with the sledge whips:

> And what a wild carouse old Toodla-mik, the leader of his Arctic sledge-hacks, would have with him in the frosty mornings of their last winter's [1855–1856] fellowship! It was a rough communion, and not quite a complete one. Toodla was an "Injin," every inch of him,—hyena, wolf, and slave in a mixture,—fierce as the boldest of the types, and cowardly and treacherous as the worst.
>
> At the first call he would look out of his kennel; then, without the usual all-hail of the civilized canine,—for he had not learned to bark,—with a bound he was upon the doctor's shoulders, looking a sneaking compound of felony and fondness. Then for the play: the whip was the attraction, not the compulsion. It looked Arctic and Esquimaux enough to see him springing like mad to receive the lash wherever it fell; no fear of the cracker. There was no place exposed to it except the eyes, nose, and fore-feet. Under defence of such a coat of hair, nothing but a cudgel could reach his sensibilities.
>
> Toodla had his virtues, whether he intended them or not. He had rendered services made high and noble by their appropriation. His name is connected with many memories which will not soon perish; and he stands now [1858], his own monument, preserved in

that Westminster Abbey of representative animals, the Academy of Natural Sciences of Philadelphia.

Kane's book was launched with great success, selling 65,000 copies the first year, while he continued romancing Maggie Fox, even "marrying" her in a quasi-Quaker ceremony. But this happy interlude at home was over. Kane left for England, with Morton, to visit Lady Franklin on October 11, 1856. With ever-worsening health, he traveled on to Cuba, where, following a series of strokes, he died on February 16, 1857. His funeral entourage was the largest the nation had known, to be eclipsed only by that of Abraham Lincoln. Maggie Fox emerged from a state of collapse to spend the rest of her life as his "widow," battling the Kane family (the "Royal Family") for financial support, though eventually returning to spiritualism to support herself.

Kane remained powerful in death—and a great commercial opportunity. His family, fiercely protective of their heroic son's reputation, and ready to take advantage of the opportunity to enhance it, engineered a campaign. With their support, Morton became part owner and narrator of a panorama—a series of moving painted scenes that predated the moving picture. The Kanes also gave Morton use of various paraphernalia, including the whaleboat *Faith* and one of the dogs Kane brought home. This might have been Toodla.

With Kane's popularity growing, several other similar panoramas sprang up, moving from city to city, sometimes in direct competition, sometimes merging with one another, and sometimes produced in multiple copies. The audience reached tens of thousands. One panorama even traveled to England, where it was visited by Queen Victoria and Lady Franklin. As pointed out by historian Russell A. Potter in *Arctic Spectacles*, Charles Francis Hall experienced one in his hometown of Cincinnati; inspired, he would soon abandon his work and family to follow his hero Kane into the high latitudes and the same glorious search for Franklin. It is tempting to say we can pick up the trail of Toodla and Whitey with these popular entertainments, a number of which claimed Kane's dogs. (One of the last panoramas to advertise an original Kane dog named him "Whitey.") But, according to Potter, it is unlikely any of these shows included any of Kane's original dogs: There were many more dogs involved than had made up Kane's team and, from what Kane has told us, only Toodla and Whitey came home to Pennsylvania.

Elsewhere, there is but a faint scent: William Hoyt Coleman, in an 1859 letter to *Robert Merry's Museum*, reported that, while on board the *New World* the preceding year, "my attention was drawn to a powerful, foxy-looking dog, which, to my surprise and delight, proved to be Toodla, the survivor of Kane's famous dog-team. Poor fellow! It seemed as if he must long for his snowy home again, during the sultry days of summer."

We don't know why Toodla, in the summer of 1858, was on this ship, the largest ever built in an American shipyard at its launch in 1846; but as it was owned by Moses and Henry Grinnell's Swallow Tail Line, there was undoubtedly some connection with the shipping magnate who had played such a large role in underwriting Kane's exploits.

Toodla must indeed have longed for his snowy home. It is Dr. Hayes, writing in *An Arctic Boat Journey* in 1861, who gives us the final snapshot of the lead dog. He fell victim, Hayes says, to a Philadelphia summer: "His skin, stuffed and set up with lifelike expression, now graces the gallery of the excellent museum of the Philadelphia Academy of Natural Sciences." (According to Elder, Toodla was an exhibit by the time his book was published in 1858.)

According to Academy records, Toodla's skin and skull were dismounted and added to the study collection in 1940. A full, taxidermied mount of Whitey was also housed at the Academy, but now the remains of neither dog can be located. And so "big yellow" Toodla, the Greenlander, and "little black" Whitey, the Newfoundlander, have been found and lost far from the icy tracts of their homes in a place meant to be safe.

6

Henry Bergh

Saving the Dogs of New York, Not Knowing the Dogs of Greenland

When Elisha Kent Kane mentioned the Society for Preventing Cruelty to Animals, he was referring to the British organization called the Royal Society for the Prevention of Cruelty to Animals, which had been established in 1840. It was not until 1866, more than ten years after Kane's epic voyage and nine years after his death, that Henry Bergh (1813–1888) founded a similar organization in New York, the first of its kind in the United States.

Once focused on the problem of animal cruelty, the "Great Meddler," as Bergh was known, was unstoppable. As soon as the New York legislature had incorporated the charter he proposed and had passed an anticruelty law to support it, Bergh and his American Society for the Prevention of Cruelty to Animals were out on the streets confronting mistreatment of animals in all its forms, especially in regard to horses, but also in regard to dogs, cats, goats, fish, turtles, toads, cattle, milk cows, and even pigeons, for which he developed the substitute clay pigeon for shooting. Nor was his work an intellectual exercise.

An impressive, tall figure in top hat and frock coat, he would accost and stop any cartsman he found beating an exhausted horse or any butcher he found handling sheep like cords of wood, their legs bound together. He would stride into slaughterhouses and burst into pit fighting scenes. He would barge into stables to find horses with raw flesh wounds. He would lecture, write letters, debate, confront, or intrude—whatever would serve his cause. Though he had neither pets nor children, Bergh would go on to found the Society for the Prevention of Cruelty to Children, as well.

At one point he took on P. T. Barnum for feeding live rodents to a boa constrictor in front of paying customers at his "museum." Barnum parried with him through letters to the editor for some time but eventually became a great supporter and friend, serving as a pall bearer at his funeral and providing a monument in his honor in Barnum's hometown of Bridgeport, Connecticut. Barnum, indeed, announced that he was the "Bergh of Bridgeport."

While sledge dogs in the Arctic were being subjected to huge loads, whipping, starvation, thirst, exposure, and what we would generally consider abusive treatment, dogs in America were being fought in pits, forced to bait bulls and fight rats, used to power treadmills in factories and to entertain in circuses, and substituted for horses to pull carts. Often these working dogs were not fed but forced to scrounge for food on their own at night. Broken-down horses and mules were abandoned in the streets. Chickens were plucked and boiled alive, while cockfighting was a popular sport.

In the Arctic, dogs held a special place in Inuit cosmology: A dog, said to be her husband, guarded the underwater home of Sedna, goddess of the water and its creatures. In America, dogs held no mystical power; they were chattel. In the Arctic, dogs meant the difference between life and death; they were partners in the dance of survival. In America, they were expendable, a source of income to be exploited as long as possible; or, if they were lucky, cherished pets. In the Arctic, everything depended on the interdependence of people and animals and the mutual needs of both. When a hunter killed a seal, he would give it a drink of fresh water to satisfy its thirst and acknowledge its spirit.

Consciousness of animals as something other than property had not yet manifested, but the idea of protecting animals from cruelty expanded during Bergh's life. By the time of his death in 1888, humane societies had taken root across the country and thirty-seven of the thirty-eight states at the time had enacted laws prohibiting cruelty to animals. One of the first shelters, a private organization, was established in 1867 in Philadelphia, Kane's city.

If Kane had lived to see it, he would have been pleased with the shelter and given it support. Clearly, he felt an emotional bond with dogs and recognized their need for companionship and decent care. As a medical doctor, he knew what that care required; yet, knowing that salted meat would kill the dogs, in extremity he fed it to them, perhaps because he could not bear to witness their hunger.

His profession was conflicted. At the time, doctors generally supported vivisection, a practice Bergh fought hard against. In 1881, according to *The New York Times*, Bergh gave an illustrated lecture on the subject including an account of a dog that was "operated upon, his sciatic nerve being laid bare, and he being kept under the most horrible torture for 10 hours, his breathing being done artificially through a bellows, operated by an engine, and the dog left alone in his agony through the night, with no sound but the cruel clanking of the engine." In another instance, in 1885, he declared, "It don't hurt men to have a dog's bowels ripped open; they smoke their cigars and go to the theatre after the operation."

It was no better with the law. Police officers and firefighters enjoyed the entertainment of dogfights, while the *National Police Gazette* supported the practice and provided information on it.

Bergh, who felt no emotional bond with animals but considered cruelty a moral issue and a matter of justice, would have been appalled by the treatment of sledge dogs in the high latitudes. But the nineteenth-century Arctic was all-demanding, a place of unique circumstances requiring a unique code. Among the Inuit people, there was no word for "goodbye," only the term *Terbouetie* as a general greeting. Death ruled. Death by cold. Death by drowning. Death by starvation. Death by polar bear. Death by custom. Unless they committed suicide or were hanged, the terminally ill and the elderly were left alone to die in igloos specially constructed for them. Sometimes when traveling and out of food, a group would leave a woman or an old person who might slow their progress walled up in an igloo; if the party succeeded in securing food, they would return for the deserted one, perhaps in time. Baby girls were often killed—literally thrown away (and sometimes eaten by dogs that would then be shunned for a few days)—and defective children abandoned. Dogs, the most valuable property, were eaten in times of dire need, and cannibalism was not unknown.

Funerary rites were quick and simple, the body put in a shallow grave or simply covered with rocks. The whole—the tribe—had to survive, not the individual; and the only way the tribe could survive was to keep moving—wherever game led. That meant the sledges had to keep moving, whether a bitch was whelping or an exhausted dog had to be pulled from

the harness and left behind on the trail for the wolves that were already
close behind. There was no time nor opportunity for the luxury of sentiment. Dogs had to participate in the kill or be killed. There was no looking
back; already the moving ice might have cracked and opened up, return
impossible. Perhaps a dog, or a whole group of travelers, on that ice might
have been cut off from salvation. Perhaps a sheet of ice broke and carried
them away, and there was no rescue. Abandonment and harsh treatment
were not acts of cruelty; they were necessary acts of survival.

At the same time, Charles Francis Hall, especially, recounted instances
of arbitrary treatment of dogs:

According to his interpreter Tookoolito, in her land of Baffin Island,
lightning struck only red dogs and, as a result, they were always killed
when young.

An old woman in the area of Repulse Bay named Evitshung demonstrated how she disciplined her dogs: One day, finding them asleep while
tied up to rocks, she started pelting one with stones while berating it. The
dog's offense, apparently, was howling and barking at night and disturbing
her sleep. Her aim was good and the dog cried with each assault. So serious
was the woman in her lecturing that Hall couldn't keep from laughing.

While traveling in Frobisher Bay, he spied through his telescope his
companion Koojesse "most unmercifully punishing his dog, probably
because the poor animal could not locate a seal igloo." Hall commented,
"The Innuits, when they do punish dogs, beat them cruelly."

There were far worse examples of discipline. Hall's friends Armou
and Ouela of Repulse Bay had beaten several dogs to death with an oar and
one with a hatchet. Armou, after starting on one trek, stopped his team
and beat each dog, "just to warm them up and prepare them for their hard
work." As Hall noted of the dogs:

> Their tenacity of life appears plainly in the midst of their sufferings
> when drawing such heavy loads while half famished, and in their
> endurance of unmerciful poundings. A case is cited, too, in which
> an animal pierced with several rifle balls recovered his full strength,
> although sick when shot.

Lieutenant Francis Leopold McClintock remarked that "[e]ven [Carl]
Petersen, who is generally kind and humane," thought little of beating dogs
about the head with any implement, no matter how heavy. When taken to
task for breaking a whip handle over the head of a dog, Petersen replied,
"That was nothing at all." A friend of his in Greenland, he said, had learned
that he could hit his dogs on the head with a heavy hammer and stun

them but then revive them by laying them down with their mouths open to the wind.

Eivind Astrup, traveling with Robert Peary on his expedition of 1891–1892, recounts the vignette of two men who wake up to find their mittens torn to pieces. One swears, but the other, "who was of graver sort, clutched the heavy whip-handle, seized the dog he judged to be most to blame, and beat it across its lean backbone until the weapon broke into splinters lengthwise and across."

In contrast, Astrup cites the vignette of a dog seizing the last of the blubber in a lamp and its master saying that it was he, the master, who should be lashed because he had not provided sufficient food for the dog.

Beatings were not the only danger. Often a team's track would be marked with blood from paws cut on ice. Colossal fights would occur when the traces tangled or a canine hierarchy had to be sorted out. When not running, the dogs were sometimes restrained from escape by having one of their forelegs tied to their neck; when running, they sometimes had their mouths tied to keep them from eating the harness and lines. Sometimes during a storm, an outer igloo would be built for the dogs, but usually the dogs slept outside, burrowing into snow; and sometimes they froze to death. A dog's tongue could stick to metal it might encounter. Little time was spent nursing sick or injured dogs, and those who could not keep up were simply left behind, often with wolves closing in. When dogs were killed, it was usually by knife; ammunition had to be saved for game.

The dogs were nearly always starving. The Kinnapatoo dogs of the Repulse Bay people, Hall noted, could survive on little food because they were brought up eating only once a week. When full grown, they were inured to hardship.

In hungry times, feedings were meted out in relation to how much work was needed: A certain amount of food given at certain periods could produce a certain amount of pulling power—just as we might fill a car with expensive fuel only to the extent we need its energy. Instead of filling the tank, we might put in ten dollars' worth.

During feeding periods, draconian measures kept order: In one instance related by Hall, the dogs had not been fed in five days. A forty-pound piece of whale beef was cut up and buttered with seal blubber and oil for them. One by one they were led into an abandoned igloo where Hall doled out the portion for each. An assistant stood inside, by the opening, ready with a club to beat off any but the one being fed. A short time before, Armou had almost killed one of his best dogs by throwing a hatchet at him for stealing at such a time.

Hall learned tricks to speed up dogs worn down with hunger: He sent some of the men ahead with a deer bone and knife and had them make strokes as if they were cutting off meat; he also had men cut up small pieces of a sledge made from walrus hide and throw them into the air, letting the dogs see what they were. Hall noted that these experiments worked even for an exhausted dog brought up from the rear and put in the front and were practiced at times when the weather was particularly thick.

But the dogs were not treated harshly for the sake of harshness. Their owners valued them beyond any other possession, fed them as best they could, let them rest when they needed rest, and provided what help they could, running alongside the sledge instead of riding and, if necessary, pulling it up over rough places. At times they rigged tents as sails for the sledge. During his second expedition, Hall commented: "The half-starved dogs were so ferocious as to be almost unmanageable, but their loads were borne forward by the help of a sail, rigged lug-fashion and spread to the southerly winds. They moved rapidly along." When it was necessary to lighten the load, every member of the party ran along with the dogs—men, women, and children. They ran in front of them as well to encourage them and to mark a trail, "tracking" for them around hummocks and other obstructions. Hall commented that women were particularly adept at this, especially in stormy weather. When he set out on his first long-term sledge trip on January 10, 1861, Tookoolito was out in front, tracking for the dogs.

Puppies were brought up by the women and, as pets, played with the children. According to Astrup, there was no place where puppies received more love than among the Inuit people: "The father of the house plays with them and christens them, the mother of the house makes handsome white neckties of bearskin for the dark-skinned little ones, while the children pat and caress them all day long."

Women could own dogs as well as drive them and track for them. In his notes, Hall comments on a dog named Elephant owned by Tookoolito.

Hall always showed particular and detailed concern for his dogs. On October 10, 1871, in what was to become his last will and testament, the commander of the *Polaris* wrote instructions to his crew before departing on an exploratory sledge trip:

> Have the dogs well cared for, feeding them every other day. Look out [for] some good warm place in the ship for the puppies, and have them well nursed.
>
> Have Mr. Morton get and open one can of pemican, and deal that out economically to the puppies. I have great hope of securing many

musk-cattle on my sledge-journey, and then we can spare much of
our ship's provision to the dogs.

...You will have plank and boxes so placed under the [ship's]
poop that the dogs cannot get to the raw-hide wheel-ropes.

On October 24, Hall returned to the *Polaris*, drank a cup of coffee, and
fell ill. On November 8, he died.

It is significant that, in his last orders, Hall remembered the dogs.
Henry Bergh, laboring back in New York to establish justice for animals,
would have approved. Possibly Bergh attended a lecture by Hall, or even
Kane. Possibly he experienced one of the panoramas celebrating the explorers' arctic adventures. He might have even seen one of the dogs exhibited at a lecture or a show. (It was late 1862 when Hall, Tookoolito,
her husband Ebierbing, their child Tukeliketa, and Hall's dog Barbekark
were entertaining New Yorkers at Barnum's American Museum, and 1863
when Bergh left for Russia to take up a diplomatic post at the court of
Czar Alexander II.) Certainly he read the reports of the arctic explorers
in the papers. He might well have discussed the subject with his adver-
sary-turned-friend, P. T. Barnum. But whether he gave thought to the needs
of the sledge dogs can only be guessed. There were problems enough in
New York, where all too many dogs and children were regularly abused
and neglected.

It was the city where municipal dogcatchers, paid by the dog not the
hour, rounded up as many as 300 dogs a day—some stolen from their
owners' yards or even from inside their houses—put them in a cage, and
swung it out and dumped it over the East River.

7

Oosisoak and Arkadik

King and Queen of the Sledge Dogs

Traveling with Isaac I. Hayes, 1860–1861,
in Search of the Open Polar Sea

Elisha Kent Kane's young surgeon, Isaac Israel Hayes (1832–1881), had just graduated from the University of Pennsylvania Medical School when he joined Kane's expedition of 1853–1855 in search of Sir John Franklin, but what he lacked in experience he made up for in energy and ambition. Like Kane, he was an enthusiastic proponent of the fabled Open Polar Sea and was determined to find it. To launch an expedition, however, was a daunting task.

Hayes had to compete not only with the looming problems of the Civil War but also with the upstart would-be explorer Charles Francis Hall, who had an equally strong sense of mission to penetrate the Arctic. But Hayes succeeded, with private backing that came largely from Henry Grinnell and fellow members of the American Geographical and Statistical Society of New York. When he sailed on July 6, 1860—six weeks after Hall—Hayes was in full command of his 133-ton schooner, the *United States*. Second in command was August Sonntag, the astronomer. Meanwhile, the under-capitalized Hall traveled as a nonpaying passenger on a whaler bound for its fishing grounds, an indigent one-man expedition.

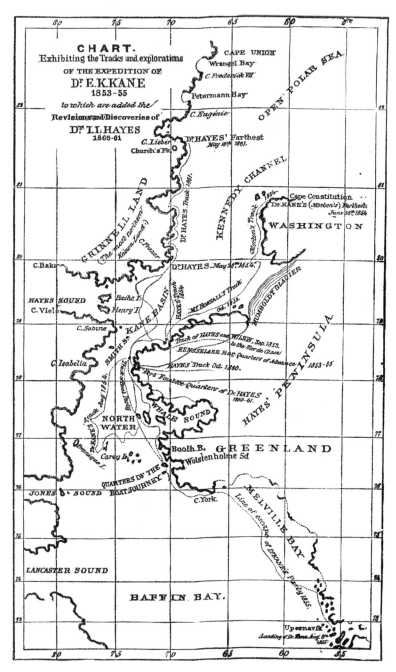

Chart exhibiting the tracks and explorations of the expedition of Dr. E. K. Kane, 1853–55, to which are added the revisions and discoveries of Dr. I. I. Hayes, 1860–61.

Isaac I. Hayes, *An Arctic Boat Journey in the Autumn of 1854*, p. 1

As with Kane, Hayes's plans rested upon availability of dogs. His goal, in fact, was similar to his predecessor's—to sail up the west coast of Greenland, strike out across Smith Sound, and travel up the east coast of Ellesmere Island north in search of the Open Polar Sea—what was to become the well-beaten path of the "American Route."

Trouble began at Pröven, Greenland, where Hayes's schooner *United States* made landfall on August 6, 1860. It was there Hayes learned that an epidemic had wiped out half the dog population during the past year. The residents could not be persuaded to sell any of the survivors. The chief trader, Dr. Rudolph, went into action on Hayes's behalf and sent word out to Upernavik and other settlements that the Americans wanted dogs. A "half-dozen old dogs and a less number of good ones" were brought in by the summons.

The chief trader, however, provided a "fine team" and Hayes took on three local hunters and an interpreter-dog driver, Peter Jensen, who came with his own team, reputed to be the best in northern Greenland. The addition of two Danish sailors increased the number of crew to twenty. There were now thirty-six dogs on board.

But inside Hayes's cabin was one special dog, a Newfoundland puppy named General who had been with him since the *United States* had sailed out of Boston Harbor:

> We have got to be the best of friends. He knows perfectly well when the hour comes to go out after breakfast, and whines impatiently at the door; and when he sees me take my cap and mittens from their peg his happiness is complete. And the little fellow makes a most excellent companion. He does not bore me with senseless talk, but tries his best to make himself agreeable. If in the sober mood, he walks beside me with stately gravity; but when not so inclined he rushes round in the wildest manner,—rolling himself in the snow, tossing the white flakes to the wind, and now and then tugging at my huge fur mittens or at the tail of my fur coat. Some time ago he fell down the hatch and broke his leg, and while this was healing I missed him greatly. There is excellent companionship in a sensible dog.

Working their way through the usual hazards of weather, ice, and hidden reef, the untried expedition reached Melville Sound, home of the "middle ice," where they were almost immediately challenged by icebergs, floes, snow, wind, and conditions that would have tried even the most experienced of crews; but this crew was anything but experienced.

Near Cape York, at the northern end of Melville Sound, Hayes started looking out for Hans Hendrik, who had left the Kane expedition to marry, and the search was soon successful. Hans recognized Hayes and Sonntag. Happily joining the *United States*, he brought along his wife, Merkut (Hayes named her such, but she is usually known as Mersek), and a firstborn child, Pingasuk, "the Pretty One"; he also had in-laws who wanted to board but were rejected.

After the family had been scrubbed and put into red flannel shirts and other "similar luxuries of civilization," Hayes's attention focused on the coastline. Soon they were passing Booth Bay, Hayes's grim quarters during his misadventure with the Kane expedition in the autumn of 1854—a place of many bad memories—and then came the pack ice as they entered Smith Sound.

Every effort to cross the Sound was thwarted by ice, wind, and storm. Eventually—and with great disappointment—Hayes had to give up hope of reaching the Canadian side and anchored his battered vessel in a protected spot on the Greenland coast. He named the harbor Port Foulke, in honor of one of his chief benefactors. It was approximately eighty miles south of Kane's winter quarters at Rensselaer Harbor. Soon the ice closed around them and all efforts were given over to preparing for the lean months ahead.

The dogs were fed every second day, sometimes receiving an entire caribou at a single meal. "They were very ravenous," Hayes says, "and, having been much reduced by their hard life at sea, they caused an immense drain upon our resources."

The dogs soon recovered, however, and took up their duties of hunting and practice for sledge exploration. One mid-October day in the long twilight, Hayes had an exhilarating ride up a nearby fiord with Jensen driving a team of twelve. The animals were "strong and healthy"—and very fast. "They whirl my Greenland sledge over the ice with a celerity not calculated for weak nerves," Hayes commented. He clocked them at six miles in twenty-eight minutes and back over the same distance, without a break, in thirty-three minutes. He raced with Sonntag and wished some of his Saratoga friends could witness this new form of competition.

As Kane had stated before him, the whip was critical. On this particular day, Jensen decided to punish a young and recalcitrant dog by whipping the tip of one of his ears off—as precisely, Hayes noted, "as with a knife."

The dogs, Hayes said, would take off after any prey—fox, seal, bird, or bear—unless they were controlled by the whip in the hands of a competent driver. Even for a driver as experienced as Jensen, the challenge was constant. On that same day, Hayes reports, the dogs were running after a fox, and were taking us toward what appeared to be unsafe ice. The wind was blowing hard, and the lash was sometimes driven back into the driver's face,—hence the difficulty. The whip, however, finally brought them to reason, and in full view of the game, and within a few yards of the treacherous ice, they came first down into a limping trot and then stopped, most unwillingly. Of course this made them very cross, and a general fight—fierce and angry—now followed, which was not quieted until the driver had sailed in among them and knocked them to right and left with his hard hickory whip-stock.

That is the story, repeated often—but mostly by neophytes—of humiliation by sledge team. Experience was no protection. The dogs, of course, were especially ready to test a new driver, as they were when Hayes set out to take a turn around the harbor. The dogs "may, perhaps, have wanted to see what manner of man this new driver was. They were very familiar with him personally, for he had petted them often enough; but they had not before felt the strength of his arm." The dogs immediately sensed his weakness—the whip was repeatedly blown back into his face and his arm felt paralyzed with the exertion—and they looked back over their shoulders. When they saw the lash was not coming, they moved to the right and soon were careening off on their own happy course, dancing and barking with delight. Finally, after heading them into hummocky ice, which slowed them down, Hayes jumped off the sledge and capsized it, anchoring the runaways. He lashed them severely, turned the sledge up, and, when he gave them the command to start, the team trotted off demurely: a lesson learned by both sides.

No matter how difficult the dogs, however, Hayes said the Esquimaux were worse, for they could not be controlled by anything and were not so useful. He said this in spite of having been saved by them during his ordeal as a member of the "Withdrawing Party" from Kane's ship in the autumn of 1854.

The dogs were getting "a little toned down" by October 21 and did not need so much food, Hayes noted: "They are lively enough still, but not so hard to keep in hand." He remarked also that they preferred sleeping in the open rather than within the snow walls built alongside the vessel; only in particularly cold and windy conditions would they seek the shelter of the walls. Other explorers noted the same, though Kane remarked on how the dogs sought the warmth and light of human companionship. The dying bitch who had approached him and licked him proved the mutual need for contact.

Hayes found much about the dogs curious and worthy of note, especially their social order:

> They have their leader and their sub-leaders—the rulers and the ruled—
> like any other community desiring good government. The governed get
> what rights they can, and the governors bully them continually in or-
> der that they may enjoy security against rebellion, and live in peace.
> And a community of dogs is really organized on the basis of correct
> principles. As an illustration,—my teams are under the control of a big
> aggressive brute, who sports a dirty red uniform with snuff-colored
> facings, and has sharp teeth. He possesses immense strength, and
> his every movement shows that he is perfectly conscious of it. In the
> twinkling of an eye he can trounce any dog in the whole herd; and he
> seems to possess the faculty of destroying conspiracies, cabals, and
> all evil designings against his stern rule. None of the other dogs like
> him, but they cannot help themselves; they are afraid to turn against
> him, for when they do so there is no end to the chastisements which
> they receive. Now Oosisoak (for that is his name) has a rival, a huge,
> burly fellow with black uniform and white collar. This dog is called
> Karsuk, which expresses the complexion of his coat. He is larger than
> Oosisoak, but not so active nor so intelligent. Occasionally he has a
> set-to with his master; but he always comes off second best, and his
> unfortunate followers are afterwards flogged in detail by the merci-
> less redcoat. The place of Oosisoak, when harnessed to the sledge, is
> on the left of the line, and that of Karsuk on the right.

There was another contender, Erebus, king dog of Sonntag's team, who had outfought Karsuk but not Oosisoak. The balance was beneficial, Hayes noted, because a change would bring anarchy and ferocious battles until a new order was established.

The fierce Oosisoak was capable of sentiment, he said:

> He has chosen one to share the glory of his reign, to console his
> sorrows, and to lick his wounds when fresh from the bloody field.
> Oosisoak has a queen; and this object of his affection, this idol of
> his heart, is never absent from his side. She runs beside him in the
> team, and she fights for him harder than any one of his male subjects.
> In return for this devotion he allows her to do pretty much as she
> pleases. She may steal the bone out of his mouth, and he gives it up
> to her with a sentimental grimace that is quite instructive. But it
> happens sometimes that he is himself hungry, and he trots after her,
> and when he thinks that she has got her share he growls significantly;
> whereupon she drops the bone without even a murmur. If the old

Track chart of the boat journey, 1854.
Hayes, *An Arctic Boat Journey...*, p. 58

fellow happens to be particularly cross when a reindeer is thrown to the pack, he gets upon it with his forefeet, begins to gnaw away at the flank, growling a wolfish growl all the while, and no dog dare come near until he has had his fill except Queen Arkadik, (for by that name is she known), nor can she approach except in one direction. She must come alongside of him, and crawl between his fore-legs and eat lovingly from the spot where he is eating.

Winter deepened and ventures beyond the schooner became more difficult, but hunting was always a possibility. One early November day, Sonntag was returning from an exploring trip when bear tracks sent his two teams, driven by Jensen and Hans, on a wild chase. The prey turned out to be a sow and cub, which took off toward open water. Sonntag was thrown off his sledge into the hummocky ice, but no obstacle could stop the dogs. In fifteen minutes they were only a few hundred yards from the bears, which were by then close to the water. The cub was having a hard time keeping up, the mother crying piteously. As the mother approached the water, she would repeatedly rush back to her cub to encourage it to hurry. At fifty yards, the drivers slipped the knot that bound the traces, and the dogs, running free, bounded toward the bears.

Oosisoak led the attack, Arkadik close beside him, the twenty other dogs behind them. One young dog rushed the sow and was crushed by her paw. Oosisoak came in on her flank while Arkadik tore at her haunch. Karsuk flew at the cub, but the cub fought back. A small dog named Schnapps was doubled over with a blow. Erebus then came to the assistance of Oosisoak, leading his minions to the opposite flank. The cub was bleeding to death as Jensen and Hans drew their rifles and fired at the sow. The dogs, leaving the cub, put their full attention on the mother. More rifle shots brought her down though she continued to fight off the dogs. As the cub fell down at its mother's feet, she forgot the dogs and, leaning down, licked its face and tried to coax it up. Realizing that it was dead, she then returned to furious battle with the dogs. She was bounding after Hans, whose rifle had misfired, when Sonntag and Jensen succeeded in killing her.

Exciting hunts soon gave way to somber thoughts. Early in December the strange disease of the south Greenland dogs—which Hayes was confident to have escaped—struck his team. The victim dogs showed great restlessness, running haphazardly around the ship, raising and lowering head and tail, then running off barking, returning to the ship with bloodshot eyes and froth running from the mouth, snapping at everything in their way. After a few hours, the stricken dogs weakened, staggered, and collapsed in a series of fits. Death followed in less than twenty-four hours from the onset of the symptoms. Hayes dissected the first victims but could find no cause and thought, since the affected dogs desired, rather than shunned, water that it was not "hydrophobia," or rabies.

During the first four days, seven dogs died. Hayes looked on in horror at "my fine teams melting away and my hopes endangered." Among the first victims was the noble Karsuk, the second leader:

> I have never seen such expression of ferocity and mad strength ex-
> hibited by any living creature, as he manifested two hours after the
> first symptoms were observed. Thinking that confinement might do
> good, and desiring to see if the disease would not wear itself out, I
> had him caught and put into a large box on the deck; but this seemed
> rather to aggravate than to soothe violence of the symptoms. He tore
> the boards with indescribable fierceness, and, getting his teeth into
> a crack, ripped off splinter after splinter until he had made a hole
> almost large enough for his head, when I ordered him to be shot. At
> this moment his eyes were like balls of fire; he had broken off one of
> his tusks, and his mouth was spouting blood.

During December, eighteen dogs died. With other losses (which Hayes does not explain), the expedition was now down to twelve dogs. Within a week, there were nine fit to travel and one recovering from an injury.

Hayes had reached a crisis: "it became very evident that, unless I should be able to supply the loss, all of my plans would be rendered abortive." He and Sonntag decided they had to open communications with the residents of Whale Sound, to the south of them, in order to obtain dogs. The distances to various settlements where animals might be found were approximated to be 100 to 150 miles. But the effort had to be made, and as quickly as possible. As soon as the new moon appeared in late December— and if there were still dogs enough alive—Sonntag and Hans would start on their desperate mission. On December 21, the two men set out with the nine remaining fit dogs.

In darkness and worry, the year turned from 1860 to 1861. During that long, anxious period, Hayes suffered yet another loss, of whose cause he gives us no details. On January 5, he wrote:

> I have no longer a dog. The General was the last of them, and he died
> two days ago. Poor fellow! I had become more than ever attached to
> him lately, especially since he had quite recovered from the accident
> to his leg, and seemed likely to be useful with the sledge after a while.
> It seems strange to see the place so deserted and so quiet. In the early

Attacked by dogs.

Hayes, An Arctic Boat Journey...., p. 168

winter I never went out of the vessel on the ice without having the whole pack crowding around me, playing and crying in gladness at my coming; now their lifeless carcasses are strewn about the harbor, half buried in snow and ice....There was a companionship in the dogs, which, apart from their usefulness, attached them to everybody, and in this particular we all feel alike the greatness of the loss.

Anxious for that companionship, Hayes had Jensen catch him a blue fox for a pet, and the young four-pound female captive settled into his cabin quite happily. He named her Birdie and quickly became attached:

Birdie has become quite tame, and does great credit to her instructor. She is the most cunning creature that was ever seen, and does not make a bad substitute for the General. She takes the General's place at my table, as she has his place in my affections; but she sits in my lap, where the General never was admitted, and, with her delicate little paws on the cloth, she makes a picture. Why, she is indeed a perfect little *gourmande*, well bred, too, and clever. When she takes the little morsels into her mouth her eyes sparkle with delight, she wipes her lips, and looks up at me with a *coquetterie* that is perfectly irresistible....She has her own fork; but she has not yet advanced sufficiently far in the usages of civilization to handle it for herself, so I convey the delicate morsels to her mouth.

When she ate too greedily, Hayes would tap her on the nose with the fork. He watched with delight as she cleaned herself—"She is everlastingly brushing her clothes"—and washed in a bath of snow, barking with happiness. She would run loose in his cabin, bounding over the shelves, until lured down by a piece of raw venison, for which she would beg by creeping into his lap. Then, he said, she "puts out her little tongue with quick impatience, and barks bewitchingly if the beginning of the repast is too long delayed."

Like Kane, who had also had a pet fox, Hayes found temporary consolation. But Birdie could not dispel the worries that deepened as days went by without word of Sonntag and Hans.

The terrible news came a month after their departure when two Inuit visitors appeared at the ship: Sonntag was dead. He had died of hypothermia after falling into seawater and being rescued by Hans. Hans arrived two days later, with Mersek's brother, father, and mother, and five dogs. Four dogs had broken down along the way and were left to die. The exhausted five, who had to be carried almost lifeless from their last stop, were the survivors of the original thirty-six.

According to Hans's account, he had done everything he could for Sonntag; but Hans had not insisted that Sonntag change clothing after his immersion and before returning to their previous shelter. Hayes never forgave Hans, wrote bitterly of his perceived failures, and, forever after, suspicion clung to the hunter's reputation.

Hayes took on another, larger fox as a pet, this one a white one, but it proved "thoroughly wild and untamable."

On February 18, the sun reappeared and prospects seemed far cheerier. The five dogs had recovered, but these were not enough for the work of exploration. If more could not be found, men would have to take up the traces.

Suddenly a party of three visitors driving two sledges with eight dogs turned up at the ship. To Hayes's delight, it turned out to be friends (though with a complex past) from the Kane expedition: Kalutunah, considered the best hunter of the area, who was also an *angakok*, or shaman; Tattarat; and Myouk. News revealed that Kalutunah's enemy, Sipsu, had been killed, but also that many of the local people had died. It was learned, too, that the same outbreak of canine disease that had swept through Hayes's team had decimated the teams of the whole area. But in exchange for presents, Kalutunah said, he would supply some dogs: two of the four that composed his present team. From Tattarat Hayes acquired one of his three and from Myouk, one, the only dog he possessed. When the visitors left after several days, they promised to return with friends and dogs. Almost immediately, two more visitors arrived—Amalatok and his son of Northumberland Island. They had four dogs, and after Hayes had cured the father of a malady, Amalatok insisted on giving the doctor his best dog and then sold him another. Now there were eleven dogs. Once more, the kennels were filling up, much to the relief of Hayes.

After several days, Kalutunah returned, with his family. He had with him six dogs that he promised to lend to the doctor in exchange for food for his family. Myouk arrived next, on foot, with his wife in a ragged coat and a baby on her back. They had walked 150 miles. Hayes now possessed seventeen dogs—as well as a growing list of dependents.

In spite of his initial joy, Hayes soon discovered that the new acquisitions were far inferior to the old teams and that they needed as much rest and good food as he could supply. And, along with seventeen dogs, there were now seventeen Inuit guests in residence, the women sewing clothes and boots and the men hunting for the benefit of the expedition: a colony of interdependence. Kalutunah had moved with his family to a hut at Etah but remained in contact.

As the *United States* settled into its new routine, it was time to retrieve and bury the body of Sonntag. Hayes sent the mate with two teams, Kalutunah driving one and Hans the other. When returned to the ship, the body was placed in the observatory that Sonntag had managed and spent much time in until a coffin could be built. Sonntag's remains were buried with solemnity in a grave dug out with difficulty from a frozen terrace, then covered with stones.

On March 16, Hayes started for the north with two sledges, one driven by Jensen and one by Kalutunah with his six dogs. There would have been seventeen dogs altogether, but one had died and one had been crippled in a fight, bringing the number down to fifteen fit for service.

The goal of this intermediary journey was to determine whether it was best to continue on up the Greenland coast, as Kane had done, or to strike out west across Smith Sound to Grinnell Land (Ellesmere Island) as the point of departure for the Pole. Five miles out, Jensen, along with his whole team and sledge, fell into open water. All were saved and rushed back to the ship for a quick drying-out and change of clothes. In a matter of hours, they started out again.

A visit to Kane's Rensselaer Harbor revealed chaotic ice in the bay, while Fern Rock, where Kane's observatory had stood and Sonntag had watched so many hours, was almost hidden by the ravages of an avalanche. There was no sign of the *Advance* but one small bit of a deck plank, and even Kalutunah could not give a definite account of what had happened to the ice-locked brig after Kane's party had abandoned it. Hayes visited the graves of Baker and Schubert.

After a stop at Cairn Point—from where he planned to cross the Sound to the Canadian side—Hayes returned to the *United States* with utmost speed. The dogs had been able to feast on a caribou. A gale was blowing. The temperature was 52° below zero. Drifting snow was lashing them cruelly. But the dogs were turned toward home. They covered the last thirty miles in three and one-half hours.

On April 3, Hayes set out on his spring exploration, accompanied by twelve crew members. Jensen drove his team of eight, and Knorr, the commander's secretary, a team of six. A group of eight men was harnessed to a sledge that carried the twenty-foot metallic boat with which Hayes planned to navigate the Open Polar Sea.

Conditions did not cooperate. The temperature, at the outset, was 32° below zero, while in the hut the first night it stood at 1° above zero. At Cairn Point, the designated jumping-off place for Smith Sound, Hayes decided to leave the boat; it was too difficult to get it over the broken ice.

Instead, cargo alone would be carried across the frozen sound to Grinnell Land on the other side. But even with the boat jettisoned, the going was daunting. As the party attempted to cross the tumultuous ice, conditions only worsened. At one point, Hayes wrote,

> The poor dogs were almost buried out of sight. They had all crouched together in a heap; and as the drift accumulated over them they poked their heads further and further up into it; and when I came to count them to see if any had left us and run back to the ship or been frozen to death, it was truly counting noses. There were four-teen of them.

The men gave out before the dogs and Hayes experienced only hope-lessness and despair. Smith Sound, he says, "has given me but one succes-sion of baffling obstacles."

Sending back most of the men, he continued on with three assistants, one of them Jensen, and the fourteen dogs. Shortly after starting out, Jensen's sledge tumbled over a decline and injured a leg of one of the dogs. The dog was turned loose and hobbled along to camp. The whole team, exhausted, needed to be nursed. They were fed a special warm supper. Only the night before, they had torn apart Jensen's sledge, eaten the lash-ings, and scattered pieces of the sledge around the camp, trying to tear open the tin cans of meat; one ate a pouch of tobacco, another the only bar of soap.

The dogs were starving. As frozen dried beef was being chopped up for them, "the wolfish brutes fill the air with the most hideous cries." They would eat their masters, Hayes stated, if given the chance. While feed-ing them, Knorr had stumbled among the pack and "had not McDonald pounced upon them on the instant, I believe they would have made a meal of him before he could rise."

Ravenous, they were also worn out. Hayes blamed himself. He had cut down on their food—their last meal had been only one and a half pounds each; and if they failed, all would be lost.

After thirty-one torturous days, Hayes and his party succeeded in crossing the Sound, but there was scant energy left to explore possible routes to the Polar Sea. One of the reasons the dogs were so spent, Hayes noted, was that walking, as they had had to do through the contorted ice, is as distressing to their spirits and energies "as the hauling of a dray would be to a blooded horse." And they had not only had to walk, they had had to drag their heavy load up and down over an enormous jumble of hummocks.

Good cheer.

Hayes, *An Arctic Boat Journey....* p. 253

At the end of the second day of struggling up the coast, the party camped near the farthest point north reached by Hayes during the expedition with Kane in 1854. They continued on, Jensen disabled by a leg injury and a strained back. McDonald and Knorr were worn out, too, but Hayes would not give up: "I have yet my dogs in fair condition; and that is the best part of the battle."

Hayes left Jensen with McDonald and five dogs and went on with Knorr and nine dogs. Soon he passed the position reached by Morton in 1854 and pushed on to reach the open water on which he had pinned all his hopes and efforts. It was no time to celebrate, however. Rough ice, deep snow, and fog frustrated their attempt. At one point, crossing a frozen bay, they were saved by the "unerring instinct of the dogs" warning them of rotten ice ahead. The men doubled back and tried a different route, walking in front of the dogs to encourage them. All efforts failed, however. Every time they came to soft ice, the dogs refused to proceed, and Hayes had to retreat from the bay and return to land.

There, he climbed a cliff to survey the ice-held landscape. He saw a headland and surmised it to be at 82° 30' and approximately 450 miles from the North Pole. The sea below him was mottled with open areas. Hayes was confident: "Suffice it here to say that all the evidences showed that I stood upon the shores of the Polar Basin, and that the broad ocean lay at my feet. . . . and that the little margin of ice which lined the shore was being steadily worn away; and within a month, the whole sea would be as free from ice as I had seen the north water of Baffin Bay."

The journey was ended. Now Hayes had to make his way back to Port Foulke and prepare his schooner to sail across the Sound and up into the Polar Sea. First, he planted flags in token of the discovery. One was that of the United States Exploring Expedition (1838–1842) under the command of Lieutenant Charles Wilkes. This epic voyage was marred by contentious relationships between Wilkes and his officers and ended in court martial charges. This problematic symbol had previously been carried by De Haven and Kane (and would later be carried by Hall).

On May 19, 1861, Hayes determined his observation point to be 81° 35' N, midway into Lady Franklin Bay, and claimed "the most northern land that has ever been reached" (though not matching William Edward Parry's 1827 record of 82° 45' and doubted by those who have studied his calculations).

The return trip started in a fierce storm that broke down the reserves of the dogs:

The poor beasts fell in their tracks the moment the whip ceased to be applied. I had never before seen them so much broken. To halt was of little use, as rest, without food, would do harm rather than good; and as we had no shelter, and in the item of food were as badly off as the dogs, there was nothing for us to do but to hold on and get through to Jensen's camp, or perish in the storm.

They did reach it, after extraordinary effort. Hayes recalled only "an endless pounding of the dogs, who wanted to lie down with every step." Once refreshed, they continued on, struggling from cache to cache. One of the teams fell through the ice but was extricated with great difficulty. At one point the party was floating on a floe.

Finally, they had crossed Smith Sound and made landfall at Cairn Point, but the dogs were decimated. One collapsed and died in a fit. Two others followed. Another, incapacitated, was shot. For this last, it was a grim end: "Much to my surprise, as soon as the bullet struck the animal, wounding him but slightly and causing him to set up a terrible cry, his companions in the team flew upon him and tore him to pieces in an instant, and those who were lucky enough to get a fragment of him were tearing the flesh from his bones almost before the echo of his last howl had died away in the solitude."

Below Cairn Point, the sea was impassable and the party kept to the land ice, climbing over the mountains. The sledges had to be abandoned and the dogs let loose: "Most of them sneaked away as soon as loosened from the sledges, and would not follow us." Three stayed by the men: Oosisoak and his queen, Arkadik, as well as Nenook, the "finest" of Kalutunah's dogs. Later, three others returned, but four were missing when the journey of 1,300 miles ended at the ice-held *United States*.

When he had recovered from the rigors of the trip and surveyed the schooner, Hayes discovered it was far too damaged to proceed farther north. He was forced to abandon his long-held plans to cross the Sound and sail up the coast of Grinnell Land to the Open Polar Sea. To limp home was the most that could be hoped for.

Hayes visited Kalutunah at Etah and returned to him his dog. (Was this Nenook? He does not say.) He apologized for returning only one dog of the eight provided him, but Kalutunah seemed satisfied with the largesse Hayes had been providing and, indeed, seemed to fear that the return of the dog would cancel Hayes's hospitality.

On July 13, 1861, with the battered schooner almost free of ice, Hayes went ashore to say goodbye to his Inuit friends. As he noted, they had given him, with alacrity, their greatest gift and treasure: dogs—and without these dogs, he said, "I could have done absolutely nothing." In spite of all he had given the Inuit people, nothing, he said, could replace a lost dog; and now, out of all those he had been given, he was able to return only two.

Were these King Oosisoak and Queen Arkadik? Hayes does not say—only that the people took consolation from his hope of a speedy return.

On his way back to Boston, the commander stopped at Upernavik. There he made arrangements with a local family to prepare for his return the following season. They were to construct sledges and to rear and accumulate dogs for him.

But, of course, what Hayes returned to in the United States was the Civil War and military duty. Upon his return, a *Harper's Weekly* article declared that in spite of Hayes's not having advanced knowledge of the Arctic, "the romance and the heroism are always the same, and every voyage does us the great service of destroying the terror which invests the silent world of ice." But the romance was wearing thin. The terror had moved from the silent world of ice to the deafening battlegrounds of the Civil War.

Eight years would pass before Hayes could get back to Greenland, a journey he would chronicle in *The Land of Desolation: Being a Personal Narrative of Observation and Adventure in Greenland* (1872). This was a very different venture. Traveling with artists on a scenic cruise, he provides a dull travelogue strangely disconnected from what had gone before. There is almost no mention of the animals on which he formerly depended for his life except one in which he describes "packs of howling, vicious dogs." But he saves his real venom for Hans Hendrik. Meeting him again, he presents him as a savage reprobate: "I am fully convinced that he was instrumental in causing the death of two of my command." Hayes makes this charge in spite of the fact that the first death of a crew member occurred before Hans had joined the expedition.

We can only hope that Hayes reserved some time for happier memories of flying across the snow behind an eager team, a team with its own king and queen, a team ready to pull until it burst, the frozen air split with the crack of the whip, the laughter, the encouraging "Ka! Ka! Ka! Ka!" of the driver, and somewhere up ahead an igloo, with perhaps something warm to eat and drink.

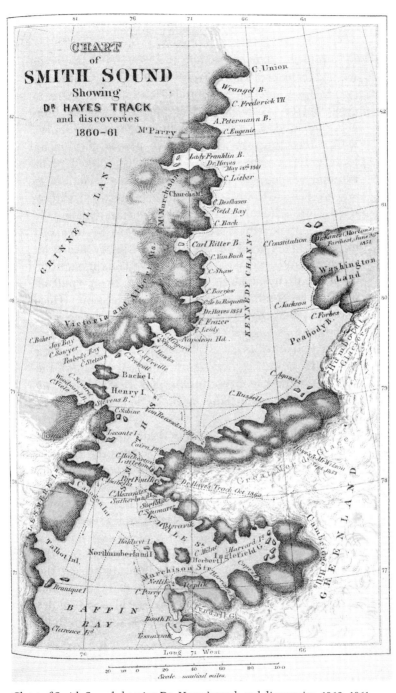

Chart of Smith Sound showing Dr. Hayes's track and discoveries, 1860–1861.

Hayes, *The Open Polar Sea: A Narrative of a Voyage of Discovery in the Schooner* "United States," p. 72; Semi-Rare Book Collection, Alaska and Polar Regions Collections & Archives, Rasmuson Library, University of Alaska Fairbanks

Rounding Cape Alexander on the ice foot.

Hayes, *An Arctic Boat Journey. . . .*, p. 318

An arctic team.
Hayes, *The Open Polar Sea*, p. 104)

A bear hunt.
Hayes, *The Open Polar Sea,* p. 174

Crossing the hummocks.
Hayes, *The Open Polar Sea*, p. 322

8

Disease and Diet

The sledge dogs' diet consisted of whatever—if anything—was available: in good times, walrus, seal, whale, caribou, or bear meat. In bad times there was "condemned" and miscellaneous canned, salted, and dried food (including, Carl Petersen remarks of Elisha Kent Kane's voyage, "half-corrupt lard"); leather artifacts including harnesses, shoes, and mittens; cornmeal and beans; bread and bread dust; scraps of anything approaching edible, including fellow dogs, often cooked in a "soup." In the worst of times they ate nothing.

Francis Leopold McClintock stated that Esquimaux dogs will eat anything but fox or raven, but there were exceptions: "One of ours, old 'Harness Jack,' devoured a raven with much gusto the other day." Birds of all manner, indeed, seemed desirable. Just before his comment on dogs not eating ravens, McClintock described how a "wearied" ptarmigan alighted near the ship only to be caught and devoured by the dogs, "and scarcely a feather remained by the time I could rush on deck." Kane harangued his dogs for eating birds' nests he had collected. August Sonntag remarked in his journal that the dogs "are fed on the offals, principally of birds."

William Barr refers, giving an earlier example, to Franklin searcher Emile Frédéric de Bray as shooting some seabirds for his dogs.

A universally popular item was pemmican, a staple of dried meat mixed with lard and sometimes with dried fruit—a sort of mincemeat. (Grapes, raisins, and currants are now considered toxic for dogs.) Each explorer took pride in his recipe. Of his pemmican, Charles Francis Hall said, "I used the best of beef and beef suet in the place of what is generally used, to wit, beef and hog's fat." He also gave clear, precise directions for the manufacture of what he considered a high-quality product. Frederick Cook gave his recipe as "pounded dried beef, sprinkled with a few raisins and some currants, and slightly sweetened with sugar . . . cemented together with heated beef tallow." Robert Peary, who lobbied the army to include pemmican as part of its rations, said his concoction was composed of "lean beef dried at an equable temperature till nearly all of the water had been expelled, then ground up and mixed in large cauldrons with hot beef suet, in the proportion of two-thirds of ground beef and one-third beef suet. A little sugar and a few dry currants were added, and the pemmican run into cans and sealed up." Whale meat, he argued, could be substituted at great cost savings. Pemmican aged well. Peary, who claimed pemmican was the most essential item of any serious sledge journey—and all that was necessary for dogs—bought what was left of the supply intended for Adolphus Washington Greely and used it for his first two explorations. It did not matter, he said, that some cans had gone bad; the dogs would eat it anyway.

Dogs, however, did not always have access to this much-touted delicacy and would ingest whatever they could find—often with fatal results. Bones are sometimes mentioned as the cause of death and sometimes tin cans or fiber such as oakum, used for caulking; but, undoubtedly, the most dangerous item was salt meat such as pork, always found in great quantity on the nineteenth-century ships of discovery.

Fridtjof Nansen, while reading Kane's book on board the *Fram*, took the doctor to task for "miserably inadequate" preparations. "Almost all the dogs died of bad food," he claimed. His statement might apply equally to all arctic expeditions.

Feedings typically ranged from every other day to twice a week. Frederick Schwatka, after a series of strenuous marches, remarked that his dogs are "averaging eight days between feeds." During summer seasons when they were not working, dogs were often put on an island to fend for themselves. No matter what the schedule, the dogs were nearly always starving, ready to do anything to find something other than wood or stone that they might eat. They would attack sledges to get at their precious cargos, sneak into tents, igloos, and cooking areas to carry off what they could—a hanging hare, a slab of bacon, biological specimens, that night's supper for the men, human hair after a barbering, harnesses, clothing made of skin, paper that had been wrapped around some item of food, human waste left in an igloo just before it was abandoned. The only edible item they could not take hold of was frozen walrus meat. The thick skin was simply impenetrable.

Hall, during his first voyage, told the story of the dog Merok, brought into the igloo one night because he was starving, who leapt at a hunter coming in through the door with seal blubber strips, seizing the meat. Although Hall thrust his hands into the dog's mouth and Tookoolito and another woman tried to fight him off, Merok succeeded in devouring what he had grabbed.

As Kane pointed out, starving dogs would readily eat puppies, and puppies would eat puppies. Any animal exhibiting weakness would be in danger. J. B. Mauch, captain's clerk on the *Polaris*, described how the bitch Smarty was devoured by other dogs soon after giving birth. McClintock told the story of a bitch who, when muzzled overnight to keep her from eating her harness, was attacked and killed by her *"amiable* sisterhood." Instances are given, too, of a whelping bitch in harness dropping her puppies on the trail to be eaten by teammates running behind. Nansen gave us the bad news "that 'Job' is dead, torn in pieces by the other dogs. He was found a good way from the ship,—'Old Suggen' lying watching the corpse, so that no other dog could get to it." In another act of compassion, McClintock's Harness Jack positioned himself uncomfortably on top of the cask where a bitch was whelping to protect the puppies from otherwise certain attack.

Dogs would not tolerate weakness any more than their human keepers. Hunger and cold were snapping at their heels. To look back was to turn to a pillar of ice. But, at the same time, they were not without the capacity for devoted protection of a friend.

Scenes of their feeding usually involve violence to keep order. Hall, at the beginning of his first arctic saga, presented an idyllic picture of shipboard feeding as he threw small fish one by one to the dogs waiting patiently in a circle around him. Other vignettes, however, show the dogs being led up a gangplank or into an igloo one by one to be fed separately, crew members standing by with clubs to keep order, and on numerous occasions we are told the men found this work exciting. Margaret Penny, wife of Captain Penny, in her diary of a winter at Baffin Island, 1857–1858, provided a scene of dogs being fed from the refuse of whale oil: "They were like a pack of wolves. The man was obliged to throw the tub from him or then they would have trampled him down, so hungry were they." Later, she describes how the dogs tried desperately to get into the hut where the oil was boiled, only to be beaten back. When they tried to get into the cauldron of boiling oil itself, the whalers had to cover it with a weighted lid and tie it down with ropes.

Diet and disease are inextricably linked. Starvation, "binge" eating, consumption of toxic materials, and lack of nutritional value and necessary vitamins and minerals would predispose dogs to a host of ailments. Combined with severe weather, unsanitary conditions, crowding, vermin, and lack of shelter, bedding, and water—not to mention attention, affection, and medical care—a poor diet such as the nineteenth-century sledge dogs suffered would weaken defenses and lead to dangerous health conditions. As omnivores, dogs can survive on a strictly vegetarian diet and without carbohydrates but must receive protein levels of eighteen to twenty-two percent and essential fatty acids of five to eight percent.

Salted meat, undoubtedly, was the most injurious item and explains much of the odd behavior—the "fits" and "madness"—of the afflicted dogs mentioned over and over that led to the indistinct diagnoses offered at the time, such as Kane's "arachnoidal effusion."

Even though salted meat was known to be unhealthful—fresh meat was necessary to protect against scurvy in people—it was still fed to dogs. Greely, for instance, mentions that during his second winter he had no food for his dogs but salted meat and fish, though it was always soaked and "freshened" for them as well as fed in an unfrozen state.

In acute salt (sodium ion) poisoning, there is a sudden increase in sodium and chloride. Salt in blood serum is at a higher level than that of other body fluids and pulls water out of the brain. As the brain shrinks, small vessels within it tear, rip, and release blood, leading to intracranial hemorrhage. Abnormal neurologic signs result—anything from seizures to odd behavior such as wobbly gait, falling over, aggression, disorientation—as well as death, which can also come quickly without warning signs.

In the chronic form, with less ingestion of salt and over a longer period of time, the dog appears normal until it drinks a large amount of water; then, with more salt in the brain than in the serum, fluid moves in the opposite direction, into the brain, causing swelling, abnormal neurological signs, and perhaps death. It may be that this metabolic derangement was the cause of many of the dogs' ailments, from *piblokto* to the rabies-like "madness" when dogs were still drinking water. (At the time, it was thought that rabies manifested "hydrophobia," or fear of water, when the virus actually was causing such painful spasms of the throat muscles that the victim could not swallow in spite of severe thirst.)

Raw meat and spoiled food could also introduce harmful bacteria that led to food poisoning and some of the symptoms described.

Aside from an irregular, insufficient, often tainted, and nutritionally poor diet and the salted meat that whalers and explorers introduced, the dogs of the far north were endangered also by virulent, contagious diseases, including rabies and distemper, two viral infections affecting the nervous system that can produce similar abnormal neurological signs. Before the advent of vaccination, distemper at times wiped out whole villages of dogs, rendering their human keepers vulnerable to starvation. Today, in spite of vaccination programs, distemper continues to be a serious threat across northern areas.

Rabies outbreaks occur in arctic foxes in the spring following an increase in lemmings and other prey. But foxes that appear to have rabies often are suffering from canine distemper, which can produce a wide variety of abnormal neurological symptoms. (In 1994, dogs were banned from Antarctica, in part because of the danger of infecting seals with such diseases.)

A more rare disease among dogs is tetanus, known commonly as lockjaw because of the facial spasms and muscle rigidity it causes. When a bacterium found in soil called *Clostridium tetani* gets into a deep wound without oxygen available, it can cause the disease by releasing a neurotoxin. Death can result from respiratory paralysis, though now tetanus can be treated with penicillin.

Most ship's surgeons were not concerned enough with dogs to keep records. An exception was Belgrave Ninnis, Fleet-Surgeon of the British North Polar Expedition of 1875–1876, who tracked twenty-five healthy dogs brought aboard in July 1875, with two young ones soon added. "We were given to understand," he said, "that feeding twice a week was amply sufficient; that the worst possible personal treatment was too good for them, and meat in any stage of decomposition a perfect luxury to their fastidious palates." Close confinement on board, he maintained, soon led to disease; within twenty-five days a bitch had a fit and died in thirteen days. Others succumbed. One was shot. One ran away. Two were accidentally drowned. Seven died from disease. Six recovered. One died mad. In summation, he stated:

> Of the whole number twelve only were under medical treatment; one had rabies and died; one so far recovered as to have two litters of pups, and then died ten months after her first fit and two or three days after her last litter; two fell into the water when in fits and were drowned; two died notwithstanding everything that was done to cure them, and six recovered and were landed at Disco. . . . The treatment found most beneficial was calomel, followed in some cases by croton-oil and solution of morphia, the best of water, and good food.

They were not kicked or cuffed, and they behaved as sociably and decorously as if brought up in a cottage.

Of rabies, he said, there was no knowledge of anyone in Greenland being bitten by a rabid dog and suffering the disease; nor did the recovery of some of the dogs seem consistent with the usual progress of the disease. Later, Ninnis published a report based on his expedition study: *Diseases Incidental to the Eskimo Dogs of Smith's Sound: Diagnosis and Treatment.*

Rarely was such attention given to working dogs. Until the arrival of whalers and expeditionary ships, even severely injured or sick animals would be left to heal by themselves. If a dog could not lick itself back to health, it was abandoned or killed. In a number of recorded instances, such dogs reappeared after absences when they were presumed dead. Doctors and captains, bearing a new cargo of scientific curiosity into the Arctic, often intervened, stitching up wounds, applying remedies, and performing autopsies, but their reports are casual and random, with little cohesion.

Danger was everywhere, starvation at its heart. But all the while, the dogs pulled, crossed thin ice, leapt across leads (breaks in the ice), waited out blizzards by burrowing into snow, provided warmth to those who might have frozen otherwise, scaled huge hummocks, found their way home in storms, warned drivers away from the edge of the ice, woke up those who fell asleep in killing temperatures, alerted people to an approaching bear, found seal holes, chased prey for miles and held it at bay—all to serve those with whom they had forged a bond—and, it would seem, to receive very little in return. Even in death they continued to serve, their short lives often evolving into food, gloves, clothing, and equipment.

There is no equivalent today of the experience of the nineteenth-century sledge dog. Dogs participating in races such as the 1,000-mile Iditarod and Yukon Quest, though running huge distances under grueling conditions, are pulling lighter loads over generally easier terrain—not broken sea ice—and are carefully trained and monitored, with mandatory rest periods, veterinarian checks, and a high fat and caloric diet for which they are gradually prepared before the race. These dogs require between 8,000 and 10,000 calories per twenty-four-hour period, sixty to seventy percent from fat and at least thirty percent from protein. Only ten percent, at most, is derived from carbohydrate. They are also provided three to four liters of water per day,

A dog traveling with Kane or Hall, lucky to be fed two or three times a week and seldom given water, knew nothing of such largesse. Yet they served willingly, these "camels of the north," often noted as "faithful companions." Was their willingness based on a bond of mutual benefit, or was there something more?

9

Dogs and Driver:
The Essential Team

As a member of the "Withdrawing Party" abandoning Elisha Kent Kane and the *Advance* on August 28, 1854, Isaac Hayes learned a bitter lesson about dog driving: Not just anyone can do it.

The eight secessionists had been experiencing terrible conditions. They took none of Kane's dogs with them, though some tried to follow them. According to Carl Petersen, Hans Hendrik even shot at them, wounding one seriously in the neck, but still they chased after them. (We are not told for how long.)

Later, as the secessionists' situation became more desperate, they tried to acquire dogs from local hunters but could obtain only five, not enough for them to be able to progress 800 miles south to Upernavik, as they had planned. Stuck at Booth Bay with one member of their group too sick to travel, they gave up, decided to retreat, and sent two men back to the *Advance* to seek help. The remaining six settled down to total misery in their collapsing hut with the temperature at zero, no food but walrus hide, and only enough fuel for two hours of lamplight a day.

On their fourth miserable day, three hunters arrived from the settlement of Netelik, to the south of Etah. One of them was Kalutunah, the powerful, unreadable shaman/hunter. The visitors offered only a small amount of meat. Hayes now pressed Kalutunah for help, either transporting the men back to the *Advance* or renting them the necessary items to make the trip on their own. Kalutunah did not soften; he could clearly see the weakened state of the white men and was ready to take advantage. Hayes, moreover, found that the hunters had large quantities of meat on their sledges that they had hidden—for no reason other than keeping it from the starving strangers.

Hayes was now desperate. He proposed to his runaway group that they drug the hunters with opium, then seize and make off with their sledges and dogs. His comrades concurred.

First they had to reassure the hunters that they had only friendly intentions, offering presents such as combs and pages torn from books, while cooking the meat that had been brought into the hut. Hayes then slipped the opium into the stew and fed it to his guests, who soon became sleepy. Fearing that the hunters were not sufficiently anesthetized, Hayes took the next step in delaying the inevitable chase: He removed the sleepers' boots, coats, and mittens. Then, after placing a slab of meat from the sledge inside the hut, Hayes and his men got ready to flee, barricading the door on the outside with blocks of ice, then mounting the three sledges. The harnessed dogs, terrified by the sudden movements of these strangers, dashed off "at the first crack" of the whip.

After an erratic start, the dogs gave much trouble. Unaccustomed to the voices and actions of their inexperienced new masters, they ran helter-skelter in different directions. Hayes's team twice took him back almost all the way to the hut. Another team ran way out on the rough sea ice half a mile from the coast.

Even when Hayes thought he had his team under control, he did not. With the dogs running in opposite directions, they overturned the sledge, threw Hayes and his companion out, and rushed off. Hayes, managing to hold on to the sledge, was dragged through a ridge of hummocks until the point of one of the runners caught on a block of ice. All but two of the traces broke and the dogs raced off, back to the hut and their sleeping masters. Hayes managed to grab the two dogs that remained, attaching one to each of the other two sledges and abandoning the third sledge now jammed in the ice. Eventually, the two teams quieted and made good speed.

The first stop, at Cape Parry, was to repair the two whips, without which the new drivers would have been unable to proceed. Hayes and his party were just getting ready to leave when a sledge came into sight: It was the three opium prisoners. They had broken out of the blocked hut entrance, collected their two dogs, found and repaired the broken sledge, and made their way to their tormentors. Hayes now knew that fear was his only refuge: He and Sonntag faced the hunters with a rifle. The three men begged them not to shoot.

Hayes and his men now grabbed the hunters. Hayes made Kalutunah understand that if he and his companions did not drive them back to the ship (where dogs, sledges, and clothes would be released), that he would shoot them forthwith. Kalutunah had no choice but to agree.

The three prisoners wore, as ponchos, the blankets in which they had been wrapped in the hut. One was red, one blue, and one white. One escapee had appropriated an old pair of discarded boots; the other two had wrapped their feet in pieces of blanket. Hayes returned their clothes to them. "A more grateful set of fellows I had never seen," he remarked. The plan appeared to work extraordinarily well. His prisoners, he noted, did not attempt to touch dog, sledge, or whip unless asked to. At least once, while crossing treacherous sea ice, Hayes brandished his pistol to push on the drivers when they wanted to turn back.

On December 12, the six secessionists returned to the *Advance*, where Kane welcomed them warmly. (The two sent ahead had already arrived.) They had just traveled 150 miles in forty hours with the temperature at 50° below zero.

The next day the captive drivers, to whom everything had been returned, left with their dogs and sledges and some presents; and they left, Hayes noted, "well pleased."

No matter which way the story might have turned out, Hayes would have been lost without dogs—and the ability to drive them. To know how to control a team was as important as having a team, and driving was not a skill easily learned. Moreover, it was not just a matter of skill. There had to be a bond between driver and dogs—an invisible line as powerful as any whip. This was the lesson visitors to the Arctic had to learn—one by one, expedition by expedition. Teams would run away and sledges overturn until a two-way trust was established between dogs and driver. This was the harness of respect that all must willingly put on in order to achieve balance and survival.

As anthropologist Franz Boas pointed out in *The Central Eskimo*, there were definite rules for success. There had to be a strong and spirited lead dog, on the longest trace, able to run in advance of the others, and, next to the leader, two or three strong dogs with shorter traces of equal length, with the weaker and less manageable dogs closer to the sledge. A team must know and accept its leader, allowing him or her all rights, and a dog must know his or her teammates. If a dog is put into a strange team, he is likely to throw himself down and refuse to run. Likewise, if he is sold or given away, he will frequently return to his old home: "I know of instances in which they even ran from thirty to sixty miles to reach it." To prevent its running away, a dog on loan would sometimes have its front left leg tied up with a loop that passed over the neck.

The language and protocol of sledging were specific. The driver would start with a "whistling guttural sound that sounds like h!h!" He would follow with other words of stimulation and words to indicate turn left or turn right, while throwing the whip lash to the opposite side. To stop the team, the driver would call out "Ohoha!"

Aside from the appropriate matching of dogs and calling of orders, there had to be confidence running both ways up and down the traces. The dogs had to know that when one of them was called, that was the dog that would receive the whip; otherwise a fight and potential chaos would ensue. And the driver had to know what each dog was capable of and which dog, at any moment, needed correction. Sometimes the driver had to trust the dogs to find their way home in a storm or to avoid open water. Sometimes the dogs had to trust the driver to get them over weak ice or an opening in the ice; they had to be able to respond to the calling of their name, no matter what that calling asked of them. Wayfinders and translators of ice, both dogs and their drivers had to depend on one another; there was no margin for error, no salvation beyond themselves. Rescue could come only from partnership. Experience, skill, trust, self-confidence, patience, teamwork, and cooperation all added up to the magic of synergy. But synergy in driving was hard won.

Visitors to the Arctic carried on endless arguments as to which race could produce the most competent drivers and who were the true masters. From the British and American perspective, highest honors went to Johan Carl Christian Petersen (1813–1880), a Danish resident of Upernavik, the northernmost Danish settlement in Greenland, who served three famous Franklin searchers as interpreter and sledge drive master (Captain William Penny, 1850–1851; Elisah Kent Kane, 1853–1855; and Francis Leopold McClintock, 1857–1859) plus Hayes in his quest for the Open Polar Sea, 1860–1861. During Kane's expedition, Hayes led the "Withdrawing Party" in their aborted break for freedom.

Dr. Pavy of Adolphus Washington Greely's party insisted that Eskimo drivers were the best, not only because they were experienced and skilled but also because, inured to cold, they could perform many duties with bare hands. Greely disagreed strongly (perhaps because Pavy, who threatened to abandon the expedition at the outset, was so bothersome to him): "Our Eskimo drivers could not be excelled in their race for bravery, energy, and activity, but Lockwood and Brainard [who made the most successful sledging explorations of the expedition] would never have reached their farthest point had they depended on the courage and activity of their dog-driver, whom it was needful to incite to continued exertions."

A quarter of a century later, Robert Peary would maintain that his African American assistant, Matthew Henson, "can handle a sledge better, and is probably a better dog-driver, than any other man living, except some of the best of the Eskimo hunters themselves." He also stated that "he had not, as a racial inheritance, the daring and initiative of Bartlett or Marvin, Macmillan, or Borup." Peary's theory was that Henson could manage perfectly well under his tutelage but not on his own.

Finally, it was for the dogs to decide who was competent and who was not. Their safety and well-being depended upon the answer to the questions, Who was that behind them, lashing the whip and calling out the orders? Do we know him and can we trust him? Do we follow him to the edge of the ice?

10

Seeking Companionship:
When Dogs Were Not Available

Captain Hatteras had his Duke. Possibly a greyhound traveled with the John Franklin expedition. (Charles Francis Hall hinted of this in a letter to Henry Grinnell published in a number of newspapers in late 1869 and early 1870.) Albert Hastings Markham, commander of the George Strong Nares British North Polar Expedition of 1875–1876, sailed into the ice with his beloved pet dog, Nellie. Charles Wilkes of the United States Exploring Expedition, 1838–1842, kept his Newfoundland dog Sydney close beside him as bodyguard. Elisha Kent Kane had Toodla and Whitey and also took on a fox to domesticate. Isaac I. Hayes had his beloved Newfoundland puppy, the General. When the General was gone, he also acquired a fox, and Birdie, as he named her, became a good and rewarding pet, providing unexpected delight. A second fox, however, proved unsuccessful as a companion. William Godfrey, Kane's nemesis, captured and maintained a blue fox he named Jack, that "conducted himself with the strictest propriety" and excelled at rat-catching. Indeed, Godfrey maintained, Jack killed more rats in half an hour than had Kane's two-day fumigation of the ship (which put them all at great danger) and became a great favorite. Adolphus

Washington Greely of the Lady Franklin Bay Expedition, like Hayes, took on two foxes; his first, Reuben, made a good pet, but the second was never able to be tamed. Men aboard the whaler *Emma* overwintering in Cumberland Sound during 1859–1860 captured a fox and kept it in a cage. There is a reason foxes were chosen as pets.

According to animal behaviorist John Bradshaw, writing in *Dog Sense*, dogs are quite different from the popular view of them as small domesticated wolves with the need to dominate. They *do* derive from the gray wolf but are profoundly changed by thousands of years of domestication. They bond with people to the point, research is now showing, that they prefer human contact over canine. Wolves, he maintains, are also misrepresented: They travel in family groups, not random packs, and seek cooperation, not dominance.

Animal science professor Temple Grandin agrees. Dogs are so tuned in to people, she says, that "they are the only animals that can follow a person's gaze or pointing finger to figure out where a piece of food is hidden. Wolves can't do it, and neither can chimpanzees.... The natural state of life for dogs," she maintains, "is to live with people."

No animal is more thoroughly domesticated and people-oriented than the dog, but a genetics program in Siberia reveals how domestication works and can alter the behavior of another form of canid. On a farm outside Novosibirsk, a fox-breeding program has been producing silver foxes with doglike qualities for more than half a century. The result is foxes bred for tameness that crave human attention, wag their tails when they see people, and seek to be petted and carried. Although the ice-bound adventurers exploring the Arctic were simply taming wild animals, their foxes showed the potential for transformation into companions.

But foxes were not always available for the bereft wanderers, and some of these lonely beings concentrated on decidedly undoglike companions. Cats, lemmings, and various species of birds skitter through the ice journals. Both Sir John Ross, searching for Franklin aboard the *Felix*, and whaling captain William Penny carried and dispatched carrier pigeons— certainly not pets but domesticated and trained birds that required careful attention. (According to *The New York Times* of December 21, 1890, one of Ross's pigeons established a record in October 1850 by flying from Assistance Bay, west of Wellington Sound, to Ayrshire, Scotland—2,000 miles—in one week.) Salomon Andrée also traveled with carrier pigeons on his doomed attempt to reach the Pole by balloon. Private Francis Long of the Greely expedition caught and raised six owlets, whose appetite surprised Greely: "I remember one bolting whole a sandpiper about half his own size. Over a hundred and fifty skuas (robber gulls) were killed and fed to these owls." In spite of not having used their wings, they all flew off. Long released them, Greely noted, the same day hunter Jens Edward shot a large snowy owl. In the appendix to his work, under *Nyctea nyctea*—Snowy Owl, Greely stated: "The bird bred abundantly in the vicinity of Fort Conger, and as many as fifteen or twenty fine young birds were raised by us until approaching winter compelled us to release them."

Arctic owl.
Greely, p. 550

William M. Davis, in his composite view of whaling life titled *Nimrod of the Sea; or, the American Whaleman*, spoke not only of cats, game hens, and pigs, but also of a monkey.

Charles Edward Smith, surgeon aboard the whaler *Diana* of Hull, England, during its disastrous voyage of 1866–1867, had a "rough-haired Scotch terrier" named Gyp, while Bill Reynolds, the harpooner, had one of Gyp's puppies, named Murphy. The captain, John Gravill, had a canary, and the engineer, Emanuel Webster, had both a linnet and a dog named Spring. By the end of the ice-locked voyage, Gyp and Murphy had been shot for "madness" and the starving Spring was drowned, for fear he, too, might go "mad." The linnet survived, as the engineer tells us; apparently, the canary did as well, described as singing along with the linnet three weeks before the crippled *Diana* reached port.

Frederick Cook, spending his desperate winter of 1908–1909 in an underground den, befriended a pair of blue rats, which "made a picture of animal delight which really aroused us from stupor to little spasms of enthusiasm."

In 1910, Robert Scott's ship, *Terra Nova*, carried not only dogs and ponies but also a cat, a parrot, and a pregnant rabbit to Antarctica. In 1914, Mrs. Chippy, a male tiger-striped tabby cat, rode to Antarctica on Ernest Shackleton's *Endurance*, tormenting the dogs and surviving a fall overboard—but not the voyage. Two cats were prominent survivors of two different expeditions of Vilhjalmur Stefansson: Nigeraurak ("Little Black One") on the ill-fated voyage of the *Karluk* (1913–1914) and Vic of the disastrous 1921 Wrangel Island venture.

Francis Leopold McClintock, searching for Franklin aboard the *Fox*, also carried a cat:

HELD

Musk calves at Conger, four months old.
Greely, p. 320

Our messmate Pussy is unwell, and won't eat; in vain has Hobson tempted her with raw seal's flesh, preserved salmon, preserved milk, etc.; at length castor-oil was forcibly administered. Puss is a great favorite.

Puss recovered but met her fate four months later when, seeking sun on a warm May day, she ventured out on deck and was seized and killed by the dogs.

The doomed *Polaris* also carried a cat, while crewman Robert Kruger captured a live lemming that was put into a box and "carefully fed." He added another, followed by two more, for which "the sailors rigged a cage on top of the galley. This cage had glass sides and many little retreats; and much interest was shown in watching the little creatures and in feeding them." The crew also tried to take on board a musk ox calf, while Greely's party attempted to domesticate four musk ox calves. Peary, too, attempted a musk ox calf; one was taken aboard his ship, the *Roosevelt*, just before returning home, "but the little creature died the next evening, though the steward nursed him carefully in an effort to save his life." Various whalers captured polar bear cubs for commercial reasons; cubs could be sold to zoological gardens for up to twenty British pounds.

Some choices of companion were even stranger. Whaler George Tyson, who would go on to lead the *Polaris* ice-floe party, once tried to tame a seal. It was the winter of 1851–1852 in Cumberland Sound—a hard and desolate winter as he waited for the whales to return:

We had not many opportunities of making pets of any thing out there; the dogs were too fierce, and small animals of any kind were scared; but one day I saw a young seal; it looked so pretty, with its pure white coat (the young of the Greenland seal is entirely white) and bright hazel eyes, that I took it up in my arms like a baby, and carried it along, talking and whistling to it by the way. The little creature looked at me, turning its head round to look up in my face without any apparent alarm, and seemingly soliciting me to give it something to eat. I thought I should take a great deal of comfort with my little pet, for I had not then got accustomed to seeing the young ones killed, much less eating them myself. Arrived at our house, I carefully deposited it outside in a suitable place and went inside to get my supper, hurrying through my meal to get and look after my treasure. I looked around, but it was not where I had left it. I began to suspect mischief, and, sure enough, there it was, a little way off, *dead*, with its back broken by the heavy heel of a whaler's boot; one of the men, with a malignancy impossible for me to understand, had pressed the life out of my only pet simply to gratify a brutal nature. Had I been quite sure who was the perpetrator my indignation would have found other vent, I suspect, than words.

During a subsequent winter when Tyson was again in Cumberland Sound, another whaler, Joseph Faulkner, noted the attempt on his ship to make a pet of a captured young seal: "This little fellow, so plump and sleek, with such a silken pelt and such bright globules of eyes so intelligently blinking always, was soon installed as a prime favorite on board." His destination was Barnum's Museum in New York, but he escaped. Live seals were also captured for zoological gardens in England, where they soon died of starvation. Charles Edward Smith remembered:

> Many years ago Captain Gravill took home some seven or eight young seals. During the voyage they seemed lively and active enough. They were supplied with food but did not seem to eat much of anything. They were sent to the Zoological Gardens at Hull, where they lived in a pond until all the fat on their bodies was absorbed, and then died. Thousands of people went to look at these seals.

Seals appear to have human qualities and to connect, in a mystic way, with human beings. They are large-eyed, curious, sociable, given to vocalizations, and are said to be fond of music. The female seal constructs an "igloo," similar to the human version, in which to give birth and raise her pup. Seals can be charmed into a near trance-like state by the talk of a human hunter sidling toward them on the ice—or by the vocal wiles of a polar bear. The male bearded seal is said to produce a particularly evocative underwater song. When sailors saw a large shoal of ringed seals springing up together for air, they would call the phenomenon a "seal's wedding."

When Hall helped Ebierbing haul up a speared seal, he looked into the "beautiful, eloquent eyes of the victim" and felt a shuddering remorse. Lacking tear ducts, seals can appear to be crying. In Celtic lore seals appear as selkies—half-human, half-seal beings who engage people in entanglements of romantic tragedy. As creatures of water they are unable to bond permanently with creatures of land, though each species would seek the other out. It was said that a woman, standing alone on the shore, had only to shed seven tears to bring one to her. And so with the solitary wanderers of the frozen sea: A seal, no matter how imploring or tearful its eyes, no matter how sweet its song, could never fill the hole in a lonely ice-held heart; it could only rip it deeper.

Kane, the pragmatic but romantic adventurer, was caught himself in a selkie-like entanglement. Before he left for his second arctic voyage, he sent to his beloved, medium Maggie Fox, a copy of his favorite book, *Undine*. This is Friedrich de la Motte Fouqué's 1811 novella of the water sprite who must marry a mortal in order to gain a soul. Kane was convinced it was his duty to save Maggie in a similar way but fell short in his efforts. The two worlds of these impossible lovers—one of physicality and one of spirit—would never merge but circle one another in haunted orbit. In the hurried weeks before he left for Greenland, he wrote to her as "pet," "pet lamb," "sweet pet," "dear pet," "dear darling pet," and "my own sweet pet." After embarking for the north, he sent letter after letter to her until there were no more ships to bring his letters home, only the silence of the ice.

And what of the Polar Inuit who spent not months or years but their whole lives in stark and lonely conditions?

According to Hall's traveling companion and informant from the Repulse Bay area, Ouela, his people did not try to domesticate wild animals from the belief that to do so would bring death to the tribe. There were exceptions. The mother of Nukerzhoo, another friend, once captured a young wolf to which she provided the most attentive and affectionate care. She hoped it would grow to become a more serviceable hunter than a dog. However, when the wolf was half grown, her dogs discovered that their playmate was a different species—and an enemy; they pounced upon him and tore him apart.

Ouela also told Hall the traditional story of the old woman who raised a polar bear cub, Koonikjooa, as a pet. He was so successful as a hunter, the local people, grown envious, decided to kill him. The old woman told him he must leave in order to save his life but asked that he stay near enough that she might go to him when in need. One day, hungry, she went to him to ask for help. He killed a companion bear and they shared its body. The faithful Koonikjooa continued to serve the woman and she to love him.

The Inuit people, with no leisure to create and maintain pets, were dependent on wild animals for their food, clothing, shelter, and hunting implements. It was essential to live in harmony with these animals and in balance with the deities who made them possible, especially with Sedna, goddess of sea mammals, whose dog-husband guarded her home. Taboos had to be strictly followed. Though a seal could never be thought of as a pet, it must be treated with utmost respect. Before it was butchered, it was to be given a drink of water to thank it and assure its return.

Only a puppy could be a pet—for a short time. Raised indoors for several months, puppies were taken care of with tender attention by women and children. When the puppies were very young, children would harness them and attach them to toy sledges. But all too soon—when they reached the age of about four months—it was time for them to enter the working world.

To pat and caress an animal was a luxury sometimes won by the crews of discovery ships and whalers while they served time in the prison of the frozen sea. It was a luxury that brought moments of peace and thoughts of home, minutes of distraction in the seemingly endless polar night, and freedom from the stress of imprisonment. It was a pleasure sought by commander and crew alike in the democracy of ice, a country where every human heart was stretched tight with longing.

11

Barbekark

The Hunter

*Traveling with Charles Francis Hall: The First
Expedition in Search of Sir John Franklin, 1860–1862*

The early life trajectory of Charles Francis Hall (1821–1871) showed no indication it would lead to arctic exploration and could not have been more different from those of Elisha Kent Kane and Isaac I. Hayes, who preceded him. Born into rural poverty in New Hampshire and uneducated, Hall started out as a blacksmith's apprentice before moving to Cincinnati, where he learned engraving, became a printer, and then became a newspaper publisher. At some point he began reading whatever he could find on the Arctic. Perhaps inspired by Kane's death in 1857—and his subsequent fame—he became more focused, and then obsessed. Driven by inexplicable forces (including sympathy for Lady Franklin), Hall determined he would save the remaining members of the Franklin expedition. He was convinced they yet lived and threw himself totally into the task of putting together an expedition to find them. King William's Land, he maintained, was the place to look, an island to the north and west of Hudson Bay.

Hall got a slight head start on his rival Hayes, who departed Boston on July 6, 1860, to find the Open Polar Sea. Hall left New London, Connecticut, as a passenger on board the barque *George Henry*, a whaler, on May 29, 1860.

Barbekark killing the reindeer.

Charles Francis Hall, *Life with the Esquimaux: The Narrative of Captain Charles Francis Hall, of the Whaling Barque "George Henry," from the 29th May, 1860, to the 13th September, 1862,* vol. I, p. 238; Semi-Rare Book Collection, Alaska and Polar Regions Collections & Archives, Rasmuson Library, University of Alaska Fairbanks

An Esquimaux and his seal dog.

Hall, Vol. I, p. 263; Semi-Rare Book Collection, Alaska and Polar Regions Collections & Archives, Rasmuson Library, University of Alaska Fairbanks

Captain Sydney O. Budington of Groton, Connecticut, was sailing master; theirs was to became a long and tangled relationship. They were accompanied by a tender, the *Amaret*, formerly the famous *Rescue* of Kane's first arctic voyage (the First Grinnell Expedition). Hall also had on board a twenty-eight-foot expedition boat. They were headed for the whaling grounds at the south end of Baffin Island.

As soon as he reached Greenland, Hall, the solitary commander of no ship or men, put together the best dog team he possibly could. Although he arrived at Holsteinborg with a minimal outfit—little but a driving desire to find and rescue the long-lost Franklin men—he did have a small expense account. For five dollars, he was able to purchase six dogs chosen personally by Governor Elberg, and these he immediately named Kingo, Barbekark, Ei (pronounced Ee), Melaktor (the leader), Merok, and Melak or Kiokoolik (later called Flora).

For twenty-five cents he purchased two bushels of little dried fish, or "capelins" (a small smeltlike fish of the North Atlantic), for their food.

All this he did before writing letters home to the family he was deserting and to Henry Grinnell, the benefactor who had gotten him this far. The letters would go by way of Copenhagen a month hence.

Soon after Hall and the *George Henry* had left Holsteinborg and entered Davis Strait, the dogs proved themselves stronger in one regard than their master: They were not afflicted with seasickness, a scourge to this unlikely explorer as well as to his predecessor, Kane.

The dogs were glad to get ashore, however. With the first landing, they happily dug into the snow and played exuberantly, stopping only to greet Hall as he disembarked after them. In his own words, they greeted him "with much joy." Already the bond had been forged: "They skip, they run, they come and look, as if grateful, in my eye, and then bound away again in the wildest exuberance of animal spirits."

They paid much attention to him as well at feeding time. He would place them in a circle around him and throw them, in turn, a capelin apiece until each dog had received ten. One day, the precocious Barbekark tried a new trick: He would grab his fish, back up, then move several places forward and force his way into the line again. Because his master seemed impressed, Barbekark then repeated the act, securing three fish per round. Then the fun ended. Hall turned the tables. When he came to Barbekark, he threw no fish; even though Barbekark changed his position quickly three times in a cycle, he got no fish. Since no amount of changing his position worked, Barbekark withdrew from the circle and stood between Hall's legs, looking up at him. His expression of repentance worked.

The *George Henry*, having sailed west across Davis Strait to its destination, settled into its moorage in what the party called Rescue Harbor, Cyrus Field Bay, at the south end of Baffin Island. Hall immediately began working with his dogs.

Barbekark quickly became his master's favorite, sharing his travels and adventures. He was particularly well known for his hunting abilities. On one occasion, during a caribou hunt, Barbekark, leading the other dogs, bounded toward the prey. Following the herd in a direct line, Barbekark was not distracted by the myriad tracks or evasive actions of the animals as were the other dogs. Barbekark's chase continued for two hours.

Hall and his companions feared that the dogs, led so far afield, would not be able to find their way home. Three hours after the chase began, however, Barbekark returned to the *George Henry*, showing blood around his mouth and over his body. Although nothing much was made of his bloody return—dogs were considered worthless in *tuktoo* (caribou) hunting—his behavior forced attention. Fidgety and whining, Barbekark went from one crew member to another, as if asking for something. Captain Budington noticed him jumping about and running back and forth to the gangway stairs. When one of the men, Spikes, left the ship to visit the wreck of the *Amaret* (the *Rescue*), which had been destroyed in an autumn storm, Barbekark followed. When Spikes went no farther, Barbekark bounded off to the northwest in the direction of the hunt, trying to get him to follow. Spikes, convinced Barbekark was trying to tell him of success in the hunt, returned to the ship and got a party together to see if Barbekark really had killed a caribou.

Two hours later the group returned with a butchered tuktoo and the remarkable story—told by snow and blood—of how Barbekark had indeed taken his prey. The fallen caribou, being guarded by the happy dog, was found to have had its throat slit by Barbekark's teeth as effectively as if it had been done with a knife. The windpipe and jugular vein had both been severed and a piece bitten out from both.

Later, when the skin was being dressed, it was found that a bullet from Hall's rifle, fired by his hunting partner Koojesse, had penetrated the flesh of the hindquarters and had been flattened by striking the hip. Hall kept the flattened ball as a memento of the event, noting the "keen sagacity and almost human intelligence, allied to great bravery, of my faithful Greenland dog Barbekark."

As the *George Henry* settled into its winter quarters, Hall sought from his new Inuit friends all the information he could glean on King William's Land, his goal—many miles to the northwest—for the Franklin search. Most important was his meeting and immediate connection with

Tookoolito, the extraordinary woman who became his translator, and her husband, Ebierbing, who became his guide and hunter. The couple would remain his steadfast friends and supporters until his death—and long after.

At this time, the autumn of 1860, Hall was also learning what it was to cope with the almost constant emergencies of life in the Arctic. When the *Amaret* and his one-masted twenty-eight-foot expedition boat were wrecked in a gale, he was left with no vessel and dashed plans. The *Amaret* was a particularly keen loss. Hall had considered it a personal connection with his hero, Kane.

Then, there was the wreckage of lives. Word came of the death of a woman he had befriended—Nikujar, the wife of Ugarng. As Hall sought to comfort the woman's first husband, Blind George, news came of the loss and death of one of the crew members, John Brown, who froze to death while returning to the ship from Frobisher Bay. Brown's death, it seemed, was assigned to the wrong choice of dog.

Brown and another crewman from the *George Henry*, James Bruce, had been sent to live with the Inuit people of Frobisher Bay in order to have the fresh meat they required to recover from scurvy. Hall had allowed his six Greenland dogs to join six other dogs to make the trip. Now it was time for the two men and the dogs to return. In a hurry to get back to his ship and the more ordinary food he craved, Brown insisted on going ahead alone. Koojesse and Charley, with whom he was traveling, required that he take a dog and chose for him a proper guide. But, for unknown reasons, Brown exchanged this dog for a younger, less experienced one that was not familiar with the trail.

Charley and Koojesse returned to the ship at midnight and, exhausted, went immediately to sleep. The next morning Hall learned that Kingo, one of his Greenlanders, had been the subject of a cruel punishment: An Inuit driver had cut off his left ear as punishment for biting harnesses. That driver, it turned out, was Koojesse! His excuse, according to Hall, was that his companion Charley had first severed the ear of *his* dog, making Koojesse think he must do the same to Hall's dog. "As I have said before in my journal," Hall remarked, "let a dog offend an Innuit, and woe be to the dog!"

But these "cruel and savage" acts paled in comparison with the story of Brown. There was no sign of the man, and the temperature had dipped to 57° below zero during the night. Ten crew members joined Hall in the search, along with Koojesse, but one by one they fell back in the grueling conditions as they crossed the hummocky frozen sea. After covering six miles in one hour and forty-two minutes, Koojesse picked up Brown's wandering and contradictory trail. Exhaustion and thirst—the great enemies of those who cross ice—wore out the searchers. Twenty men had joined in the effort, but by noon, only five remained. Hall tried to suck on a piece of ice from an iceberg only to have it freeze to his mouth and tongue. The temperature was at 10° below zero. The group rested for fifteen minutes and started up again at 1:30. Some protested they could not continue. And all the while the tracks led to the open sea of Davis Strait. At 2:15, Hall proceeded on alone, only to have crew member William Johnston overtake him. "John was my shipmate," he said, "and I loved him. I shall ever regret, perhaps, if I return now."

But John Brown's tracks—a monochromatic portrait of fear, panic, and bewilderment—circled round and round, crossing every compass point and themselves. At 4:30, help arrived: Captain Budington had sent a sledge, dogs, and three men. Soon, Captain Budington appeared himself, with Charley and a sledge. Hall was persuaded to take Charley's place on the sledge while Charley did the tracking. Shortly after five o'clock, at a point ten miles from the ship, Charley and Johnston encountered the body. John Brown was frozen solid, the snow around him showing a last struggle to get up and move. He was buried where he lay on the ice, covered up with more ice and snow. At half past five, the mourners turned their backs on their fallen shipmate. It took the team of twelve dogs, driven by Charley, until 9 p.m. to reach the *George Henry* with the sad news. During the trip, the men had to struggle against cold and frostbite. Captain Budington, in his haste to get out on the search, had rushed out in his "civilization" boots and one foot began to freeze. He had Johnston pull off that boot; as he did, ungloved, some of Johnston's fingers froze. Hall himself ran along the sledge half the way in order to keep from freezing. The temperature was 17° below zero and the distance traveled during the search was fifty-one miles.

Waiting on the ship were seven Inuit visitors from Frobisher Bay, along with Bruce, Brown's recent companion. They had with them the dog Brown had been so mistaken to choose—a young black one belonging to Captain Budington. When they first encountered the dog, running back to the igloos of Frobisher Bay from where he started, Bruce had been startled, thinking it was a bear. Later, as they traveled with the dog, they came across the place where the dog had lain down to sleep. When he had arisen, he had walked around in circles, then struck out in the opposite direction from the ship. He had known no better than his young human companion which way led to safety.

John Brown was eighteen at the time of his death. His parents were said to reside in France.

Ugarng, Ebierbing, and Tookoolito now came to visit the *George Henry*. They brought not only their hunting, guiding, and tracking skills but also stories of exploits and tragedies, especially of those swept out to sea on ice floes. Ebierbing told the story of the winter of 1859 when a party of sixteen Inuit walrus hunters was carried out to sea. The cold was so intense, most of the dogs perished. Two survived for some time but finally had to be eaten. For thirty days the men floated but finally reached shore, so skeletal that their friends could barely recognize them. Being washed out to sea was a constant danger for those whose living came from ice. No matter how careful or adept the hunters, there was no telling when the sea would heave under them and cruelly play with its shattered surface and any living being unfortunate enough to be riding on it.

As Hall spent more time with the local people, he learned just how important a hunting dog was. A good sealing dog could sniff the wind and tell exactly where a seal's breathing hole was and lead his master there. The hunter would then stand guard at the hole waiting to hear the seal's "blow," at which point he would strike with his harpoon, penetrating the unseen seal's head. This partnership of dog and man, requiring exquisite timing and patience, could determine life or death—and often did.

Meanwhile, Bruce had once more traveled to the Inuit settlement at Frobisher Bay, where he had been a guest with the late John Brown. As if no lesson had been learned, he started back to the *George Henry* alone. But a resident, Bob, concerned and unable to leave himself, hired a woman the whalers called Bran New to accompany Bruce and make sure he got back safely. (Women were recognized as competent trackers, especially in bad weather, and in many instances Tookoolito led the team.)

The next day, mate Rogers started on a trip from the ship to Frobisher Bay. He had a sledge and dogs driven by Koojesse. Among the dogs was Barbekark. At the outset, the weather was clear, but it soon gave way to a gale and snow. Fifteen hours later, Rogers was back, exhausted. When he was sufficiently rested to speak, he told how he had convinced Koojesse, after seven hours of traveling, that they needed to return to the ship—not stop for the night as Koojesse urged—and how the lead dog, belonging to Charley, had lost his way and confused the others. The men as well as the dogs were nearly blinded. Barbekark, however, was clearly struggling to set a different route. They let him have his way and he soon returned them to the ship. Hall asked Koojesse what he would have done if Barbekark had failed. He answered that they were to have thrown themselves among the dogs and cover themselves with the two bearskins they had and thus survive until first light. This was not the last time Barbekark was to be credited with saving a life.

Among the Inuit people, a relationship with dogs began early. As Hall made ready for an exploratory trip in Frobisher Bay, the twelve-year-old son of one of his companions insisted on taking with him a young puppy, called Pink, harnessed to a toy sledge. Hall made no more mention of the arrangement, though the trip was strenuous and clearly made more complicated by such encumbrance. It was a trip particularly noted for thirst and a too-small igloo. But how could one complain of the responsibility of a puppy and young driver in training when future generations depended upon the bond they would establish?

By early May 1861, Hall had returned to the *George Henry*, and there he was joined once more by Ebierbing and Tookoolito, who had been off on their own following a precarious course of sealing. It was a time of high expectation and activity. The ship was gradually being freed from its icy prison and Captain Budington was preparing to refit it and enter the spring whaling season. Hall, meanwhile, was awaiting his long-planned exploratory trip to King William's Land, still convinced he would find survivors of the Franklin expedition.

Captain Budington's immediate need was to feed the dogs properly for the hard work that lay ahead transporting the whaleboats and supplies from the ship over to the whaling depot at Cape True. He planned to take the dogs to Oopungnewing, an island where there was a plentiful supply of walrus skin and meat. When the Inuit men refused to go because of weather, Captain Budington determined to do the task himself, taking with him two assistants who finally consented to accompany him, Charley and Jim Crow. Twenty-five dogs, including Hall's six Greenlanders, were harnessed to a sledge.

Hall, who drove the dogs part way, commented:

It was amusing to see my Greenland dogs, with the others, weaving and knitting, braiding and banding their traces into knots and webs that apparently would defy human devices to unravel. One dog would leap over the backs of a dozen others; another dog, receiving the snap of the thirty-feet lash in the driver's hands, thinking it was the work of his nearest neighbour, would seize him, as if to repay it by a ten-fold severer snap; then the rest would join in the fray, till all became involved in a regular dog-fight.

Such was the everyday process of travel by sledge, and only the ever-optimistic Hall could consider its complications amusing.

Captain Budington returned from Oopungnewing the following day with a load of walrus meat. The storm continued unabated, but he had not wanted to stay in the igloos that were beginning to melt with wet and warmer conditions. It was the time of year when the Inuit inhabitants moved from igloo to caribou tent (*tupic*), such domestic labor being the responsibility of the women.

And now Ebierbing and Tookoolito, living in tupics on an island near the *George Henry*, invited Hall to meet Ebierbing's aged grandmother, the remarkably clear-headed Ookijoxy Ninoo, who was able to give him, through Tookoolito's translation, much oral history of the Frobisher expeditions of 1576, 1577, and 1588. The old woman, Hall estimated, was at least 100. In spite of bitterly cold weather, Tookoolito sat outside the older woman's small tent so that Hall could be inside conducting the interview.

Shortly afterwards, Tookoolito became ill, perhaps, Hall opined, because of the heavy work of having moved her tupic from one island to the other the previous day.

By the end of May, travel over snow and ice by day was difficult, and travel by sledge a challenge. Temperatures were warmer and the ice was breaking up, but the weather was no less volatile. At one point on a trip to Oopungnewing, Hall was traveling with a gale at his back. The wind was sometimes driving the sledge faster than the dogs could pull it, sometimes pushing them along behind it. Hall, who had been walking, tried to jump on the sledge as it went past but missed and found himself disoriented and alone in the snowy chaos. He caught up with his party only when it had to slow down because one of the dogs gave out and had to be unharnessed and placed on the sledge. Casting this dog off, Hall took his place upon the "*living* snow-bank." Later, two more dogs gave out and were cast adrift, following behind as best they could. Nine dogs remained and these, Hall said, "made a good team."

A few days later, on a trip to the "Dreaded Land" (an area between Frobisher Bay and Cyrus Field Bay from which many years before a large group of Inuit people had been swept out to sea), Hall's sledge was drawn by only six dogs, "just half the number that such a journey required," he noted. And these dogs became very excited—they *flew*, Hall said—when they scented and sighted seals. Indeed, they and their Inuit drivers, Koodloo and Ebierbing, became obsessed when a seal hunt manifested, rushing in among the seals to deal death in every direction; there was nothing Hall could do to dissuade them. Suddenly the "Dreaded Land" was not nearly so fearsome. It was rich, and its bounty all for the taking. Hall's notes, written on the sledge, turned red with blood.

And there was more success to follow on this trip. Ebierbing and Koodloo came back to camp one night with news that the six dogs had succeeded in stopping a bear, keeping it at bay, barking and biting, until Ebierbing could shoot it through the heart. Back in their traces, the dogs carried home the skin and meat of the bear as well as pieces of a particularly large bearded seal shot on the return trip.

On the way back to Rescue Harbor and the *George Henry*, a furious gale developed, so strong the men had to hole up as best they could in a tupic for three days. By the time they could set out again, the sea ice was cracking and moving all around them. A thick mist settled over them: "and there we were," Hall noted, "three men, the dogs, and sledge, on the broken ice, in the middle of a bay wide open to the sea." Koodloo and Ebierbing, frightened and confused, wandered off course. Hall insisted on using the compass. Finally, after a correction of three miles, the party made it back safely across the ice to the ship.

It was now the middle of June 1861. The *George Henry* was still caught fast in the ice of Rescue Harbor, though in the outer bay the ice was breaking up. Furious winds continued, wrecking the tupics of the Inuit visitors camped nearby. Ebierbing and Koodloo continued to hunt seal, killing more animals than could be used. Koojesse came in from the whaling depot at Cape True, where Captain Budington and his crew were waiting for favorable conditions and scouting in the meantime for their prey.

On June 21, Hall set out with Koojesse on his return trip to the whalers, thirty miles away. They had a sledge and a team of eight dogs, including Barbekark and his brother Merok. During this passage Merok demonstrated one of the hunting methods a clever seal dog might use: Having scented and spotted a seal, Merok darted toward it as fast as he could pull his companions. Simultaneously, Koojesse set up a loud cry. The tumult of flying dogs and human noise so startled and frightened the seal that it froze in place. Only when the dogs were within a few paces of it did the seal regain its senses and dive safely into its hole. The stratagem had not worked this time, but Koojesse explained that it often succeeded with young and inexperienced seals.

Koojesse then demonstrated a means Inuit hunters used: He lay down on one side and crawled toward a seal he had spotted resting on the ice. When the seal raised its head, Koojesse stopped, then pawed with his right hand and foot while making "seal-talk." The seal, charmed, raised and shook its flippers and rolled over on its side and back, then dropped its head to sleep. Koojesse then inched along, getting ever closer; but if he got too near too quickly, the charm would break and the seal would escape.

The whale depot was a hive of activity in preparation for the season ahead. But Hall had one thought in mind and that was his long-awaited trip to King William's Land. Captain Budington had promised a whale-boat but now said no. The specially designed twenty-eight-footer had been appropriate but now it was gone, along with the *Amaret*, and a whaleboat was not sufficient, Captain Budington declared; he could not allow it, especially as whaling season was about to begin.

Once more, the very Christian and optimistic Hall declared himself in God's hands: If he had to delay for another year by returning to the United States and re-outfitting, that is what he would do. In the meantime, he could explore some of the places made famous by Frobisher.

One day, returning from an egg-gathering trip in Frobisher Bay, he met Captain Budington, who had been out prospecting for whales, and joined up with him. The broken, slushy ice made the journey difficult, with the men having to slog through much of it by foot. On the way back to the *George Henry*, Hall and Budington, with Koojesse as their driver, stopped at the place where John Brown had met his death three months before. They found his body as they had left it, except that foxes or bears had nibbled at his skin clothing. The snow monument over his body was gone, and soon the icy platform beneath him would melt away, lowering his remains into the deep, into what Hall referred to as "the world's great grave-yard."

The Fourth of July—always an event to celebrate—came and went with the carefully executed explosion of an old cast-off gun. As summer progressed, grasses, flowers, and mosquitoes made their appearance, and Hall carefully noted them.

Finally, on July 17, 1861, the *George Henry* broke free, but only at its moorage. Ice still blocked the way to open water and the whales. Hall, increasingly frustrated, tried to keep himself busy, walking, surveying, examining, writing, and visiting his Inuit friends, learning all he could in preparation for his long-projected travels.

One day he was out with Ebierbing when the dogs noticed a seal and took out after it with an enormous burst of speed and energy. As the seal plunged, to make its escape, the remarkable dog Smile grabbed it by its tail and flippers. Aided by the other dogs (all still harnessed to the sledge), Smile was able to drag it out of its hole and take control—without any human help. Smile, said Hall, was the "noblest-looking, best leader, seal, and bear dog I ever saw." He certainly rivaled Barbekark's prowess with caribou.

By the end of July, the ice in Rescue Harbor had broken up further, and the wreck of the *Amaret* was floating free, in and out with the tide,

Dog 'Smile' captures a seal.
Hall, *Vol. II*, p. 42)

spooking the crew of the *George Henry*, who considered the hulk nothing but bad luck. In spite of dangerous circumstances, the *George Henry* managed to get out of the harbor, poised to do its work.

In the meantime, Hall had committed himself to his Inuit friends. He had moved into the tupic of Tookoolito and Ebierbing and was preparing for a summer of exploring in Frobisher Bay while the *George Henry* pursued whales. He had managed to get a boat—he does not tell us how—although one "not as good by any means as I should have wished." He would be traveling with a surprisingly large Inuit crew, including Ebierbing and Tookoolito. He planned to be gone for two months, returning to the *George Henry* at the end of the whaling season. The dogs were left behind. This was boat season, not sledge season.

Gales persisted. The *George Henry* was forced to retreat to the inner harbor. Ebierbing became seriously ill and was attended to by Jennie, Koodloo's wife, an *angakok*. Hunting failed and starvation loomed. Hall was reduced to breaking into supplies reserved for the Frobisher Bay trip— pemmican and coffee, augmented by kelp. The stormy weather continued, halting all work. The ghostly remains of the *Amaret* drifted out of the harbor toward the open sea.

On August 9, Hall started out with an Inuit crew of six. Ebierbing, convalescing, and Tookoolito stayed behind. Captain Budington cheerfully saw him off.

During the summer weeks that followed, Hall would satisfy his longing to explore the area first visited by Frobisher, to verify Frobisher's findings and to correct his misunderstandings. Frobisher's *straits*, Hall determined, was instead a *bay*.

Hall, as much an anthropologist as an explorer, also learned much of the ways of the people with whom he traveled and with whom he would be increasingly bound for years to come. He learned to respect the skills of women as rowers and cartographers, as he had already learned their skills in tracking for the dogs, especially in storms. Thanks to Tookoolito's language abilities, he had been able to discuss not only history but also mythology and cosmology with the people he met and to record customs that might otherwise have gone unnoticed.

A month passed. On September 6, at the insistence of his companions, Hall headed back to Rescue Harbor and on the 27th reboarded the *George Henry* to great acclaim. Those on board had presumed Hall's party was lost. As for the summer travels of the ship—not one whale had been secured.

The greatest surprise was in finding that Tookoolito had given birth to a boy, her first child. She was no less surprised at the meeting, having

Hall on his exploring expedition.
Hall, Vol. II, p. 239

assumed she would never see Hall again. Ebierbing, who had recovered from his illness, recounted the critical state Tookoolito had entered upon the birth of their child. He also reported the loss of his remarkable seal and sledge dog, Smile, as well as another dog.

"Lose our dogs," Ebierbing is quoted as saying; "sick and unable to go tuktooing [caribou hunting]; no tuktoo skins for winter; never mind; we alive and together; got fine boy, and are happy." The baby's name was Tukeliketa, "Little Butterfly."

In early October, Hall made another try at exploring Frobisher's territory but was halted by bad weather. At one point, when searching for driftwood to make a fire, he found a piece of the long-lost *Amaret*, another haunting. The storm that now blew up was as bad as the one that had smashed the *Amaret* the year before. Hall had no choice but, when weather allowed, to turn back. At least there was good news on their return: Two huge whale carcasses rested alongside the *George Henry*.

It was now time to leave for the United States. Captain Budington had set the date of October 20. But the ice had its own plans and once more was setting up its prison walls. Another whale was secured, but there was little joy, only a growing sense of doom, as the ice grew thicker around them and another ice-bound winter loomed.

Once more Hall, his plans dashed, turned to a positive, Christian view: Surely what was happening "is all for the best." But it was Captain Budington who now had to make the hard decisions to get his ship and crew through another nine months of killing cold and potential starvation. As of October 27, he ordered that only two meals would be served a day instead of three. Hall turned over to the captain the supplies of pemmican, meat-biscuit, and ammunition he had brought along for his exploration of King William's Land. His benefactors, he was sure, would concur.

The aurora burned, the temperature dropped, and igloos replaced tupics. Once more, the *George Henry* entered into a marble tableau of hunger and cold.

A visit to the grave of Nukertou, Hall's friend, showed that the previous winter starving dogs had eaten her body, as they would search *this* winter for any abandoned flesh.

But now it was time for the dogs to be working. Through the darkening months, Hall made a number of small excursions as he continued learning all he could about Frobisher Bay. On December 15, he set out with a sledge, eight dogs, and two Inuit drivers to explore Jones's Cape. The temperature was 20° below zero with a wind from the northeast. Shortly after starting, while traveling through snow saturated with seawater, Hall experienced a unique phenomenon: The dogs' paws brought forth a "flood of molten gold"—a manifestation of phosphorescence—that spread out some distance from the sledge.

At Jones's Cape, he was received warmly by the resident Inuit people as he sought information about Frobisher. Three days later, he headed back to the ship. The dogs had not been fed since leaving three days before and were growing tired. Making the ascent of Bayard Taylor Pass—over a mountain—was particularly hard: Going down a steep descent can be even more difficult than going up. In this case, it involved one person at the top holding on to the sledge by an attached rope while a second person kept ahead of the dogs, whipping them back. "Notwithstanding all our precautions," Hall commented, "the sledge occasionally bounded away over snow-drifts, down steep pitches, now and then plunging dogs and men into one general heap."

The "little camels of the north" had once more proved their hardiness and soon would be needed more than ever.

January of 1862 brought severe cold and starvation to the Inuit villages as well as to the *George Henry*; neither populace was able to help the other. Crew members who had been sent out to live with the Inuit people returned with dire tales. One came back with frozen feet and Captain Budington was forced to amputate all his toes as well as part of one foot. One group returning from Oopungnewing related a sad tale: The wife of Jim Crow, reportedly sick and unable to care for herself, had been left to die.

Although such was the custom, Hall could never accept it. On February 21, accompanied by five volunteers, a sledge, and four dogs including Barbekark, he set out to save the woman. Traveling in a storm through soft, thigh-deep snow proved so exhausting, the volunteers gave up one by one until only Hall and mate Lamb were left. In spite of the gale lashing them with glasslike sharpness, they struggled on. Then Lamb gave out. The dogs were floundering. Finally, Hall gave up and turned around.

The trip back to the ship was the hardest Hall had experienced to that point. Lamb was at the point of death and Hall had to throw himself down on occasion to rest. It was Barbekark who saved them:

> During this hard passage back to the vessel my noble dog Barbekark was like a cheering friend; as now and then I lay almost exhausted upon the snow for a moment's rest, he danced around me, kissing my face, placing himself by my side, where I could pillow my head upon his warm body. No one who knew his characteristics could fail to perceive that he realised the critical situation of Lamb and myself.

He would bound toward me, raise himself on his hinder legs, place
his paws upon my breast, and glance from me toward the vessel,
from the vessel to Lamb, then leap away, leading the sledge-team on
a distance ahead, there to wait till we again came near, the few dogs
and the soft state of the snow preventing us from riding.

Four days later, Hall made another attempt to reach the abandoned
woman. First, two missing dogs had to be found and corralled. Hall walked
over to the island where Ebierbing and Tookoolito had recently lived. After
lengthy and strenuous exertions involving much cajoling, Hall was finally
able to capture one of the strays hiding inside Ebierbing's collapsing igloo.
As he dragged that one back to the ship, its comrade followed.

Seven dogs, none of them Hall's, were now harnessed for the mission.
Hall regretted not having his Greenlanders, upon which he felt he could
depend in any emergency, but the team he had was "an excellent one, trac-
table, strong, and of great speed wherever and whenever the travelling
would admit it." Ebierbing's leader, moreover, showed rare skill. He was
able to pick up the tracks, almost obliterated, from the previous trip, and
get the team to the last journey's final point in just two hours.

Temperatures of more than 30° below zero forced the men to take
turns running alongside the sledge in order to keep warm. As the sea ice
gave way to land and the area where the woman had been reported, all
previous markings were gone, and Hall wondered if they had made the
correct landing. The leader kept vigilant, however, finding the way with
no visible signs. Soon they were in the midst of the abandoned village.
Ebierbing eventually located the buried igloo and Hall cut through its roof
with a knife, only to find the woman he sought as still and cold as marble.

More bad news arrived at the ship. Starvation was streaking through
the land like a pack of wolves. Hall went to visit Ebierbing and Tookoolito.
Ebierbing was away from home. Hall found him where he had remained
immobile at a seal hole for two and a half days and two nights. During that
time he had had nothing to eat or drink. And he had caught nothing. Hall
brought the couple and their baby back to the ship. He planned to take
them with him back to the United States.

But first, there was to be another exploratory trip up into Frobisher
Bay. Hall started on April 1, accompanied by four Inuit helpers and four
crew members. The dog team, a "good one," numbered nineteen, including the Greenlanders. In spite of the usual difficulties of the pass, they
reached Oopungnewing in the remarkably good time of nine hours.

As the trip continued, Hall discovered there were two puppies in the
entourage, the offspring of an "excellent" sledge dog. They were carried in

the legs of a pair of fur breeches on the sledge while their mother did her job of pulling. At every stop they were taken out and given to her for nursing. At night a small snow hut was built for the family. Hall noted, "The Innuits take as much care of their young dogs as they do of their children, and sometimes even more."

No matter how excellent the dogs, they could at times misbehave and cause delays. One day some of the Greenlanders were missing, having returned to Oopungnewing on their own, and Hall had to wait until they were rounded up. Shortly after that, there was great excitement when a woman, out sealing with a dog, managed to capture a baby seal. Everyone rushed to her assistance, forgetting the dogs back at the igloo. As Hall noted, they "made sad havoc with our walrus meat and blubber, and other things in general."

But then, the very next day, the dogs offered the rarest of gifts in an arctic blizzard: warmth. Sharkey and Koojesse were off seal hunting while Hall and his attendant, Henry, took a side trip to explore an unknown bay. After some hours, the dogs became fatigued and a snow storm whirled up around them. There was no time to get back to camp. Caught without a snow knife, Hall and Henry had to construct a makeshift igloo around the sledge. They pulled the dogs in and slept comfortably with them: "I had one dog for my feet-warmer, another for my pillow, while a third was arched at my back. Henry was also comfortably provided for." The snoring of one of the dogs completed the picture of friendly domesticity. Hall commented in his diary:

> Now within a few minutes of midnight. Hark! A singular noise strikes the ear. Perhaps it is a polar bear! We listen. Again the same alarming noise. Another sound, and we determine its source. It is the snoring of one of the dogs! So good night to all the sleeping world. Heaven bless all those who need it; none needs it more than myself.

The dogs were exhausted, however—strangely so. The next day brought a gale with temperatures at the zero mark, heavily drifting snow, and next to no visibility. When Hall inquired of Henry, he learned that Sharkey and Koojesse had been feeding their own dogs while neglecting Hall's Greenlanders. By the end of the journey, two of them could not pull at all and one repeatedly fell down. Hall had to lead the way by compass, arriving at his encampment to find Sharkey on the lookout for him, while Koojesse was out in the storm searching for him. His Inuit friends, all through the previous night, had kept Hall's lighted lantern suspended on a pole for a beacon; and soon the women had a hot supper ready. Friends,

Hall learned over and over, could be both outrageously selfish and heroically generous.

The explorations of Frobisher Bay went on, with ever-present need for food for six travelers and their dogs. Gradually igloo weather was giving way to tupic weather; sometimes the two forms of habitation merged. At one point, while an igloo/tupic was being constructed and everyone was distracted, the ravenous dogs sprang in a pack upon the sledge, each snatching a piece of meat or blubber. Hall with a club and Henry with a seal spear waded into the confusion, striking at the dogs as hard as they could. But hunger was stronger than fear of blows. As a piece of meat was rescued from one dog, another—or two others—would seize it. Blows flew as did dogs. Five minutes passed before the battle came to an end, only because Koojesse leaped over the walls of the igloo under construction and came to the aid of the two men. In the process, Koojesse's seal spear broke—the worst of calamities for the enraged owner.

The dogs' hunger was not abated and their poor condition continued to slow progress. (Lucky was the dog, such as one Hall observed while visiting with an Inuit family, that was allowed to lick clean the seal soup bowl before it was filled for the next person in line.)

In spite of all the difficulties, Hall, as was his nature, pushed on, continuing his studies of the bay and its first foreign visitor, Frobisher. Sharkey and Koojesse made every effort at hunting—seals, white whales, and ducks were all in abundance—but were unsuccessful. Men and dogs were now living on *kow*—walrus hide with hair on it.

Then, one day, success! They bagged one seal and the next day, two seals. Finally, the dogs could be fed.

As April turned to May, the weather continued to warm. Excursions continued to reach out across the bay, and the dogs to weaken. The team now numbered ten, and progress was slow, only three and a half to four and a half miles per hour.

A sudden victory in hunting gave Hall the confidence to set out on yet another quick exploration up the bay. On this venture, traveling with companions Koojesse and Sharkey, he experienced a dramatic effect of the dogs' hunger. Spotting a seal, the dogs bounded off "at a rate of not less than twelve miles an hour." The seal plunged into its hole, escaping, and the dogs flew by; but, as the scent of the seal reached them, they turned so sharply the left sledge runner caught in the snow crust and split in two, hurling Hall off the sledge. Happily, Koojesse and Sharkey were able to repair the twelve-foot-long runner and keep the party on the move.

Gales blew. Koojesse became sick. There was no food for the dogs, who became increasingly voracious. They ate a whip, thirty feet long. One swallowed a piece of *kow* one and a half inches thick and six feet long in seven seconds: Hall timed him.

Suddenly, as they traveled, a polar bear and cub appeared. The dogs were cut from their traces and raced toward the bear, which moved with her cub onto the mainland and high ground. One dog attacked the cub, separating it from its mother. Another dog sprang at the mother, then tumbled with her down a cliff. The mother pulled out of the fight and tried to regain the cliff and her cub. Eleven dogs took after the cub until one seized it and tumbled down with it. As the cub raced toward Hall, he speared it and killed it, while the mother ran off. Only later did Hall realize what a mistake he had made: Inuit hunters would never kill a cub before its mother and thus increase her dangerous wrath. Later, Barbekark got loose from the sledge and found and ate the buried liver of the cub: Inuit hunters never ate the head or liver of a bear or allowed their dogs to.

On May 21, Hall returned to the *George Henry*, where he concentrated all thought and effort on return to the United States and preparation for the next and ultimate exploration—of King William's Land and the mystery of the Franklin expedition.

On June 14, Hall set out by himself for the whaling depot. As no other sledges were available, he took a small one and two dogs, one of them Barbekark, which "by dint of hard blows" Hall managed to keep in proper position. Along the way, seven Inuit friends joined him along with their two large dog teams and sledges. Such was travel in the Arctic—always fluid, always dependent on the vagaries of weather, food supplies, availability and ability of the dogs—and the needs of the people met along the way. A sudden illness or injury, an unexpected kill, or discovery of a cache could throw all timing off. A spontaneous feast, or a storm, might require days of staying put. At the same time, a death would be dealt with quickly, the body placed in whatever monument was possible—often the place where the person fell—and left to the care of the elements and the attendance of animals while the mourners moved on to the next encampment.

All at the whaling depot were well and Hall planned for a last sledge trip through Cornelius Grinnell Bay, to the north. Already conditions on the melting ice were becoming dangerous, however, and Hall had to curtail his plans. The season of boats had replaced the season of dogs. The ice, which imprisoned, also required a price for freedom. When it let go its hold on ships, it took away its highways for sledges.

The *George Henry* was ready to leave. On August 9, 1862, the anchor was raised and the whaler was towed down the breezeless bay on the long way home. Hall was on board with his "faithful" dog Barbekark, which "could not be forgotten nor left behind." Tookoolito, Ebierbing, and Tukeliketa were also with him, along with their "fine seal dog," Ratty. The Inuit couple's only concern was that they would lose their child; many visitors from the cold climates did not return from their voyages to England and America.

Tukeliketa would be dead in New York on February 28, 1863, at eighteen months. He is buried in Groton, Connecticut, in the Starr Burying Ground within a little village of Inuit travelers including his mother and adopted sister.

Barbekark also would die in the United States as Hall campaigned for his second expedition.

No record remains of Ratty; but he, too, undoubtedly did not long survive the heat and stress of his American visit.

The bear hunt.
Hall, *Vol. II*, p. 271

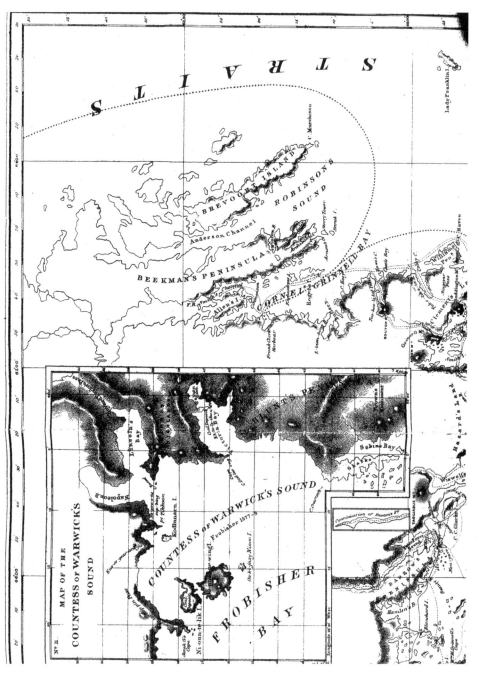

Top right half of map of Frobisher Bay.
Hall, *Vol. I*, back papers

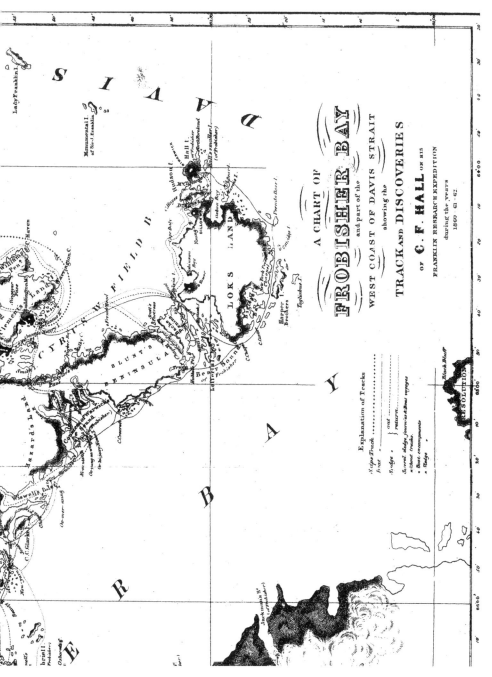

Bottom right half of map of Frobisher Bay.
Hall, *Vol. I*, back papers

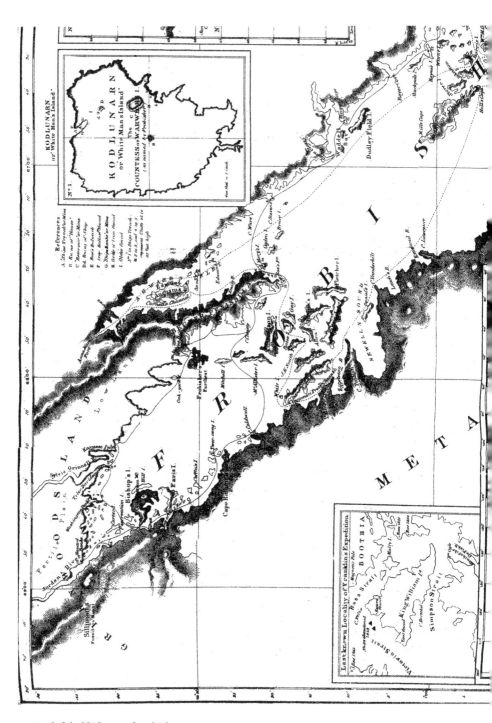

Top left half of map of Frobisher Bay.
Hall, *Vol. I*, back papers

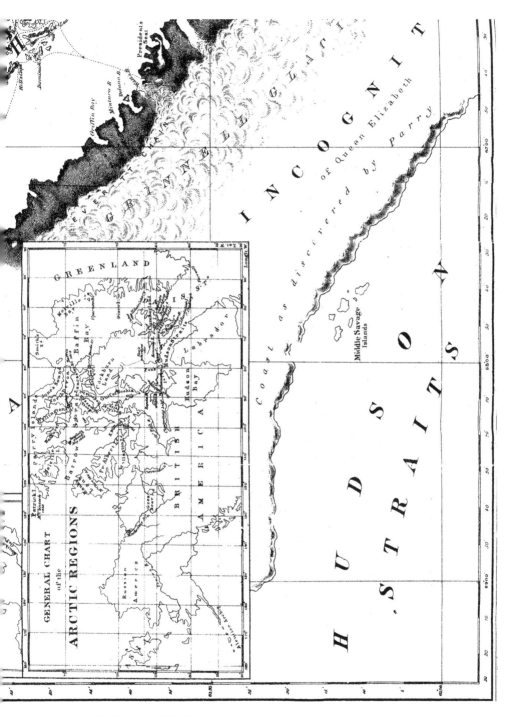

Bottom left half of map of Frobisher Bay.
Hall, *Vol. I*, back papers

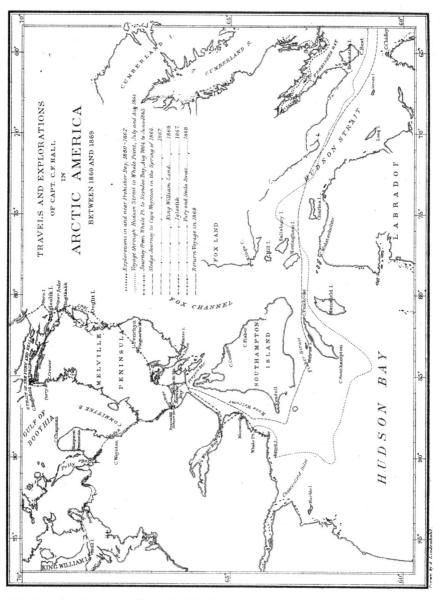

Travels and explorations of Capt. C. F. Hall in Arctic America between 1860 and 1869.

C.H. Davis, editor, *Narrative of the North Polar Expedition, U.S. Ship* Polaris, *Captain Charles Francis Hall Commanding...*, p. 195

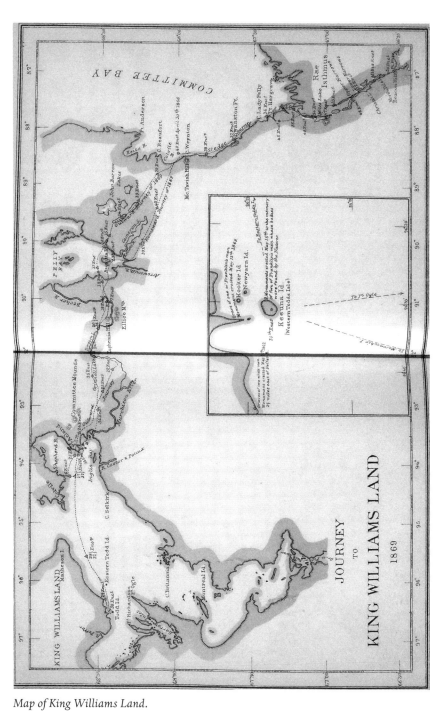

Map of King Williams Land.

Hall and his expedition crossing Frobisher Bay.
Hall, *Vol. II*, p. 277

12

Dogs as Showmen

When Toodla and Whitey came home with Elisha Kent Kane, and when Barbekark returned with Charles Francis Hall, they began a new life as entertainers. In both cases the quest for fame and finances necessitated public appearances for their masters. Kane, already immensely popular, was working toward publication and promotion of his book on his second arctic expedition, 1853–1855. In the case of Hall, the motivation was funding for the next trip, for he was determined to return to the search for Franklin—and perhaps pursue another goal as well.

Writing and editing a book describing his first trip while lecturing and pursuing every possibility to gain support for the second trip, Hall pushed himself—and Tookoolito and Ebierbing, who accompanied him—to exhaustion. The Baffin Island family, especially, were worn out by the demands, crowds, and heat of their hurried schedule of exhibitions, including a two-week engagement at P. T. Barnum's American Museum in New York and a similar commitment at Cutting and Guay's Aquarial Gardens in Boston.

Barnum's Museum, which opened in 1842, was enormously popular. At its peak it was open fifteen hours a day and had as many as 15,000 visitors a day. A newspaper ad for Barnum's from November 20, 1862, under the classification "Amusements," promotes "Esquimaux Indians Which have just arrived in this country FROM THE ARCTIC REGIONS... Being the first and only INHABITANTS OF THESE FROZEN REGIONS ever brought to this country, they are objects of universal interest; but they can remain only this week. SEE THEM NOW OR YOU'RE TOO LATE. They are on exhibition from 10 A.M. till 12 M, from 2 till 4, and from 7 till 10 P.M." Another ad touts the presence of "their FAITHFUL dog, BARBEKARK."

Finally, on the advice of friends, Hall curtailed the family's engagements, limiting them to his own lectures. These lectures, in the winter of 1862–1863, took place in a number of cities including Providence, Norwich, Hartford, New Haven, Hudson, and Elmira. At Elmira, the Inuit family took sick with colds. Late in January, from his quarters on Fourth Street in New York, Hall wrote to Captain Budington in Groton, asking him to "take the Eskimos into your family." But before that could happen, the colds had turned into pneumonia. On February 28, 1863, Tukeliketa, eighteen-month-old Little Butterfly, died. Tookoolito slipped into unconsciousness and delirium, almost succeeding in her wish to join him in death.

We know that Tookoolito, several weeks later, following the custom of her people, placed her child's playthings on his grave; but we do not know what happened to Barbekark and Ratty, which came to join Barnum's ranks of Chang and Eng the Siamese twins, the Feejee Mermaid, flea circuses, dancing bears, and a loom run by a dog.

The final words on Barbekark are Hall's. Writing in his *Life with the Esquimaux*, published in 1864, he says of his dog, "He shared all my labours with me, and was here as my companion in the States, until he died a few months back."

13

Wolf, Smarty, Bear, Shoemaker, Tiger

Riding a Doomed Ship

Traveling with Hall's North Polar Expedition,
U.S. Ship Polaris, *1871–1873*

In spite of everything working against him, especially the specter and financial drain of the Civil War, Charles Francis Hall managed to scrape together enough funds to return to the Arctic for a second expedition in 1864–1869, visiting Repulse Bay, the Straits of Fury and Hecla, and King William's Land. Tookoolito and Ebierbing traveled with him. Once more, he was seeking the lost Franklin expedition, and once more he met insurmountable difficulties—first and foremost a lack of dogs; second, an unwillingness on the part of his Inuit helpers to travel to a place where they feared hostile inhabitants.

During Hall's aborted effort in the spring of 1866, Tookoolito suffered the most profound of losses—her second son, the infant Hall had insisted on naming Little King William. The eight-month-old baby, ill for some time, died on the return trip and was buried on an empty hilltop in bitter weather.

When he did finally manage to get to King William's Land for a hurried visit in the spring of 1869, Hall discovered artifacts of the missing men—a mahogany writing desk, silver spoons, parts of a boat, and so on.

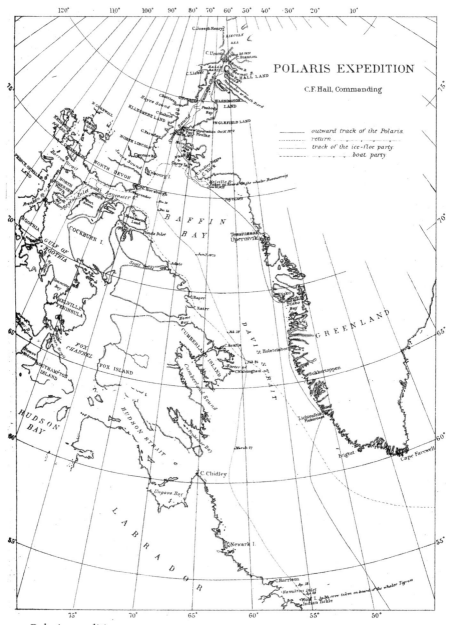

Polaris *expedition.*
Davis, facing p. 46

He also found a thigh bone and a full skeleton that he managed to return to England and that was later identified as that of Lieutenant Henry Le Vesconte of the *Erebus*.

From the local people he pieced together a narrative of the Franklin victims as they fled their ice-bound ships and, dragging huge weights behind them, sought safety. Some of the last survivors, led by Lieutenant Francis Crozier, apparently were abandoned by local bands who were, at the time, starving themselves. Increasingly disillusioned by the vagaries of these northern people, Hall was unable to forgive them for this lapse.

After his five-year saga—one of endless frustrations—Hall returned to New Bedford with Tookoolito and Ebierbing, along with Punny, the daughter they had adopted; but this time there was no Barbekark or Ratty.

Hall had his notes but did not live to write them up. The record of this lengthy and extraordinary adventure comes to us as *Narrative of the Second Arctic Expedition Made by Charles F. Hall: His Voyage to Repulse Bay, Sledge Journeys to the Straits of Fury and Hecla and to King William's Land, and Residence among the Eskimos during the Years 1864–'69*, edited by J. E. Nourse of the U.S. Navy. Lacking Hall's personal attention and interest, the story of the dogs grows faint, though their importance is never understated.

Once home, the period after his second expedition was similar to that after his first: Hall plunged into lecturing and lobbying in order to raise funds to return to the Arctic. This time his goal was clearly stated: the North Pole. In spite of pressures from Lady Franklin, Hall was ready to relinquish his search for the lost explorer and move on to the yet unclaimed Pole.

With the Civil War recently passed and the Franklin search largely dismissed, the American public had lost interest in the Arctic and Hall had to work particularly hard to find support for his North Pole quest. As before, he threw himself into lecturing, writing letters, and buttonholing members of Congress. Isaac I. Hayes, his competitor, arrived in Washington, D.C., at the same time to argue that he deserved funds for an arctic expedition more than Hall did.

After much delay, Congress finally awarded Hall $50,000—half of what he had requested. On July 20, 1870, President Grant wrote to him that he was to be in command of "the expedition towards the North Pole," reporting to the Secretary of the Navy and the Secretary of the Interior.

Hall spent the next eleven months hurriedly putting together his crew, his equipment, and his ship—too hurriedly, it would turn out.

The *Polaris*, formerly the U.S. steamer *Periwinkle*, fourth rate, steamed out of New York on June 29, 1871, with commendations from President Grant and instructions from the U.S. Navy to reach the North Pole by whatever means Commander Hall should deem most appropriate—vessels, boats, and sledges. Sailing and ice master was Captain Sydney O. Budington, formerly of the *George Henry*. Also on board were George Tyson, formerly a whaling captain, as assistant navigator and master of sledges, and William Morton, Elisha Kent Kane's personal assistant. Tookoolito, Ebierbing, and Punny were there also, to be joined by Inuit hunter Hans Hendrik and his family, which now consisted of his wife Mersek and three children. Hall named these children as Augustina, Tobias, and Succi. (Hans, who had previously served Kane and Hayes, would go on to serve the George Strong Nares expedition of 1875–1876.) An otherwise oddly mixed crew— from Prussia, Germany, Russia, Sweden, and Denmark—would prove to be strangers indeed, fractious and unreliable. As if underscoring contentious relationships, the *Polaris* carried, as had its predecessors, the Wilkes flag from Antarctica.

Because Hall did not survive the trip, his account comes to us from his notes edited by Rear-Admiral C. H. Davis of the U.S. Naval Observatory.

Among the expedition's orders was one to procure dogs at ports in Greenland, but Hall did not wait that long. At St. John's, Newfoundland, he took on six Newfoundland dogs, three of which were puppies, and capelin with which to feed them. When Hans, who was to be dog-driver, came aboard at Upernavik, Greenland, with his family and goods, he also brought puppies whose eyes had barely opened.

At Upernavik, twelve dogs were taken on board, "increasing the certainty," Hall's editor notes, "of the night's being made hideous by interminable howlings." Also added were ninety seal skins and 100 dog skins. At the next stop up the coast, Kingitoke, there were further negotiations for dogs and skins, but none could be had. The governor of the little settlement had a large number of good dogs but nothing could induce him to part with any of them. It was only through the efforts of Governor Elberg of Holsteinborg, and with much difficulty, that eleven dogs were obtained from some of the inhabitants. At the last and most northern stop, Tasiussaq, Hall was disappointed by Peter Jensen, the Greenlandic Inuit who had served Hayes as hunter, dog-driver, and interpreter. Hall had hoped to entice him to join the expedition. Jensen refused, citing family need, but did help by furnishing dogs and skins.

Now it was time to leave human habitation and set forth into the unknown Arctic. At three in the afternoon of August 24, 1871, the governors of the settlements who had been traveling with them took leave in their boat, carrying Hall's last dispatches home. One letter stated, "The *Polaris* bids adieu to the civilized world." There were thirty-three men, women, and children on board—and an unstated number of dogs (a lapse of narrative detail Hall would never have allowed).

Less than a week later, on August 30, the *Polaris* reached its northernmost point—by Hall's calculations, 82° 26'—and, blocked by ice, was attached to a floe that was moving south. The overriding need was to find winter quarters. Before that could be done, the ship was "nipped"—pinched by ice severely enough that it was thought to be in danger of sinking. Supplies were unloaded on the floe. But *Polaris* escaped and chugged off—only to be in sudden danger of catching on fire: Problems in the engine room had almost gotten out of hand.

The double deliverance from fire and ice brought prayers and an expedited choice of anchorage. The harbor selected, on the far northwestern coast of Greenland, was to become known as Thank God Harbor and the iceberg to which the ship was anchored as Providence Berg.

Only now, with the ship settled in for the winter, did Davis, editing Hall's notes, give us news of the dogs, news that sounded reassuringly similar to previous postings: Housed on shore, the dogs found the ice between them and the ship sufficiently strong to bear them and they hunted around the ship in search of food. During their searches they managed to knock over a barrel in which the sextants and the artificial horizons had been placed for safekeeping. With the barrel overturned, the dogs broke open the carefully packed boxes and dragged out some of the instruments, though fortunately doing no serious injury.

To keep the dogs from disturbing the sleep of the crew, and to provide some shelter for them, one of the ship's boats was turned on its side on shore and prepared as a kennel. Until they had been put ashore, the dogs had been a danger to anyone on board who had anything resembling food. It had been particularly difficult for John Herron, the steward, who was a man of slight stature.

Soon their work began. In spite of high winds and heavy snowfall, two of the Newfoundland dogs were harnessed to a sledge and pulled to shore the materials for a house Hall wanted to build for recreational purposes. The house was built entirely of boxes and barrels containing clothing and provisions.

More serious work began on September 18 with a hunting party going out in search of musk oxen. A sledge drawn by eight dogs, driven by Ebierbing and Hans, carried the tent, sleeping bags, and provisions needed for seven days. Another reason for this venture—and the overriding plan—was to hunt for a feasible route to the north.

Although the plain the party crossed had insufficient snow for the sledges, the dogs more than earned their keep. As soon as a musk ox was spotted, the dogs were loosed and quickly brought it to bay, enabling the four hunters to kill it with just a few shots. It weighed 369 pounds and was considered a rarity on the western coast of Greenland.

Hall, of course, was eager to set forth to reconnoiter and select a route for his spring journey to the Pole. When he realized there was not enough snow for the sledges, he ordered the carpenter to construct a wagon. He would travel over open ground if need be.

On September 28, final preparations were made. The dogs were selected and carefully fed. The sledge and harness were examined and repaired. Heavy snow had just fallen and there was hope the dogs might be put to good use. Provisions were stowed in bags for people and dogs, with duplicates of perishable items provided.

Suddenly, in the midst of preparations, it appeared that the *Polaris* might be nipped, and, after that temporary crisis, other delays ensued. Finally, on October 10, Hall set forth on his journey, but not before leaving explicit instructions with Captain Budington as to the management of the crew, ship, and dogs, and particularly the puppies.

After the instructions had been given, Hall set out with first mate Chester, Ebierbing, and Hans. He had one sledge, heavily loaded, with a team of twelve dogs. At the start, he had to have the men who were working on shore help pull the sledge up the hill and through the deep snow for a distance of approximately half a mile. The next morning, Hans returned to the ship for another sledge, more dogs, and a few items that had been forgotten. Hall had made only five miles: not a favorable beginning for his aim of a highest northing, but Hall was accustomed to inauspicious beginnings.

When Hall returned to the *Polaris* two weeks later, he complained of not feeling well. He said he had not been able to run before the sledge and encourage the dogs as on previous trips but had been compelled to ride.

He was able, however, to report much news: No seals had been secured, and although tracks had been seen, no musk oxen or foxes had been seen. A large litter of pups had been devoured by the team as soon as born. The dogs' paws became sore as they broke through crusted snow over ice. At one point, Hall and Chester had an adventure with one of the Newfoundlanders, named Wolf, when the two men became separated by a steep ravine and Hall feared that Chester was lost. But Chester and Wolf reappeared on the other side of the ravine, and all three went on to survey a series of gorges, the rugged summits of which took them

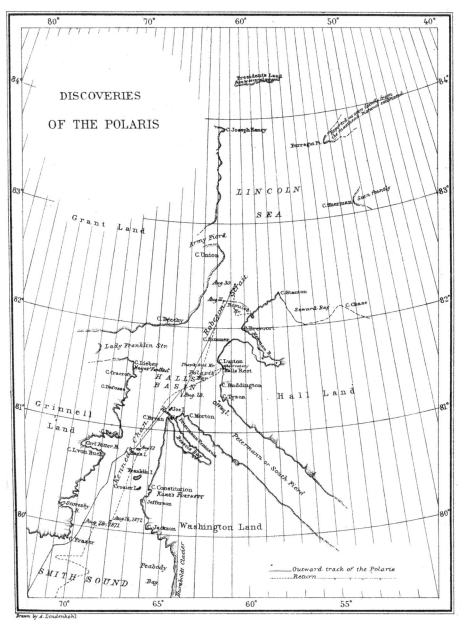

Discoveries of the Polaris.

to high vantage points. They reached 82° N and observed the last few rays of pre-winter sun. A fierce storm delayed their return. While storm-stayed, Hall deposited records in a cairn elaborately designed to maximize secrecy. The dispatch he left for the Secretary of the Navy, at the "Sixth Snow-House Encampment, Cape Brevoort, October 20, 1871," was to be his last.

Back on board the *Polaris* on October 24, Hall drank a cup of coffee brought to him by Herron, the steward, and immediately fell sick. He was dead on November 8 and on November 10 his body was taken to shore and buried. It is reported that the only sounds after the service were the sobs of Tookoolito.

Many years later, Hall's biographer, Chauncey C. Loomis, would lead a forensics team to the grave, exhume the body, and discover that Hall had suffered from massive doses of arsenic in the last two weeks of his life. Whether by murder or self-medication, Hall was gone, and with him the hopes of the North Polar Expedition. Captain Budington, now in command, had no desire to move north. The *Polaris* would never leave Thank God Harbor, though every one of her crew would return to the United States after suffering extraordinary danger and hardship.

For almost a year, the company would stay together on board, with increasing tension and disorder bordering on madness. The tragedy, the imprisonment by ice, the long arctic night, the loss of leadership, the abuse of alcohol, and the growing suspicion and dissension among a dangerously varied crew led to a breakdown in morale and order.

And what of the dogs during this perilous time? Davis tells us that as of November 3, during the time of Hall's fatal illness, when an assessment of all supplies and stores was undertaken, there were fifty-four dogs remaining. Right along there had been fear that an epidemic, such as had plagued the plans of Kane and Hayes, would break out, but so far the dogs were healthy. Up to now, from one cause or another, thirteen dogs had been lost—six adults and seven puppies. What remained were six Newfoundland and forty-eight local dogs. The puppies had died rapidly, by a strange disease that caused their bowels to protrude. Once afflicted, they had to be killed or would be torn apart by older ones. The dogs had generally been fed every other day, or, at times, twice a week. At first they were fed on the dried fish bought for that purpose at the Danish settlements and sometimes with the old seal meat procured at the same time. The puppies were also fed with bread.

Hermann Siemens, one of the crew members, had no doubt that the dogs were starved. Writing in his journal, he noted:

My heart would almost break when I saw the poor creatures thus starved. He who caused this will have to answer for it at the last day. He who delights in the sufferings of a beast will grow cold and heartless and surely also torment his fellow-men; he never can love God.

By the middle of November, the dogs' food had given out and the dogs were being fed on pemmican. A can weighing forty-five pounds was being allotted to them every three days, and feeding them was a tricky matter with a well-established protocol: The whole pack would be brought to the ship at the same time and let in through the door in the awning over the gangway. Ebierbing and Hans would chop up the pemmican and divide it into equal shares, while two or three other men would be on hand to assist and to control the dogs. When the food was ready, one dog at a time was allowed to go into the passage and remain there until he had eaten his portion; then he would be put back out on the ice. It was, as Davis noted, "always an exciting time." Keeping the dogs in order and keeping those already fed from returning for more required the utmost vigilance. At times they would attack the door of the gangway so violently it was almost impossible to keep them back. The men who stood with clubs at the door often had to use them. It was "exciting sport" for them, Davis said, and something they enjoyed in spite of the dangers.

When weather allowed, the dogs—particularly the Newfoundland dogs—were put to work training for spring work; and the men were not without sympathy. During one severe storm at the end of November, the dogs howled so piteously that the men opened the door of the gangway and allowed them all to come on deck to get some protection from the wind. During that storm, two sledges disappeared. After the storm, two dogs also were missing and it was thought they had been lost. When the entrance to the doghouse on shore was dug out, however, they were found safely tucked away inside.

During December, concern for the dogs continued. They were still being fed pemmican. In his journal, Captain Budington remarked: "We must care for them as much as we do for ourselves. The whole success of the expedition depends on our dogs, for with our vessel we cannot hope to reach a much higher latitude."

Various exploratory excursions were made during January 1872, mostly to examine the state of the ice that surrounded the stranded party. On January 19, two crew members with a sledge and eight dogs headed north, intending to reach the second cape up the coast. (Cape Lupton was the first.) When they got to their destination, they left the dogs and sledge in a safe place, ascended a hill, and looked out over a large area of open water shining with moonlight. On the return, they had to stop several times to disentangle the lines but made it back to the ship after a total of four hours. Five days later, another group traveling with a dog team reached the third cape north and also reported seeing open water.

During subsequent days, other sledge trips were made to inspect the water, which gave hope for spring travels. A large sledge was now built that could carry a boat to launch on this water, and two boats went into construction. As the winter months of 1872 moved darkly and slowly by, there was much discussion—certainly on paper—as to how to proceed, but no one ventured north in serious fashion.

On March 3, Mauch, the clerk, wrote in his journal:

> Today I have to announce a sad loss. Our yellow Esquimaux bitch "Smarty" is no more. The poor animal had young ones yesterday, some of which were devoured by the other dogs as soon as they were born. About 9 a.m., one of the men found the dog on deck and other dogs tearing her to pieces, and swallowing her partly alive. He chased the dogs all outside, and gave "Smarty" a nice place in a corner, where she soon was stiff. Indeed, the voraciousness of these Esquimaux dogs is beyond all limit. Not satisfied with her young ones, they tried to eat her up, too, just because the poor animal in her weakness could not defend herself. We can soon tell what good these dogs will do us.

Three days later, when the dogs were assessed, twenty-five were found to be in good condition for sledge travel, with numerous others that could also be used—sufficient to equip two or three parties for exploration. A few days later, however, several of the dogs experienced "fits"—the phenomenon cited frequently throughout the ice journals, but usually with few specific details.

It was only on March 27 that Dr. Bessels, science director, who was now in charge of sledging, set forth on an exploration. Traveling with R. W. D. Bryan, the astronomer; Ebierbing; a team of fourteen dogs; and provisions for fourteen days, he headed south to survey Cape Constitution. His goal of connecting Kane's cartography with their own, however, proved impossible, their venture marked by impediments and frustrations.

Six hours after they left, one of their dogs returned to the ship with a message written on a piece of wood tied around his neck: The party had forgotten India-rubber blankets and requested that they be sent on. Hans and an assistant complied.

On April 8, the Bessels party returned to *Polaris* with a report of slow going and inconclusive mapping. With fog, heavy snow, and hummocky ice, and with the sledge heavily laden, the dogs continually needed assistance, Bessels reported. On March 30, the dogs were "going very nicely and needed no urging," but Bryan, wanting to practice with the whip, swung the lash at them and, missing his mark, struck Bessels in the face instead, "which caused great pain and called forth some remarks of a significant character."

The next day, a sledge had broken and was patched for a return trip to the ship with Ebierbing and Bryan. Bessels, with a dog for companion, stayed behind, making geologic observations. Davis reported that Ebierbing caused the sledge to break on purpose—that he had complained from the beginning that one sledge, so heavily laden, would be impossible, but that Bessels had overridden his advice. Now Hans and a second sledge were added—along with increasing evidence of the acrimony on board.

One day Bessels attempted, alone, to make a trip up a fiord, but the dogs refused to go and proved to be the masters. The next day Ebierbing succeeded with them on the same route.

When the Bessels party from the south got back to camp, they brought with them a polar bear that Ebierbing had shot—and an exciting story to go with it. According to Tyson, one of the dogs—a "very plucky" dog named Bear—had been badly injured in the fight with its outsized prey and received solicitous attention from the men when he returned to the ship. Another dog, thrown with such violence against an ice hummock that it was left for dead, showed up at camp the next day nearly recovered.

On April 17, Ebierbing and Hans had to return early from a hunt: The dogs had gotten into such a desperate fight that nothing could be done with them. One was so badly injured it had to be killed. "The dogs go in pairs, which are inseparable," Davis noted. "They often crowd themselves, while running with the sleds, and in the hustling together have, at times, long and severe battles."

On May 1, another party, out on a musk ox hunt, lost one dog and were delayed while other dogs had "fits."

As the month went on, hunts were frequent, with the dogs in regular use. One day, Davis noted, there was sudden need for a team to bring back carcasses: "Notwithstanding that two of the best teams were away, the dogs, which had been hastily collected, pulled remarkably well, and brought the party back in a short time."

On May 20, a large sledge and a full team of dogs succeeded in pulling one of the newly constructed boats to the shores of Cape Lupton, four miles north of the ship. Four days later the second boat was transported. Other sledges followed with provisions. But the once open water was now covered with ice. As May turned into June, continuing trips north brought back the same discouraging report: Every surface was solid.

At the end of May, two live lemmings were caught for the purpose of being kept as pets, and a musk ox calf was brought back to the ship but had to be killed because of a broken leg.

A trip by Bryan and Ebierbing to the south proved particularly difficult. The honeycombed nature of the ice made the dogs' paws so sore they had to be protected with skin boots.

A serious and enthusiastic effort was now made to move the small boats north toward the Pole. Much winter discussion had made the goal seem feasible, exciting the crew with the possibility. Every time scouting parties viewed open or partially open water, hope flared. But the ice held and, on June 9, one of the two boats was crushed, with the loss of almost all supplies and equipment on board.

In the meantime, the *Polaris* was leaking and suffering badly from the effects of melting ice and turbulent weather. Increasing effort had to be put into pumping. When, at the end of June, the ice opened up, Captain Budington decided to sail north (though it seems clear he wanted only to go south). He called for the dogs and anything of value stored out on the ice to be placed on board. The *Polaris* got underway. But one day's outing to the north was all that could be achieved: The pack ice turned the ship back to the refuge of Thank God Harbor and the anchorage of Providence Berg.

Second and third efforts were made. On the third return to Thank God Harbor, the ice of Providence Berg was notably altered; the berg was no longer connected to shore ice, and some of the dogs had disappeared, undoubtedly having drifted out with the missing ice. Soon the ship was grounded on the shore, heeled over so far the scuppers were under water and under attack by floes careening through the harbor.

By mid-July, winter appeared to be coming on; still, there was hope that the vessel could find a break in the ice and, with six days' worth of coal, steam out as far south as Disco. By early August, however, young ice began to take hold around the ship.

On August 5, Hans was out in his kayak hunting geese when he found a dog that had been missing for eight days. It was Shoemaker, considered one of the best musk ox hunting dogs. He was wounded, undoubtedly by one of his prey. There was a hole the size of a musk ox horn in his side between two of his ribs and another through the fleshy part of his leg; and his belly was gored, nearly all of the skin removed. As soon as Hans got back with the news, one of the seamen immediately started down the coast carrying food for the injured dog. The next day, two other crewmen, Siemens and

Peter Johnson, also went to the rescue, carrying the dog back in a blanket slung on a pole over their shoulders.

In a rare positive event, Mersek, Hans's wife, gave birth to a boy on August 12. The crew unanimously named him Charles Polaris Hendrik. He became the fifth child of the expedition.

This was also the day on which Captain Budington decided to make a run for the south. The dogs, which now numbered twenty-one, were taken on board. At 4:30 p.m., the engines were started and the *Polaris* pulled out of Thank God Harbor. Just as the vessel got underway, one of the dogs considered to be among the best, a Newfoundland named Tiger, leaped over the stern bulwarks onto the ice. His loss, Davis reported, was "greatly regretted; he was a general favorite."

The *Polaris*, pummeled by ice and commanded by currents, drifted south, passing Cape Constitution and Kane's Rensselaer Harbor. Soon the ship was caught tight in the pack and nipped by ice. Imprisonment, darkness, scurvy, hunger, and frozen shipwreck loomed.

Only on August 21 were the dogs allowed to offload and run on the floe that had become their floating port. They were being kept in readiness for the essential seal hunting. As Ebierbing and Hans went off to the edge of the floe to seek prey, shipmates kept binoculars on them. As soon as the signal of success was given, the dogs were quickly harnessed and driven off with the scow to meet them.

The *Polaris*, locked within its floe, was drifting rapidly and irrevocably south with the pack ice of Baffin Bay. Occasionally icebergs, appearing as large as mountains, passed by in close proximity, and sometimes the floe swung about in complete revolutions while the pumps—and the pumpers—worked ceaselessly. By October, gales and heavy snow were lashing its gyrating world while final preparations were made to abandon the vessel.

On one occasion the tracks of three polar bears, an older one and two cubs, appeared near the ship, but the dogs discouraged the bears from coming closer, preventing their capture.

Starting early on the morning of October 15, a heavy snow began to fall and a forty-mile-per-hour gale to blow, first from the southeast and then from the southwest. Both snow and wind continued all day. About 6 p.m., the ship was nipped severely and Schumann, the engineer, cried out that the pumps could no longer keep up with the flooding. Captain Budington threw up his arms and ordered: "Throw everything on the ice!"

Great confusion followed as goods were indiscriminately heaved overboard and moved away from the ship while the pumps were kept going and the storm raged. The ship, it turned out, was not sinking. Leaving Budington and thirteen other men on board, George Tyson went back on the ice, working alongside Tookoolito, to try to save the provisions that had been thrown down helter-skelter.

Suddenly, the ice embracing the ship cracked and *Polaris* broke free, to be carried rapidly away into the black and snowy night, farther and farther from the floe that held more than half the party. Just as the break came, Tyson pulled away some musk ox skins lying across a wide crack in the ice. To his amazement, he discovered "two or three" of Hans's children rolled up in one of them.

Tyson walked the floe all night. Only in the dim light of morning would the seriousness of the separation be known. The North Polar Expedition had now bifurcated: Fourteen expedition members and the ship's cat and lemmings rode the battered *Polaris*, while nineteen souls, along with the remaining dogs, inhabited the runaway floe. The two groups would not meet again in the Arctic, and not for many months, but every single person would survive the extraordinary adventures, including eight-week-old Charlie Polaris. Only the animals would be lost—or sacrificed. None survived.

14

Tommy the Cat and the Lemmings

Life and Death after the Dogs

The Final Voyage of the Polaris:
October 15, 1872–June 23, 1873

From the crow's nest that dark and wild night of October 15, 1872, there was no sight of the floe party. All that was clear was that the ship would need to be scuttled. Slowly, the rudderless and fatally damaged *Polaris* was eased toward shore and supplies unloaded.

Three days later, as the work continued, came the sound of dogs, causing great excitement and anticipation, but the nine-dog sledge brought Inuit visitors, not lost colleagues. The strangers were dressed in dog-skin jumpers and bear-skin trousers. Fortuitously, it was men from Etah, former friends of Elisha Kent Kane and Isaac I. Hayes and of William Morton—Awahtok and Miouk—but they had no news of the floe party. They were surprised to meet the pet lemmings and the cat, animals they claimed they had never seen before. According to the ship's fireman, W. F. Campbell, the Inuit guests "had never seen a cat before and were very much interested in it. They gave it the name we called it by, Tommy. They have a name for it in the Esquimaux language, though they have not the animal itself."

While the castoffs built a house on shore and continued to remove supplies from the ship, more visitors from Etah arrived. First, six appeared

The separation. Oct. 15, 1872.
Davis, facing p. 524

with five teams of dogs, which were immediately put to work. "Four of their dogs," noted C. H. Davis, editor of the Navy's publication regarding Charles Francis Hall's North Polar Expedition, "would trot off gaily with a weight which four of the ship's crew could scarcely move." Eventually, almost the whole population of Etah joined the *Polaris* camp. The last two families to arrive came out of necessity. They had been so hungry they had been forced to kill and eat several of their dogs. Captain Budington, as with Kane in his day, was now unwillingly in charge of an expanded community bound together by mutual need.

Miouk, who continued to live at Etah with his family, made frequent trips to the house to beg for bread and blubber. In order to care for his family he was forced to kill four "fine" dogs.

Captain Budington made use of the opportunity to gather information from the visitors. He learned, for instance, much about the previous Hayes expedition. In one account, a group of visitors sleeping in the Hayes house one night dropped some fire into a powder cask and were blown up; four or five died. One guest, Arrowtah, had a wooden leg that had been repaired by Hayes.

Not every visitor was starving. In January 1873, a party of eight men, two women, and one child drawn by six teams of dogs arrived from Northumberland Island, to the south. They were all in good shape, including the "forty or fifty very fine dogs." These people, too, had been friends of Dr. Hayes, Kane, and Morton. Prominent among them was Kalutunah. They were also accompanied by an old woman, Atkootta, the widow of Metek. She seemed, after a while, to recognize Morton.

With so many visitors and their teams, it was possible for Captain Budington to fill a request of Dr. Bessels's to buy ten dogs so that he might make a sledge trip to the Humboldt Glacier, first seen and named by Kane.

Starving or not, increasing numbers of people found *Polaris* House. By March 24, there had been seventy-seven visitors, by May 1, 102, with as many as 150 dogs. (Davis estimated that the whole population of that region—the people Kane had wanted to move to the south—did not exceed 150.) On the night of March 30, there were twenty-three Inuit people stretched out on the floor. And while guests filled the floor space, the cat frolicked among them after sleeping all day on the captain's bunk.

In the meantime, *Polaris* the ship was taken apart, board by board and nail by nail, for the construction of two small boats to carry the company down the coast as soon as weather allowed.

While the construction continued, the Etah visitors made hunting trips possible. On one, Bryan fell asleep on the sledge as the dogs were working their way through heavy snow. Suddenly he was awakened by the sting of the driver's whip on his face. Turning to yell at the driver, he came to realize that he, too, was asleep, though continually lashing the dogs to keep them going. The trip was to Rensselaer Harbor, where Bryan, staying alone with one dog for a companion, made observations at the site of Kane's observatory. On the return walk, the dog refused to carry Bryan's pack and Bryan, exhausted, finally had to jettison it. While walking across the sea ice, he and the dog simultaneously sighted a large piece of seal meat and blubber and made a run for it. The dog reached it first, but Bryan succeeded in driving him off so that he could share it. Both refreshed by their serendipitous meal, they reached *Polaris* House after a period of twenty-eight and a half hours over a distance of sixty miles.

At the end of May, just before the abandonment of *Polaris* House, Bessels and Bryan visited Port Foulke, Hayes's base. There they found Sonntag's grave disturbed, his bones scattered about. They gathered up the bones, including "his fine large skull," reburied them, and reset the headstone.

Captain Budington ordered final preparations for departure by boat. Each man was allowed to carry eight pounds of personal property. Provisions for two and a half months were packed and Hall's library was cached.

On June 3, the two boats got underway, lurching into gales and heavy weather. Four days later, Captain Budington's boat had to be beached, cleared out, and turned bottom up for repairs. When Tommy the cat was taken from the boat, he ran away and disappeared among the rocks. He had become, Davis reported, "quite wild from the excitement of the journey and its confined quarters."

Somewhere along the way the lemmings also disappeared. Now, for the first time since the *Polaris* set out, there were no animals, only fourteen desperate men.

Fighting ice all the way, the two small boats struggled south for several weeks. On June 23, 1873, they established contact with the *Ravenscraig*, a whaler from Kirkcaldy, Scotland, and by midnight were kindly received aboard.

15

Bear, Spike, and the Nameless Prisoners

Castaways on Ice

Traveling with the Polaris *Floe Party,*
October 15, 1872–April 30, 1873

Holding the highest rank, George Tyson was suddenly captain of the ice floe and its accidental passengers. He walked his strange new vessel all night and took stock in the morning of what and whom he commanded: eighteen souls, including the two Inuit families and their five children; and one of those, Charlie Polaris, was eight weeks old. There were no charts or navigational equipment, but he did have assets, aside from his extensive arctic whaling experience: two whaleboats, various food supplies, and dogs. It isn't clear how many dogs—he did not enumerate them as he took inventory, nor did he give attention to them as Charles Francis Hall would have—but it was fewer than a dozen.

Almost immediately, there was another crisis and the new captain put the dogs right to work. The runaway floe itself split, severing the party from the larger piece of the ice island—the place where they had started. This bigger raft of ice held one of their boats, the house constructed before the separation, and various supplies. Several days later, the two moving pieces came close enough that a rescue was possible. Tyson remarked, "I fortunately had five or six dogs with me." There were no sledges, but by harnessing the dogs to the boat he and his assistants were able to haul it back to the smaller ice sheet where the party was encamped. A few days later, having decided that a larger piece of ice was essential for the castaways, Tyson had the dogs harnessed and had the two boats pulled over to the larger floe, where the party now settled down for a long-term stay. All hope of rescue by the *Polaris* had been given up.

Eventually, having two boats was to make all the difference between life and death. It could easily be argued that without the dogs at that moment and their part in securing the two boats on the larger floe, Tyson would not have lived to tell his story.

Ebierbing and Hans built igloos, and the company created a working community. Tyson moved in with Ebierbing, Tookoolito, and Punny. Schedules were set up. With only minimal food available, meals were limited to two per day and everyone's portion was weighed out with a pair of scales rigged up for the occasion—eleven ounces per day for adults, half portions for children.

Right away, as the supply of chocolate dwindled, it became clear that pilfering was occurring, but it was much too cold to stand guard over the storehouse. (Tyson had come away from the ship without even a coat or long pants.) Nothing is said about feeding the dogs, but clearly there was little if anything for them. Almost immediately, Hans killed, skinned, and butchered two of them.

But soon after, two dogs that had gone missing when the floe broke apart now reappeared: The sledge came back one day from the original encampment with Bear and Spike. "I suppose," Tyson noted, "since we brought the food away, they thought best to follow it."

Seal hunting failed, and hunger stalked closer. Tyson wrote on October 28:

> In consequence of there being no seals caught, I have nothing to give
> the dogs to eat. The poor things are almost dead. I cannot afford to
> give them our canned meats. They will have to go.

Attempts to reach shore often led to drastic consequences. Early in November, while pulling a sledge, the dogs were almost driven into the water before a wide crack was spotted. Increasingly, bad weather made efforts to reach land futile; at times, even pretensions of leaving the igloos were pointless. Darkness, added to fiercely cold conditions, made outdoor activity almost impossible, while any physical effort simply led to more hunger and exhaustion.

In the meantime, there was nothing to do but wait—and hope that the Inuit hunters might be successful. On November 6, Ebierbing secured a seal. At one point, Hans got lost and, momentarily mistaken for a bear, was almost shot as he returned.

On November 15, Tyson wrote:

> Our poor dogs are suffering; they got nothing at all today. Five have been shot altogether, leaving us only four; I regret it, but it can't be helped.

Every so often, the hunters would succeed, but there was never enough meat for food nor blubber for cooking and light. The rebellious crew members ("mostly Germans"), who lived apart in their own igloo, cut up one of the two whaleboats for fuel. Tyson, ill-clad and without a gun of his own, felt incapable of stopping them. He knew that eventually only a boat could save his passengers.

Bear tracks were found on the floe but no sight of a bear. "Our four remaining dogs," Tyson commented, "are very thin and poor and unless we get more food, they will either have to be killed or must starve. It is a great pity, for they would be very useful in bear-hunting."

Tyson's account fills increasingly with dark thoughts and reveries of meals that might be, but he stopped writing every day in order to save paper.

It still was impossible to tell exactly where they were, but the "German" faction insisted they were closer to the east, while Tyson guessed to the west. The "Germans," Tyson knew, wanted to make a break for the coast of Greenland and reach Disco, where supplies could be obtained. Ebierbing feared the rebellious men would kill and eat the two Inuit families—and the families shared his fears.

On January 16, 1873, Tyson reported: "Our dogs—we have two left—came in somewhat disabled; they appear to have had a skirmish with a bear. A bear would not be a bad addition to our impoverished larder."

Two days later he gave a fuller report:

> How our two dogs live I know not. A few days ago Joe [Ebierbing] discovered where one of them had been off hunting on his own account, and had evidently encountered two bears, indicated by the appearance of the ice, and held them at bay for some time. One of the bears must have hit him, for he came bleeding to the hut. The wound is but a slight scratch, however, and will soon heal.

Eventually, the sun returned, and with it, somewhat better sealing. Dovekies—small birds (now known as little auks) that augur spring—appeared, as did bears. The temperatures remained ferociously cold; the thermometer registered more than 40° below zero (until the mercury froze), but the hunters kept trying.

In late January, Tyson criticized Hans for losing "our best bear-dog." In bringing the dog home from a hunting trip, Hans let him off harness and, released, he disappeared. Was this Bear?

The second—and now last—dog was off hunting with Ebierbing. But shortly after, the last dog was gone as well. As he returned with Ebierbing, he sickened and died. Tyson reported:

> I fed him last night on what I was eating myself, seal skin and pretty well-picked bones; it may be that the bones caused his death, as they swallow such large pieces, or it may be something has happened to him that I do not know of. Well, it is the first and only natural death that has occurred, and that, surely, is wonderful; but it is astonishing what men can endure. It must be that the *hope* keeps us alive, and the poor beasts have not that to sustain them. They feel all their present misery, and can not anticipate relief. It will be a very difficult matter to capture a bear now, without a single dog.

It was also to be more lonely.

"It is now one hundred and seven days since I have seen printed words," Tyson recorded. Books and animals were gone.

And so the drift continued, day after day, week after week, through the pack ice of Baffin Bay into lower latitudes and lengthening light. Remarkably, only Tobias, the son of Hans and Mersek, became ill, but he recovered. Little Punny is recorded as saying, every few minutes, "I am *so* hungry."

The floe began to break apart, but Disco—and the hope of reaching it—had been left behind. Tyson knew that the only possibility for a landing was on the inhospitable west coast, the Canadian side, and that the effort to reach it would have to be made before the floe was totally shattered. As usual, everything depended upon obtaining enough seal meat, and now there was no dog to find the breathing holes. A bear escaped because there was no dog to sound the alarm and hold it at bay. Only one small meal a day could be provided.

Then, on March 2, relief! The hunters secured a 700-pound bearded seal that temporarily saved the starving prisoners.

As the floe shrank and they floated farther south, they approached, on the west coast, Cumberland Sound—Tyson's former whaling ground and the home of Tookoolito and Ebierbing. The couple must have wanted to make a break for it on their own—they undoubtedly would have survived—but they stayed true to Hall and his expedition. In adhering to the group, they undoubtedly saved the lives of all.

On April 1, the entire party of nineteen took to the one whaleboat designed for six or eight men. They made twenty miles before pulling up on another piece of ice to spend the night.

Now, with almost all goods jettisoned, the prisoners leaped from floe to floe as they continued to work their way west and south. Gales blew and the ice cracked beneath them, sometimes through their igloos and tent.

There was no space to lie down, no place that was dry. There was no rest—and almost no food. At night, the women and children stayed in the boat in case it had to be instantly launched. One night, about nine o'clock, huge waves carried away most of what few items remained on the ice. Every adult spent that night hanging on to the boat to keep it from being swept away along with the tent and skins.

Miraculously, soon after that tumultuous night, Ebierbing was able to shoot and secure a bear. It was a thin specimen with an empty stomach, but a welcome and life-saving feast.

Gales continued and the slabs of ice diminished, but on April 30, rescue arrived! The *Tigress* from Newfoundland answered their signals—a flag hoisted and three rounds shot from rifles and pistols—and picked them up. One crew member, when he heard about their ride on the ice, asked incredulously, "And was you on it night and day?"

Yes, the ice prisoners had traveled for six and one-half months down approximately 2,000 miles of Baffin Bay and Davis Strait to the mouth of the Atlantic Ocean off Labrador—the longest ice drift ever recorded.

All members of the North Polar Expedition except for the murdered Commander Hall made it safely back home and to the subsequent Navy inquiry in Washington, D.C. At the hearing, no one spoke for the animals or acknowledged the role the dogs had played.

16

Toekelegeto, Ublubliaq, Miqijuk

Racing with Hunger

Searching for Franklin Records with Lieutenant
Frederick Schwatka, 1878–1880

Lieutenant Frederick Schwatka (1849–1892), like Elisha Kent Kane and Isaac I. Hayes, was a physician. Like Charles Francis Hall, he had served as a printer's apprentice. Unlike any other predecessor, however, he had also graduated from West Point and had subsequently studied law and medicine simultaneously. He was admitted to the Nebraska bar in 1875 and received his medical degree from Bellevue Hospital Medical College in New York City the same year. While stationed at army posts in the Dakotas, he read everything he could on arctic exploration and the Franklin search, especially the accounts of Hall.

During the years between Kane's expedition of 1853–1855 and Schwatka's entry into the field, the British had continued the search for Franklin, with some success. Most notable had been the 1857–1859 voyage of Francis Leopold McClintock in the *Fox*, which had turned up the only document so far found, announcing the death of Franklin. McClintock and his party had also found skeletons and a wide variety of relics. The physical aspects of the case had been largely resolved. But rumors persisted of papers not yet found. One whaling captain, Thomas Barry, brought back

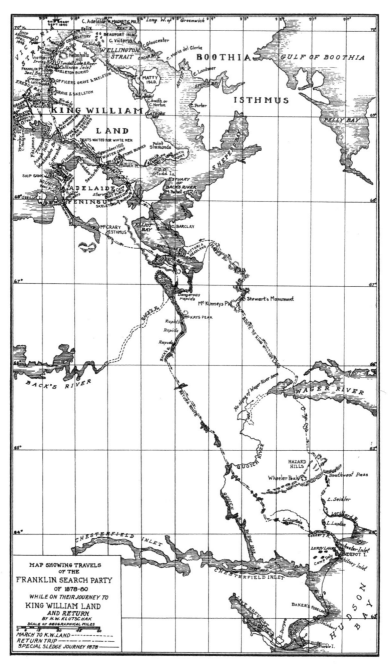

Map showing travels of the Franklin search party of 1878–80 while on their journey to King William Land and return.

Frederick Schwatka, *The Long Arctic Search: The Narrative of Lieutenant Frederick Schwatka, U.S.A., 1878–1880, Seeking the Records of the Lost Franklin Expedition*, p. 77

word from Hudson Bay that Inuit hunters had knowledge of papers deposited in a cairn on an island in the Gulf of Boothia, east of King William Island and the Boothia Peninsula. As proof, Barry brought back a silver spoon bearing Franklin's seal. Ebierbing corroborated the story. Fanned by newspaper articles, interest in the cairn and its alleged treasure swelled. When Schwatka heard that the American Geographical Society was organizing an expedition for the purpose of finding the cairn, he applied and was accepted as leader.

On August 7, 1878, the *Eothen*, carrying Schwatka's Search Party, put in near Depot Island, the small but important whaling center located in the northern end of Hudson Bay at the mouth of Roes Welcome Sound—the place that had been essential to Hall. Schwatka was traveling with Joe, that is, Ebierbing, who had covered so many miles with Hall. Tookoolito, the hunter's former wife, had died in Groton, Connecticut, on December 31, 1876, and their adopted daughter Punny the year before. With no reason to stay in the United States, Ebierbing had returned to the Arctic and remarried. He had already served on Sir Allen Young's *Pandora* search expedition of 1875–1876.

Second in command was Colonel William H. Gilder, who was to write the first account of the voyage. Also on board were naturalist Heinrich (Henry) Klutschak, who was to produce his own account, and Henry Melms, who, like Klutschak, had spent time with whalers in the Arctic. Captain Barry, whose credible reports of the Franklin papers—along with the single silver spoon—had launched the Search Party, oversaw a crew of twenty-three.

At Depot Island, the expedition secured dogs, sledges, and drivers. Though far from King William Land (Schwatka referred to it thus, not King William's Land as Hall did), Depot Island became the expedition base. The local people assured the newcomers it would make a good staging area for the search.

As with those before him, Schwatka noted immediately the need for dogs: "I felt the greatest solicitude in securing a sufficient supply of these valuable animals as in 1864 Captain Hall on these same grounds had been delayed three years on account of failure to obtain them."

On August 9, the men and dogs of the Search Party made camp on the granite shore near the *Eothen*: "What a dreary land it seemed to be." Schwatka named it Camp Daly, after Judge Charles P. Daly, the president of the American Geographical Society and the prime mover behind the expedition. It was situated a short distance to the south of Depot Island. An observatory was quickly established. The local residents settled down around the camp and caribou hunting began. By the time the hunt ended, between 200 and 300 caribou had been killed and cached. Various boat trips were made to explore the immediate area. When it became colder, in November, the party moved from a canvas tent into an igloo.

As preparations pressed forward, there were problems: Guides who had been promised did not appear and dogs were slow in coming. (The most important delay, Schwatka commented, was "the great scarcity of dogs.")

Finally, on December 28, 1878, Schwatka was able to set out on a preliminary exploration to the head of the Wager River, the quickest route to Back's River and, in turn, the quickest way to King William Land, site of the hoped-for papers. He was accompanied by two hunters, the wife and child of one, and a boy. His team consisted of nine "fine Esquimaux dogs, all my own." The sledge runners, which had no shoes, were covered with a mixture of mud and moss, frozen and iced. (Sometimes the contents of a caribou's stomach were used to coat the runners, but none of these, Schwatka noted, "will compare in value to the shoe made of long, longitudinal flat strips cut from the jawbone of the polar whale.")

Schwatka hoped, along the way, to find not only local people but also more dogs to buy. The scarcity of dogs around Camp Daly was a major concern. He had to have more.

As he searched for the Wager River, the year changed from 1878 to 1879. After sixteen days, he was back in camp on January 13. In the meantime, his assistants Gilder and Klutschak had set out with Inuit drivers on a journey to the whale ships anchored in ice at Marble Island, a hundred miles to the south. Their goal was to obtain dogs. Already, during Schwatka's absence, five dogs had been secured. Added to those belonging to Inuit hunters, there were now forty-four, a number Schwatka considered the "barest minimum number" necessary for the projected journey to King William Land. When some hunters from Whale Point stopped by, joining the "colony of beggars," Schwatka took advantage of the situation by obtaining ten more dogs: "Remembering how near disastrous a delay which Captain Hall had suffered by lack of dogs, I felt that I had anticipated such a situation, and nothing less than a dreaded dog disease could serve as an annoying delay." He also received some information about the cache of Franklin papers he was planning to search for: One of the Whale Point visitors claimed his father had found a stone cairn on the south coast of King William Land that had contained paper.

Now another problem emerged: According to local superstition, once caribou season gave way to walrus and seal, no more caribou could be eaten, at least not if one continued to live in the same igloo. Schwatka was not allowed to receive any caribou meat for himself or the dogs as long as he lived in the present igloo. Only if he built and moved to another, could caribou meat be provided. Finally, he resolved the problem by taking the dogs from Camp Daly over to Depot Island, where the residents allowed them to be fed.

By March 1, 1879, all the dogs that could possibly be begged and bartered for had been obtained, and soon after Schwatka returned to Camp Daly for final preparations. On the way, he encountered some hunters from Chesterfield Inlet from whom he was able to obtain another four dogs.

On April 1, he set forth on his search for the missing documents with a party of eighteen, including a number of women and children. One of the women was Ebierbing's new wife, "Nipschank or Hannah." (Tookoolito had also been called Hannah by the whalers.) There were three large sledges with runners shod with the bone from a whale's jaw and forty-four "very good dogs." Schwatka expected to be gone for nine or ten months. Two thousand pounds of kow was included in the cargo for the dogs. Yet the prospects were daunting: "With less than one month's provisions, we were separating ourselves by an icy desert of eight and nine leagues from all chance of rescue, with eighteen human and forty-four brute mouths to be fed in a country reported destitute of game." And they were, as Schwatka noted, "at the disposal of the angry clerk of the elements."

Traveling over land necessitated crossing through rocky portages connecting chains of lakes. Such going made it difficult to proceed without scraping all the ice off the sledge runners. The best driver, Schwatka claims, could guide his sledge "twenty feet unscratched through a rocky portage of a hundred yards in length."

Signal lights with a pyrotechnic display were fired at night to warn away wolves from a possible attack on the dogs, while the dogs, in turn, were successful with hunting musk oxen by day.

One night the howling of wolves was followed by the barking of dogs broadcasting danger. Toolooah, hunter and chief sledge-driver, thrust a signal light through a wall of the igloo: "It burned brilliantly in its varied colors of red and white, and we heard the rapidly receding howlings of the hungry pack as if they could not get away fast enough." As the party continued through the rough country on their way to the Wager River, wolves continued to follow them.

But the dogs could not always be saved. On the night of May 13, according to Gilder, "one of our best dogs," Toekelegeto—one of the leaders—choked to death on a bone:

He had eaten a piece of the shoulder-blade of the reindeer, which is thin and breaks into fine splinters. The Inuits usually hide this bone in the snow, as they say such accidents are frequent, especially when the dogs eat rapidly, as they always do when there is a number together.

On May 15, with much barking and excitement among the dogs, the Search Party came upon a band of Inuit people originally from the shores of King William Land who had lost their position there because of famine and attack by hostile tribes; now they were in great want. With Ebierbing as translator, two of the older men gave testimony that seemed to corroborate stories of the Franklin expedition, and the strangers had a number of relics of the lost ships to support their stories. One informant indicated that the cairn Schwatka sought was on Montreal Island, just east of Adelaide Peninsula and south of King William Land. Schwatka, strengthened in resolve, was more eager than ever to proceed with his search for the cairn. With the promise of a "gun and ammunition" and return to his camp during the winter, he hired one of the band, Nowleyout (the Spear-Thrower), as guide.

On May 21, in a fierce storm, the party reached Back's River, the intermediary goal toward which they had been struggling for two months. As storms continued to bear down on them, they worked their way up the river. When they reached the smoother saltwater ice, everyone rejoiced, "none more than the dogs themselves." Once they got to Montreal Island, Schwatka began searching for the cairn but could not locate it. They moved on to the Adelaide Peninsula.

They encountered a settlement on May 31, where they began hearing stories of the Franklin men, and, as word of the Schwatka party radiated out, more and more people came in to see them and provide further information. A woman about fifty-five years old was able to offer Schwatka specific memories of some of the lost party at Washington Bay, near Cape Herschel. She saw ten white men dragging a boat mounted on a sledge, she claimed. They had nothing to eat until some of her band caught several seals and shared them with the starving white men. She was able to describe three officers. Later, she saw some dead white men in a tent at the head of Terror Bay, with many belongings scattered about. Those items included a number of small books, some of which were used by the children as playthings.

Soon, inhabitants of another settlement produced more artifacts as well as stories. They also described a stone monument, which further excited Schwatka's interest.

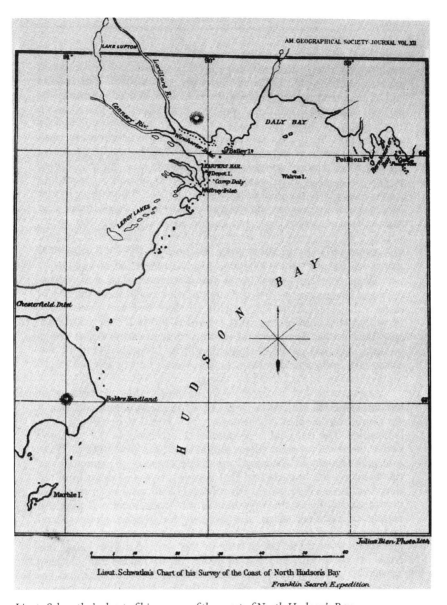

On June 5, in spite of a furious gale, the searchers, traveling with a light sledge and double team of dogs, reached King William Land and what they hoped was the long-sought cairn. What they found, however, was a terrible disappointment: The cairn turned out to be one constructed by Hall, ten years before, commemorating the graves of two of Franklin's men that he had come upon. Later, Schwatka's party found a third grave, which had gone undetected by Hall.

The next day, at Cape Geddes, they encountered a group of Inuit people that included a woman of seventy ("an old crone") who had spoken to Hall and who now gave Schwatka the information he did not want to hear and that "destroyed our fondest dreams": What "this ancient hag" told him was that there had been a central place in which the Franklin documents had been placed but that they had been hauled out by the natives, tossed to the winds, and given to children as playthings. Pages flew about for some years, then gradually disappeared. She and her son went on to tell of skeletons and a boat at Starvation Cove. And now came reports of cannibalism.

But every sad and grim detail paled beside her news: The records were gone, committed to the elements. In spite of almost overwhelming disappointment, Schwatka and his group decided to press on.

On June 12, the party split up, with some of the Inuit members staying behind at Cape Herschel with the heavy luggage, while the others continued north up the west coast of King William Land. The Inuit assistants were to stay put as long as there was adequate game but, if necessary, they were to travel down the coast or even cross over to the mainland, leaving stones to indicate their route.

Afterwards, the Search Party encountered its most difficult going. The snow was so soft, the sledge would sink and the dogs, floundering in slush, could not pull it out unaided. Still, the party made ten miles a day, because, Gilder says, of the dogs and their drivers:

> Without the assistance of dogs and natives, it is altogether probable that we would not have been able to accomplish more than two or three miles at the best; and I can well understand that Dr. Hayes had so much difficulty in crossing Smith Sound through the heavy hummocks in the spring of 1861. But at the same time I feel pretty well convinced that with plenty of good dogs and competent native drivers to manage the sledges, there is no ice in the Arctic that would prevent an average march of ten miles a day, with light loads, during the long days of spring.

Throughout his book, Gilder speaks most highly of Toolooah, the accomplished driver, who seemed able to achieve almost anything, never got tired, and never lost his positive outlook:

> There is something reassuring even in the tone in which he addresses the dogs. Many a time we have started to go through a place that seemed absolutely impassable until I heard that cheery cry, "Why-ah-woo-ha-hu-ah!" and saw him bend his own shoulder to the task. It seemed all right then. Even the dogs were more hopeful, and pulled with renewed energy.

On June 24, between Franklin Point and Cape Jane Franklin, they found a crude grave with a skull that they assumed to be that of a Franklin victim. Later, they found the grave of Lieutenant John Irving, third-ranking officer of the *Terror*, and after that they came upon a cache of relics.

On July 3, having found no further signs, they reached Cape Felix, the northernmost point of King William Land. Schwatka searched hard for the graves of Sir John Franklin and Lieutenant Graham Gore and the fourteen men who were known to have died in this area, but days of search between Cape Felix and Victory Point revealed nothing of significance.

They turned south on July 7, continuing to search the whole of the western shore as they retreated, occasionally finding artifacts.

One night while the cook stepped away from the meat he was cooking—and everyone else was asleep—the dogs took advantage of his momentary absence by tearing loose from their traces and raiding the stove. The always resourceful Toolooah jumped naked out of his sleeping bag and, rushing from the tent, showered the dogs with stones until they retreated. Their chief gain was some blubber.

By now—mid-July—the shore ice was melting and it was getting difficult to load items from land onto the sledges out on the sea ice. Still, the hunt for signs of the *Terror* and the *Erebus* continued, occasionally turning up bones, clothing, and personal items.

The simultaneous hunt for food was equally active. One day when meat supplies had run low, one of the hunters went out in a thick fog, accompanied by one of the dogs, and came back with three caribou. As Schwatka pointed out, having a dog in foggy hunting conditions is critical for the hunters, usually working in teams of two:

> The well-trained Esquimaux dog never barks when he is hunting thus. One of the party holds the animal and the other crawls cautiously forward on his victims. During the time the snow is on the ground they take several dogs and, after being successful, utilize them to drag in

the carcasses. An animal of keen scent will often detect the presence of game at two or three miles distance during a fair wind.

Of this period, Klutschak said of his team:

> Our 12 dogs are giving us the greatest concern. They have been lying here, tied to rocks for seven days now without food, and they cannot stand it for very much longer. But if we were to let them run free they would smell our last leg of caribou and renew their attack on it as they did last night.

The summer breakup of ice caused the party to separate further. Schwatka and Gilder, alone, searched Terror Bay as far west as Cape Crozier, while the others went to Gladman Point to ferry supplies across Simpson Strait with kayaks lashed together. Later, when conditions were favorable, the dogs were to be brought back to continue moving out the gear. In the meantime, Ebierbing and an assistant were exploring the Adelaide Peninsula. Schwatka was making use of every resource he had.

Two searches were always under way—one for caribou and one for Franklin artifacts. As Schwatka noted: "Without the reindeer my expedition of from nineteen to twenty-two souls and forty to fifty dogs could not have accomplished the journey it did, having only about a month's ration when it started from Camp Daly."

Happily, the caribou were plentiful, though relics and remains scant. Later, Schwatka would learn that six years before, the sea had washed away a number of skeletons he had anticipated finding in a spot indicated by Inuit informants.

When Ebierbing, disabled by rheumatism, returned to Schwatka's camp, he hobbled into the hut with a cane. He also brought in reports of having found bones, cloth, shoes, and a medal—but no records—in his search along the Adelaide Peninsula.

By the end of September, the ice in Simpson Strait, separating King William Land from the Adelaide Peninsula, was nearly strong enough to cross and preparations were made for the return trip south.

On November 1, 1879, the Search Party headed back to Camp Daly. Immediately, snow and stormy weather impeded their progress. But local people, in spite of Ebierbing's fears of hostility, added their teams to the effort and speeded up the travel across the hilly country. They reached Back's River on December 5. Schwatka's greatest concern at that point was the dogs:

> Not having seen a single reindeer during the trip from King William Land, our dogs having suffered badly in consequence. Averaging

eight days between feeds, during the last three times, and doing hard though fortunately not continuous service meanwhile, the powers of endurance of these brutes seems absolutely beyond comprehension. They bear up under this terrible strain of fasting with a fortitude that would bring compassion from the heart of a hickory tree. At our new camp on Back's River, however, we found several caches of fish and our half-starved dogs had a most royal feed.

Severe cold set in, with temperatures averaging 60° below zero. As they worked their way down Back's River, the suffering dogs got little food. Gilder, too, spoke of their not eating for eight days at a stretch, marveling that they could work at all: "I am constrained to believe that the Esquimaux dog will do more work, and with less food, than any other draught animal existing." He also mentioned how roughly they were treated, clubbed, and whipped. At best, now, Schwatka's dogs got occasional meals of fish. Klutschak described their Christmas feed, the last of this supply:

> The large lump of frozen fish which has just been unlashed and which a grown-up lad takes from the sledge in order to chop it into so-called "mouthfuls" (in fact quite suitable portions), using a pickaxe, has not escaped the notice of our largest and strongest dog, Ublubliaq (Star, in Inuktitut). First he raises his head, then stands up, and in an instant the entire unruly pack of dogs has followed his example; without any apparent effort dogs, sledges, and everything on them are racing in a wild chase to the point where the fish supplies are located.
>
> The Inuk, without any attempt at opposition, leaves it to the dogs to undertake the chopping-up of the fish themselves. The scene which now follows is of short duration but wholly typifies the Inuit dog as being the nearest relative of the wolf.

The fish was now gone and there was little new meat, while the "razor edged weather" further wore the dogs down; they were beginning to collapse. According to Schwatka:

> Before we left the river we had lost one fine dog and so drained the vitality out of the rest that we increased the mortality to twenty-two before we reached Camp Daly. It was pitiful in the extreme to be compelled to notice the silent sufferings of these faithful companions. As they slowly fell by the wayside there was an attitude of devotion, as if this sacrifice was self-imposed to aid as much as possible our uncomfortable journeyings. Ravenous as they were, tearing everything to pieces not actually wood or iron, or raiding fearlessly into

the igloos in quest of food, they are faithful respecters of their human companions. Not even once did I ever observe them attempting to harm the little children that wandered innocently among them, petting them with their toy whips, when a half an hour afterwards they would be savagely tearing a dead starved companion limb from limb to secure the hide which was nearly all that was left of him.

Gilder claimed that twenty-seven dogs were lost, all but four from hunger and cold. Klutschak corroborated much of what Schwatka said of the faithfulness of the dogs and their deference to people. If, he said, a dog ever did bite a child or an adult, it had to be killed immediately. He also described how a failing dog would keep going until it collapsed and died. There was no way to spot exhaustion, he maintained. A dog would run with the team, pulling well, until the moment it gave way. Even when the fallen dog was loaded on a sledge, it was hopeless. Subsequently, he said, "we simply removed the harness and left them lying; fifteen minutes later we would hear a pack of wolves quarreling over the animal we had left lying." One of those who gave out was Miqijuk ("He Is Little"), whom Klutschak called "our favorite dog."

The year 1879 came to a grueling end as the Search Party left Back's River and headed for Depot Island and Camp Daly. With the loss of dogs— Gilder said it was common to lose one or two a day—the men were helping to haul the sledges. The temperature was still 60° below zero, and it would go lower, even to 71° below. On January 3, 1880, a vigorous and unsuccessful musk oxen chase took place at 65° below zero. The dogs ate Schwatka's morocco valise and two gun covers one night.

There were only twenty-seven dogs left, nine to each of the three sledges, and wolves were moving in closer. At night they would drive the dogs from their food right at the door to the igloo. On the night of February 9, a driver was feeding fresh caribou to the dogs when he saw what he thought was a larger dog taking food from a smaller dog. He tried to kick it away, when it snapped at him and he realized it was a wolf and shot it. Another night, Ebierbing had a close call when he went to rescue a dog from a wolf that, in turn, seized him by the breast of his caribou coat. Ebierbing knocked it off with his gun and shot it before it could spring at him again. But that same night, the wolves attacked and tore apart four of the dogs.

The Inuit hunters would stand for no more. The next night, they built a special igloo for the dogs and locked them up for safekeeping. Ebierbing then smeared caribou blood on two sharp blades and buried them in the snow with the blades up and blood showing. When the wolves arrived and started licking the blood, they lacerated their tongues, then continued to lick their own blood until they bled to death or died of the wounds. Three wolves thus met their end.

But that wasn't all. Ebierbing had another method to apply. He cut strips from a piece of baleen, fastened little triangular blades to their ends, and filed them to sharp points. He then rolled up the strips and tied them in a spiral coil with caribou sinew and hid them in meat that was then frozen solid. These deadly pieces, scattered about the camp, were quickly found and eaten by the wolves. As the meat thawed in their stomachs, the baleen would spring open as fatal and agonizing weapons.

On one occasion, unsuccessful at the hunt and starving, the party was happy to find a carcass left by wolves.

By the end of February, cold, hunger, and wolf predation had taken their toll. There were now only sixteen dogs left (Gilder said nineteen) and two sledges; one had been used for fuel. But the party was almost "home."

On February 28, Schwatka started on the final push. "The non-emotional Innuits," he noted, "caught something of the inspiration of the hour and be-labored the poor dogs harder and talked a great deal louder than usual."

Twenty miles out, Gilder said, the dogs sensed home and "coiled their tails over their backs and ran along barking until we halted for the night."

The next day, March 4, the struggling, starving party reached the out-skirts of their home base, Camp Daly, where they learned that the winter had also been a hard one for those who had stayed behind at the whaling center. At one point residents had been reduced to eating their starving dogs and their seal and walrus lines.

Worst of all, when the party reached Camp Daly, they discovered that Captain Barry and the *Eothen* had sailed without them, taking all their supplies. Schwatka could not provide the feast he had planned for his Inuit friends; indeed, he and his returning party were now dependent on the largesse of his generous but ill-supplied hosts, and soon famine set in.

Although deserted by their captain, the Search Party found another American whaler overwintering at Marble Island that provided welcome, comfort, and—most importantly—a ride home: the *George and Mary* of New Bedford, captained by M. A. Baker. Ebierbing and his new wife de-cided, at the last moment, not to accompany Schwatka back to the United States, as did Toolooah and his wife, who had learned from Ebierbing just how dangerous it was for Inuit people to visit that faraway country.

There is no more mention of dogs—they fade away into the barren landscape of Hudson Bay—but the story ends with a hunt that ordinarily would have been done with dogs: As the ship moved south through the pack ice, a sleeping polar bear sow and cub were spied on a cake of ice a quarter of a mile away. A boat was lowered as the sow swam off with her cub on her back. When the bears climbed up on ice, Schwatka shot and dropped the sow, soon killing her with another bullet. The cub, trying to cover its mother's body, licked her face and wounds, then growled fiercely to warn off the enemies. Schwatka, out on the ice, threw a rope over the cub's neck and had it towed back to the ship. Hoisted on deck with its mother's body, it continued to growl and rush at anyone who approached. The Search Party wanted to bring the "handsome little rascal" home, but Captain Baker said there was no room and ordered it shot.

The incident is reminiscent of Hall's and Ebierbing's adventure with a polar bear after leaving Repulse Bay on the *Ansell Gibbs* in September 1869, at the conclusion of Hall's second expedition. While the captain cruised for whales, Hall and Ebierbing hunted on shore. One day they spied and followed a bear, weighing the danger of pursuing it without assistance from a dog or even the protection of a spear, but pursue it they did, managing to kill it, before sailing for New Bedford.

On September 22, 1880, the *George and Mary* brought the Schwatka Search Party into New Bedford to broadcast their news. The world would soon learn of their exploit—a sledge trip of more than eleven months covering almost 3,000 geographical miles—the longest sledge journey yet made—and completed with no human deaths. It would also learn there was no further hope that records of the lost Franklin expedition would ever be found; they had been given to the wind. In Schwatka's words, his effort "established the loss of the records of the Franklin Party beyond all reasonable doubt."

Hardly any mention was made that forty-four dogs started out from Depot Island on the epic search and that fewer than half returned. The exact number cannot be told any more than the last words of the Franklin mystery. We know little of the "silent sufferings of these faithful companions." Only a few names and anecdotes of the dogs remain. Their names and stories had been left behind in trackless, blowing snow.

Preparing for the long journey.
Schwatka, p. 48

Crossing Erebus Bay.
Schwatka, p. 92

Muskox hunt.
Klutschak, p. 55

Inuit departing.
Heinrich Klutschak, *Overland to Starvation Cove: with the Inuit in Search of Franklin 1878–1880*, p. 23

A tented fall camp, King William Island.
Klutschak. p. 122

An arctic ferry.
Klutschak, p. 115

17

The Importance of Naming

Every sledge dog, of course, was named. He or she had to be in order for the driver to be able to communicate with him or her. A name was necessary for a relationship that required demand and cooperation, willingness and patience—a relationship that could make the difference between life and death.

As anthropologist Franz Boas explained: "If any dog of the team is lazy the driver calls out his name and he is lashed, but it is necessary to hit the dog called, for if another is struck he feels wronged and will turn upon the dog whose name has been called; the leader enters into the quarrel, and soon the whole pack is huddled up in one howling and biting mass, and no amount of lashing and beating will separate the fighting team." In other instances, when dogs had to be lured across weak ice, the driver would call to them by name, calming and encouraging them.

Boas told us, too, that the "father of the house" christened the puppies as they were tended to with great care inside for their first four months.

Naming takes time and thought and can bestow significance. Naming shows respect, and respectful use of a name indicates acknowledgment and appreciation. Who does not take pleasure in being addressed properly by name, especially by someone who does not know us well, or someone in authority?

The dog held an important role in Inuit cosmology. According to the myth as related by Boas, Sedna's dog (in some versions the dog is her husband) lies across the threshold of her house, guarding it. The dead must enter her dwelling: "The dog moves aside only a little, just enough to allow the souls to pass. They have to stay in this dismal abode during a whole year."

Sometimes an *angakok*, in an effort to save a sick person, would change the patient's name or consecrate him as a dog to Sedna, the deity who ruled sea animals. In the latter case, the sick person would get a dog's name and would have to wear a harness over his inner jacket for the rest of his life. Sometimes friends would exchange names, and dogs would be called by the names of friends as a token of regard.

Names could change but had to root firmly enough to be known and accepted by the dogs. Often, however, the explorers did not tell us the names, or they told us only some of the names, and in random fashion. Sometimes the names are in Inuktitut and sometimes in English, and sometimes they are repeated, changed without explanation, and confused.

(An exception is Fridtjof Nansen, who carefully listed the name and weight of each of his twenty-eight dogs along with the specific contents of each of his three sledges in preparation for his departure from the *Fram* for his two-man trip across the Polar Sea. Nansen then closely followed the fates of the individual dogs, remarking on them specifically as they were killed one by one to feed the others.)

Early in his first journey, Charles Francis Hall introduced the six dogs he purchased, listing them by their "Greenland" names. Albert Hastings Markham, commander of the Nares expedition, offered a more informal approach. The dogs, he said,

> lived almost entirely in the fore part of the vessel, and were consequently especial favourites with the men, by whom they were fed and greatly petted. Of course they were all named, their appellations being more characteristic than euphonious. They rejoiced in such names as Ginger, so called on account of his colour; Bruin, because he was minus a tail, having been deprived of this appendage in his youthful days; Boss-eye, on account of the obliquity of his vision, or as our men expressed it, because "his eyes were rove cross-jack brace fashion"; Sore-sides, in consequence of the unfortunate dog when it came on board suffering from an unhealed wound in its side. Sallie, Topsy, Sly-boots, Jessie, etc., were the names of others.

Boats, and the sledges that carried them, were often named with more attention and ceremony than were the dogs. Markham, having noted how the boats were painted with "gay and brilliant devices," tersely stated, "The sledges were, of course, all named by their commanders."

Similarly, English names were often assigned in random and arbitrary fashion to the Inuit people. Tookoolito, for instance, was usually referred to by the whalers as Hannah, and her husband Ebierbing as Joe. (To confuse matters further, Ebierbing's second wife, Nipschank, was also referred to as Hannah.)

The original name of a place usually referred to a geographical feature or an event that occurred there that had significance to local inhabitants. Foreign names imposed on indigenous names usually referred to benefactors who made the "discovery" of such places financially possible and had nothing to do with topographical identity or history. Whalers, Christian missionaries, politicians, monarchs, and resource hunters left their imprint of irrelevant names across the Arctic, while misunderstandings and mistranslations also played a part.

As W. Gillies Ross states:

> Place-names present a formidable problem for several reasons. There were two different systems, one Eskimo and one Euro-American. No written language existed for the Eskimo names, and when whalemen, explorers, and missionaries adopted them they spelled them in various ways. No central authority existed to approve place-names, so spelling variants and duplications often occurred.

Hall claimed with enthusiasm that Tookoolito could do a better job as a translator than Carl Petersen and that, indeed, Petersen had not served Francis Leopold McClintock well. There were too many new words coming into local languages, he claimed (and some of these, introduced by the whalers, were anything but polite). Sometimes, when nomenclature failed, coordinates were substituted—a mathematical fix, but numbers do not speak with the same energy as words.

The area known to Hall, Tookoolito, Petersen, and McClintock, once part of Canada's Northwest Territories, is now Nunavut ("Our Land"). The capital city, Iqaluit, was for many years Frobisher Bay. Slowly the "modern" names are being returned to their original ones and the rash of accidental foreign names is fading.

An indigenous resident, once known as an Inuk, then an "Eskimo," is once more an Inuk. Other names have been more confusing. During the early 1940s, an Inuk, given an ancient family name by elders at birth, was then christened by missionaries with a biblical name and identified by the Canadian government with a number.

Sometimes it is hard to find a place on a map because of confusion of names or loss of names. If maps of dogs were made, the same would pertain. Canine cartography is a record of our consciousness. At what point do we decide that dogs are important enough to our geography to be set down on paper like mountains, like rivers, like oceans and continents? When we enter their world and recognize it as our own. When we find balance through respect.

Charles Edward Smith, surgeon of the *Diana*, was sure he was going to die, along with all his patients on the scurvy-ravaged, ice-locked ship. When he had to shoot his little dog Gyp, he took her collar and fastened it around his arm so that it might identify his corpse when it washed up on the coast of Labrador. This was his last hope. This, perhaps, was the first dog tag.

18

Kasmatka, Snoozer, Bingo, Snuffy, Tom, Jack, Wolf

Drifting to Farewell

Traveling with George W. De Long,
the Polar Expedition, 1879–1881

A graduate of the U.S. Naval Academy, George Washington De Long had gained his first arctic experience while on board the USS *Juniata*, the relief ship sent to find Charles Francis Hall's *Polaris* and its officers and crew. Volunteering for the dangerous task, De Long commanded a ten-day search in the steam launch *Little Juniata* from Upernavik, Greenland, into Melville Sound, considered the "nursery" of icebergs. Ice, fog, gales, cold, and hunger were his fare. He considered himself lucky to have survived but could not have imagined how much more there was to suffer.

Although the *Juniata* and the *Little Juniata* were to fail in their mission (the *Polaris* party were to find rescue on their own), Lieutenant De Long had caught polar fever. He immediately tendered to the Navy his services in the event of another arctic expedition and lobbied for such an opportunity. Some years passed, but he finally succeeded in persuading James Gordon Bennett, owner of the *New York Herald*, to underwrite an expedition to the North Pole. For De Long, it was a chance to prove himself in the Arctic. For the publicity-seeking Bennett, it was the opportunity

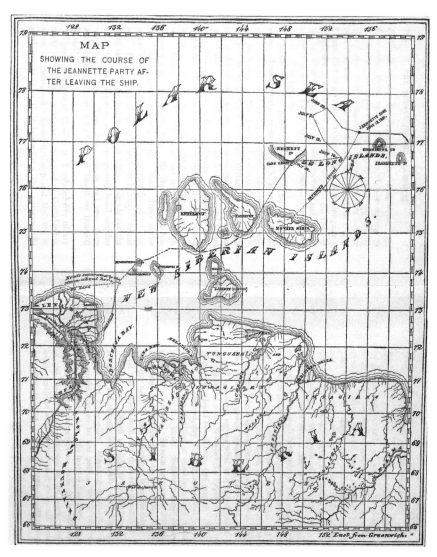

Map showing the course of the Jeannette *party after leaving the ship, 12 June–19 Sept. 1881*
(George W. De Long, *http://www.history.navy.mil/photos/images/h92000/h92140.jpg* Photo #NH 92140); Rare
Book Collection in the Alaska and Polar Regions Collections & Archives, Rasmuson Library, University of
Alaska Fairbanks

for another scoop—one to follow the achievement of his reporter Henry Stanley in locating the absent African missionary Dr. Livingstone.

For his ship, Bennett purchased the yacht *Pandora* from Sir Allen Young, who had made two voyages in it during the search for Franklin. (Young was assisted, in 1875–1876, by Ebierbing of Hall's expeditions and of Frederick Schwatka's Search Party.) Young had also served as sailing master of the *Fox*, under Francis Leopold McClintock, in the voyage that found the only Franklin document.

In 1877, Bennett had the *Pandora* refitted in England and recommissioned as the *Jeannette*. With Bennett carrying the expenses, the U.S. Navy assumed control of the ship and its personnel, placing De Long in charge as commander of the expedition.

On July 8, 1879, the *Jeannette* set out from San Francisco with orders from the Secretary of the Navy to pass through Bering Strait, searching for the missing Swedish geologist and arctic explorer Adolf Erik Nordenskjöld on board the *Vega*, and then proceed to the North Pole.

Where De Long aimed was Wrangel Land, a largely unknown area north of the Chukchi Peninsula, which he took to be not a small island but a large landmass reaching over the North Pole to Greenland. He had with him thirty-two men, only two of whom had overwintered in the Arctic—William Dunbar and William Nindemann. Dunbar, the ice pilot, had spent a winter on a whaler in Cumberland Sound, on the east coast of Baffin Island, home of Ebierbing and his first wife, Tookoolito. Nindemann, the ice quartermaster, was a survivor of the *Polaris* ice-floe drift.

On August 12, the *Jeannette* adventurers put in at St. Michael's in Norton Sound on the northwest coast of Alaska. Their expected supply ship, carrying the essential coal, had not yet arrived, and there was no word of Nordenskjöld, for whom they were to search before heading north. "This is a miserable place," De Long noted. "There are exactly four white men here, and not one white woman."

But he got the forty dogs he expected, along with five sledges and forty sets of harness. "These dogs are fine animals," he claimed, "young and active, and they took to me very kindly today when I visited them on shore." Also loaded on board were 2,290 pounds of "compressed dog food." This was to augment the 12,000 pounds of dried fish for the dogs sent by the Alaska Commercial Company from Kodiak to Unalaska, an earlier stop. Two local men, Alaska Natives, were hired as dog-drivers—Aneguin and Alexey, who also served as interpreter. De Long then pushed on to St. Lawrence Island.

While anchored there on August 25, he wrote of the dogs:

> Our forty dogs are a great item. They are all good sized and strong, and thus far roam around the deck in a happy go lucky kind of way, fighting every five minutes, and seemingly well contented. We have five dog sleds from St. Michael's, and the four we brought from England make nine altogether. I got also three skin boats. I hired two natives to go with us as dog drivers, very decent, intelligent men, and, wonderful to relate, very clean. I had them rigged out in white men's costume, and they look very swell indeed. They live with the men of course, and their duty thus far is to feed and water the dogs. The nature of these dogs is to fight at all times, and unless they are beaten well they will not keep the peace at all.

Garbled conversations with local people seemed to indicate that Nordenskjöld had come and gone. Before De Long set out, telegraphs sent from San Francisco to Washington, D.C., and from there to Stockholm and back again, indicated further that the missing explorer had last been seen at Cape Serdze Kamen on the Siberian coast, 130 miles distant from where De Long now was.

De Long determined to go there on his way to Wrangel Land. At the first settlement they came to on the cape, inadequate translation continued to cause confusion and frustration, but, after investigations in a second settlement, it was determined that the *Vega* had overwintered there and had safely left some months before. De Long was now free to steam to Wrangel Land—and on to the Pole.

Soon, the *Jeannette* had entered the ice. Off Herald Island, where De Long had planned to overwinter, the ship caught fast. "This is a glorious country to learn patience in," the commander noted. He kept hoping they could reach the island—and made many attempts; one involved exploding torpedoes under the stern.

The ship was imprisoned, but the dogs got to run free. They were let out on the ice from daylight to dark—a delight to the dogs, which enjoyed their freedom, and a relief to the men, who could clean the ship. Because bear traps were set around the ship every night, the dogs were brought back on board at the end of the day.

In spite of such precautions, however, two dogs were caught. The first, unnamed, was "one of our finest." He was caught by a front leg, the tooth of the trap catching between the bones without breaking them. For his sake, the starboard side of the bridge was turned into a dog hospital. The following day another dog, "our largest, Kasmatka," fell victim. Both dogs escaped broken bones or serious injury, but the traps were taken in.

While the patients convalesced, some of their teammates went to work. De Long organized a sledge party to visit the elusive Herald Island, where he hoped to find driftwood to use as fuel. He sent four men, including Alexey, with eight dogs that moved off, De Long commented, "in high glee, dragging the sled rapidly along after Alexey, who runs and dances before them." A day later they were back, having gotten within five miles of Herald Island. They saw no protective anchorage and no driftwood. What they did see was many bear tracks.

The two wounded dogs were released from the hospital and joined their comrades on the ice.

The *Jeannette* was now drifting inexorably north and west. As Herald Island faded away, another unknown landmass became visible. It was clear that there was no escape from the pack ice and no excess of provisions. The *Jeannette* was held tight, and for how long was impossible to say. It was time to prepare for straitened circumstances; time to measure and monitor coal and food. Two walruses were shot and secured—2,000 pounds of additional meat for the dogs; the men ate seal.

On October 29 came the first expedition death—that of a dog: Alexey and one of the men had gone out from the ship with a team to find three walruses that had slipped into the young ice after being shot the previous day. On the way, one of the dogs, variously called Dandy or Bingo, broke out of his harness and escaped. The other dogs attempted to chase him. Alexey remarked in his broken English that the other dogs would beat him up if they caught him. And they did. After failing to find the walruses, the two men returned to the ship. Half an hour later, Bingo was reported killed in a fight. Finding him a good distance from the ship, the other dogs had exacted their justice for desertion. The three or four hours that had elapsed in no way lessened their vengeance. He was so badly damaged that he was dead ten minutes after being brought back on board the ship. He was skinned, his coat saved for future wearing apparel, and his carcass stored on the deckhouse roof as a possible meal for his murderers.

In the first half of November came anxious hours, especially at night, when the ice embracing the ship cracked, split, and heaved. There was no telling what it might do next or how long the ship might survive. Emergency supplies were reconfigured on deck, made ready for instant offloading, and De Long slept in his clothes. During the early morning hours of November 13, there was a loud crack under the ship. That night, the ice broke away from the whole port side. Three dogs, sleeping on the floe, were carried with it. There was no effort made to rescue them, De Long explained, "our hands being too full in getting our things [on the intact ice] aboard to send for them." As the troublesome Tom and his two canine companions drifted off, all the other dogs were collected and penned on the quarter deck. Meteorological instruments, dinghies, and anything else left on the ice were all taken back on board.

Two days later, the ice had reestablished itself around the ship and Alexey was able to find and bring back Tom and his two friends—a threesome that was to garner much notice. Alexey reported seeing numerous bones where he had found the dogs, undoubtedly a resource buried in better times. As with Bingo the runaway, when the missing dogs returned, they were greeted with animosity—a common experience De Long was often to report. If not prevented, the stay-at-homes would have "given them a fight as a celebration, looking no doubt on the enforced separation as some new dodge for shirking work."

When the ice became sufficiently stable, De Long, once again, had the dogs housed on it. Unlike Elisha Kent Kane's dogs, which increasingly longed to be near the men, De Long's seemed to prefer the colder conditions:

> Though a few luxurious ones prefer seeking the shelter of the ship, the majority prefer living in the open air; hence our attempt to bring them on board only resulted in a series of fights and violent attempts to break away again. Once on board it would take four men to keep one dog from breaking for the ice, and there have been frequent escapes.

One of these escapees was almost shot as a bear one night. Another fell in a hole in the ice and was rescued by De Long, who plunged his hand in the water and pulled him up. The dog was "pretty far gone and remained in a dazed condition for an hour or two after I hauled him out."

All the time, through crises small and large, the ice was moving in its inscrutable way, taking the captive *Jeannette* with it. There was no rest on board. De Long continued to sleep in his clothes, ready for sudden alarm, but sleep was really no longer an option.

November 23, the dogs were brought back on board. The next day, the ship broke free from its floe and moved forward in a canal between two sheets of ice, but this was no deliverance. The ship now rocked in a cradlelike trough.

Young, tumultuous ice was in wild movement while gales blew and a new problem developed: lack of snow for drinking water. Because the ice was so treacherous, no one could be allowed to try walking on it in search of snow, even though the men began to sicken from drinking salty water. The dogs, too, had to be restrained and suffered from the confinement. When they were not fighting, De Long said, they "go moping around in a desolate way. They have regular cliques, and occupy certain portions of the quarter deck exclusively. Any trespass brings on a fight inevitably."

Once more, the ice thickened around the *Jeannette* and pressed dangerously against it. De Long lost interest in the beauties of ice scenery: "I will simply remark that the pack is no place for a ship, and however beautiful it may be from an aesthetic point of view, I wish with all my heart that we were out of it."

When the surface of the ice had settled and smoothed sufficiently, the commander ordered two hours of exercise a day—walking, hunting, or ball games. Ah Sam, the cook, and Charles Tong Sing, the steward, liked to fly kites. The temperature dipped to 24° below zero, with a number of startling effects. Ordinarily, the dogs' hair would stick to the ice, but now, one of the dogs stuck so fast he had to be dug out with a shovel.

There was no telling when the ice would move in such a way as to threaten the ship. The dogs picked up on the uncertainty and began coming up the gangplank regularly at two bells in the evening. Only a few stalwarts would stay on the ice. At times when the ice broke up, these renegades would need to be chased and corralled.

"Our surroundings are not of the most cheerful character," De Long noted on Christmas Eve. As the ice prisoners slipped deeper into the darkness, this day of special remembrances would have been appropriate for theatricals, but, De Long explained, the ship was not large enough. To compensate, he served the company three quarts of whiskey. But Christmas Day, he declared: "This is the dreariest day I have ever experienced in my life, and it is certainly passed in the dreariest part of the world."

Three days later, a dog became paralyzed. Thinking that he had frozen, De Long had him carried up to the deck house and laid on felt. Still, the dog remained motionless, his jaws locked and his eyes fixed and expressionless. The doctor, Passed Assistant Surgeon James M. Ambler, injected him with ammonia to no avail. He died during the night. In his postmortem report, De Long wrote:

> Alexey opened the dead dog, and found in his stomach a wad of oakum [loose fiber from rope, used as caulking] as big as my fist, which of course caused his death. These dogs will eat anything, and in spite of all attempts to prevent them. They are given a dried fish each daily, but all the same are prowling around day and night among empty meat cans and ash heaps, and making a rush every time a pan of dish water even is thrown over the side.

Now, at the close of the year 1879, there were thirty-eight dogs left of the original forty. One of these, De Long noted, was slowly dying, having been bitten through the nose in a fight at St. Michael's, their origin. This was Snuffy, about whom De Long would make a number of comments.

The dogs were never far away. When a minstrel show was gotten up for New Year's, Alexey posed in one of the *tableaux vivants* with a dog, aiming at an invisible prey.

The celebratory evening of imagination and cheer was soon over, however, and it was back to monitoring weather, position, and condition of men and ship. In mid-January, by De Long's calculations, the *Jeannette* was 100 miles to the north and east of Wrangel Land, drifting ever farther away from the nearest settlement on the Siberian coast. The *Jeannette* was also leaking, at the rate of 2,250 gallons per hour. As fast as oakum and tallow could be forced into openings, water found new entry.

The sledges were set to go, with forty days' provisions, the boats were ready to lower, and the two dinghies were mounted on their sleds. Every man had his gear packed, and the documents needed only to be sealed up. But as long as the pumping was maintained—largely by Nindemann and Alfred Sweetman, the carpenter—the ship stayed upright in its icy cradle. "This," said De Long, "is like living over a powder magazine with a train laid ready for firing." The ship's doctor, Ambler, operated on the eye of Lieutenant John Danenhower, the navigator, who was never to make his way off the sick list, and whose health was to be a constant worry and detriment to the commander. De Long's troubles and anxieties were crowding him just as the ice was crowding the ship; both for him and the ship, the pressure might change but never ease.

Suddenly, in the moving void, there were visitors: An arctic fox, chased by the dogs, ran up the gangplank, where Alexey met it with a rifle and killed it. Immediately after, a bear appeared, and that, too, was quickly dispatched. A meteor fell from northeast to east, and the next morning another bear appeared, drawn by the scent of his brother's body hanging in the rigging. The dogs retreated on board and, standing by the rail, barked as the bear attempted to climb up the side of the ship to get on the deck house. He fell back but then noticed the gangplank and was about to ascend it when Dunbar appeared at the rail and fired at him. Wounded, he made off, the dogs following. Bleeding profusely, he sat down to fend them off with his paws until Dunbar shot him again and killed him. The stomach of this bear had in it only a few small stones; the stomach of the first was empty.

That same morning, February 2, 1880, Alexey saw a walrus but had no rifle, and the loss of such food for the dogs was a keen disappointment. The last dried fish was finished this day, except for what had been packed with the forty days' emergency provisions on the sledges. The dogs were

A fight among the dogs, while the Jeannette lay icebound north of Siberia, circa early 1880. Fighting seemed to be the dogs' favorite recreation.
(Engraving by George T. Andrew after a design by M. J. Burns. Emma J. Wotten De Long, editor, *The Voyage of the Jeannette*, p. 341; Semi-Rare Book Collection, Alaska and Polar Regions Collections & Archives, Rasmuson Library, University of Alaska Fairbanks

now dependent on the "compressed" food, the meat and bones obtained at St. Michael's, which had to be thawed. De Long noticed that cutting back on fuel had made feeding the dogs even more challenging:

> But since the fires under the main boiler have been discontinued the dogs have had a hard time. I learned today that they were being fed on this concentrated food in its present frozen condition. I have been wondering for several days why the dogs fawned so much upon any-body who came on deck, and why the rattle of an empty meat can thrown over the rail was a call to all the dogs to rush for the ship in a body.... As soon as I learned of the issue of frozen dog food, I im-mediately conferred with Melville about putting a pipe in the Baxter boiler to carry steam into a barrelful of the dog food to thaw it, and he commenced to do so immediately.

De Long was concerned that some of the dogs had poor teeth and could eat only "on their gums." These dogs, he said, were frequently robbed of their meals by the fully toothed dogs as they tried to eat. One morning, he said, he went out on the ice and was immediately surrounded by all the toothless dogs, "who fawned upon me as if their instinct had told them I was the commanding officer, and should be appealed to to right them. I am in hopes now that the evil is remedied, and that every dog will get his food in such shape as will prove eatable."

Meanwhile, the pumping continued as the supply of coal dwindled. Steadily, the ship was getting wetter and conditions more unpleasant. Although daylight returned, intensely cold weather prevailed. For the men, there was still seal meat and bear meat. The dogs were faring less well, reduced to their condensed food, now steamed "until it makes a kind of soup hash." With less nourishment than they had with the fish, they were now constantly hungry, rummaging for whatever scraps they could find. They needed walrus. But, for their masters to secure walrus, there first had to be open water.

The end of February brought clear and pleasant weather. The dogs lay in the sunshine though their coats were stiff with frost. De Long noted:

> Their hardihood is immense. Lying right out on the floe night after night, they seem to keep warm enough, and at the same time throw out sufficient heat to thaw a hole under and around them an inch or more in depth. Ash heaps and dirt heaps seem to be especially sought for. Alliances are formed for their enjoyment, and the approach of an outside dog is the signal to clear for action. A few of the strongest dogs take post on board at the door of the cook house to intercept

any supplies, and be nearest the place of deposit if they are thrown over the rail, and a hungry or inquisitive brother is at once driven away by them.

March 1, Danenhower had a sixth operation on his eye and on March 2, a seventh. On Sundays, De Long continued to read the Articles of War, followed by muster and the reading of divine service.

On March 16, the two Alaska Natives came back with a bearskin. They had encountered a sow and cub and Alexey's two dogs had tackled the grown bear. Before she was shot, she managed to wound one dog badly on a front leg and nearly to "tear the toes off another." The cub escaped. The men skinned the sow and buried the body until they could retrieve it the next day. Now there was fresh food for the dogs.

On St. Patrick's Day, the commander thought to note the names of some of the dogs:

One of our dogs, an old one, having a comical and quizzical countenance, had long since been named "Paddy," and today he was treated to a piece of green ribbon around his neck, and placed alongside of the Baxter engine, a proceeding so unusual as to occasion him considerable astonishment. The dogs in general, and the names given to some of them, merit a special mention, which I shall give them some day. Kasmatka, Tom, Quicksilver, Jack or Prince, Smike, Snoozer, Bismarck, Paddy, Skinny, Foxy, Plug Ugly, Dewclaws, Joe and Jim, Johnny Armstrong, Dan, and Wolf.

Three days later these and the unnamed dogs were lucky: Alexey shot a walrus so large that thirty of the dogs and four men could not drag him back to the ship over the rough ice; the carcass had to be cut in two for separate trips.

April 1, the dogs had another bonanza: A bear approached the ship, the dogs encircled it and then chased it for a mile:

The dogs managed him beautifully. While about twenty of them would surround him out of reach of his paws and distract his attention, a half dozen of them would bite him, making the hair fly by mouthfuls. The bear would then throw them off, and, sitting on his haunches, reach around for them with his fore paws.

At this point Alexey and Dunbar arrived and shot the bear, which got up again and renewed his battle with the dogs, until Dunbar finished him with another bullet. This 675-pound animal also had a completely empty stomach.

A few days later, because of such generous feedings, the dogs were showing their mettle. De Long and an assistant hitched up a team of eleven for a "cruise" but could drive them no farther than a few hundred feet from the ship. They would bolt and drag the sledge and its passengers back home. If the men took hold of a leader, the middle dogs would double back. Whipping on one side would make them veer to the other. Exasperated and exhausted, De Long then had the ailing dog, Snuffy—a companion of Jack, the leader—held out in front. While Jack was distracted, the other dogs were coerced into position. Still, one of the dogs was so determined not to move that in spite of whippings he would throw himself down only to be dragged along by the team for a hundred yards or more. De Long abandoned the effort after a mile.

With warmer temperatures, the dogs were removed from the ship and bivouacked on the ice, along with the walrus and bear meat that had been put aside for their use. (The frozen walrus hide was impervious to dogs' teeth.) Although vigilant in their guarding of the meat pile, the dogs still wanted to return to the ship at night, lining the gangplank "like chickens waiting to go to roost." They had become heavy and lazy, De Long noted, so averse to work "that a sight of harness will make the whole pack skulk off."

On April 22, De Long had determined to shoot the resilient Snuffy:

> Although I know that he will never be of use again, I hardly like to have him shot, preferring to give him all of his life that he can hang on to. Occasionally he seems going, as, for instance, today, when he was lying on an old mattress on the rubbish heap, seemingly at his last gasp. Being occupied with taking sights, I postponed his shooting until the afternoon, when, going out to see that he had not died in the mean while, I found him gone one hundred yards or so, and as frisky and far from death as ever. No doubt this is a small thing to set forth at such length, but when all days are alike, and but little occurs to break the monotony, even an occurrence like the foregoing seems an unusual item.

May arrived with ever-shrinking supplies of coal but an abundance of gloomy and cold weather. Heavy snow still fell, the dogs sleeping alongside the ship appearing as small white lumps—but peaceful lumps, not given to fighting, apparently, when they could not distinguish one another. During the truce, De Long commented upon their pugilism:

> Why they fight, how they fight, and whom they fight, seem to be purely abstract questions with them, so long as it is a fight. For instance, dogs

one and two will see dog three in a good position, perhaps enjoying a meat can that has been empty for months and has, of course, no nutriment. As if by concerted plan one and two will spring on three, roll him over, and seemingly tear him in pieces. Fortunately the wool is so long and thick that an attacking dog gets his mouth full of hair before his front teeth reach the flesh, so no great damage is done generally. The vulnerable places are the ears and the belly. I have seen an attacked dog run, and, lying on his stomach, shove his head into a snow bank with impunity, while his foes were choking over the hair they tore out of his back. . . . Suddenly dog three will turn on dog two and be promptly aided by dog one, his previous foe. By this time the whole pack has gathered as if by magic, and a free and indiscriminate fight occurs, until the advent of the quartermaster with the whip and a merciless application of it breaks up the fight.

These fights, De Long explained, would also take place within groups or cliques of three or four. No matter how many dogs were involved or what the circumstances, there was a clear protocol for behavior and punishment:

It is a common occurrence to see a dog on the black list, a quarter of a mile from the ship, all alone and afraid to come in until his time is up. He then approaches fawningly, wagging his tail deprecatingly to become reconciled, and is either welcomed with wagging tails or snarling teeth, in which latter case he retires to his isolated position for another spell.

A returning team, though mourned with howling on its way out, would be attacked by the stay-at-homes out of harness, requiring two or three men to end the assault. Once the harness was removed from the homecoming team, all would be quiet again, the cliques reassembling. If a single dog had the misfortune of coming in alone, he would be attacked by all the others:

Let him be never so wary, and slink around hummocks to reach the ship unobserved, some one dog sees his head or his tail, gives the signal, and away they go. It is then a question of speed, for if the single dog but reaches his usual sunning or stopping-place he is safe; for, by some rule always observed, the getting to home base restores him to the full rights of citizenship.

Dogs did more than fight, however, as De Long pointed out:

The care they bestow on each other in distress or trouble, arising from disability, has a marked exhibition in the case of Jack and Snuffy.

Snuffy had his nose bitten into in a fight at St. Michael's last summer, and in consequence his head is twice the natural size, by swelling and diseased bone. Jack is seemingly Snuffy's brother, and he is devoted to him beyond much human fraternal affection. He stays by Snuffy, cleans him, sees that he is not molested by other dogs, follows him into enemies' camps, leads him through in safety, and guards his retreat. Let Snuffy get a tidbit, like an old moccasin or a piece of hide, Jack sees him secure it, stands by him while he chews it, and if he leaves it, chews it for him until he seems to want it again, when it is promptly surrendered. So accustomed have the pack become to this sort of thing, that they permit many liberties with their food which they would resent with a well dog.

De Long was impressed by the dogs' cunning as well as their consistent social protocol. One midnight, as he went out for meteorological readings, he encountered a dozen dogs milling about him in some excitement. The reason was quickly revealed: A large dog was headfirst in a tipped barrel of frozen walrus meat, with only his tail and hind legs sticking out. As soon as De Long drove him out, half the pack, recognizing the errant dog as no great fighter, pounced on him while the other half fought over the barrel. The dogs had been waiting, De Long surmised, for someone to come along who would solve their problem: Who was in the barrel—a weakling or a tyrant?

In mid-May six bears appeared over a three-day period. Three were secured, with great difficulty, while three escaped. The weather improved and the drift to the northwest, beyond sight of land, continued. On May 21, another bear was sighted and the dogs were loosed on him. After being hit and knocked over by three bullets, the bear got to his feet, singled out a dog, and charged him fiercely, but Dunbar and Alexey shot him again and killed him. Carting the carcass back to the ship over rough ice, even with a team of eighteen dogs and three men, proved frightening and exhausting. At one point the ice vibrated and broke under them; they were saved only because of the speed at which they were traveling. The dogs were pulling as hard as they could because they were homeward bound. One area of jumbled ice was so difficult, however, it took an hour to progress a quarter of a mile.

June 1 brought the realization that although the ice around the ship was soft and mushy, the ship was held as firmly as ever. Items thrown overboard went down and sometimes reappeared in the slush. Occasionally, the dogs would unearth treasures they had buried months before and that they seemed delighted to have found once more.

But below decks a darkness was growing. The doctor reported that one of the coal-heavers was on the edge of madness. De Long, too, was reaching his breaking point: "First a blind officer, and now a crazy man—these will be serious charges on my mind in any emergencies." And now the *Jeannette* seemed to be drifting backwards—to the southeast. De Long tried to be hopeful, even cheerful, maintaining daily and weekly routines. On Sunday, June 13, he inspected the ship, read divine service, and reported that Jack had captured a young fox, which was turned over to the naturalist.

Words like "gloomy" and "depressing" entered the reports more frequently, along with "discouraging" and "monotony." With the sameness of every day grating on his nerves, De Long took great care to note any unusual event—the discovery of mosquitoes, the shooting and collecting of a pink-hued Ross's gull. (Some years later, Fridtjof Nansen would take equal delight in obtaining three of these rare, mysterious, and beautiful birds.) Such were the gossamer hints of summer.

Only the dogs, De Long stated, were oblivious to monotony and did not change in relation to the worrisome conditions:

> They seem perfectly oblivious to all surroundings, utterly indifferent whether the sun shines or does not shine, so long as they are fed. From the liberal diet of bear meat and seals' entrails they have remained as fat as dumplings, and repudiate utterly any labor or exertion. When with the sunshine the temperature reaches 32 degrees, it is amusing to see them pant, and seek shady places, while we human beings are merely comfortable.

Danenhower's eye needed daily to be cut and probed, but the hysterical coal-heaver's condition improved.

The coal supply itself was shrinking, now down to fifty-six and a half tons, and though the crew dug away much ice from its sides, the ship still held fast in its frozen cradle; clearly, the coal would have to last far longer than had ever been anticipated.

De Long had meted out his first punishment of the expedition—to the fireman for abusive language. Now the dogs were misbehaving, especially the "hoodlum gang" of Jack, Tom, and Wolf:

> Ordinarily they lie around on ash-heaps all day in the sun, blinking lazily, and ready to head an attack on some wandering dog in search of a bone, or more particularly sallying out to meet some dog returning with the hunters, who has incurred their grave displeasure by assisting at any work. The sight of a harness, merely, reminds them of a pressing engagement elsewhere; and the moving of a dog sled in

their range of vision seems suggestive of the advisability of a change of base. Accordingly, each morning, when the ice has to be dragged in for melting, these three are occupied in surveying the work from a distance until it is completed, and then they unite in an attack on those who did the dragging. They were caught by strategy today, however, and harnessed up; but Tom slipped his harness quietly and bolted, while Wolf chewed his through and escaped. When caught they were securely tied to a rope over the stern, and kept there until ten p.m., when, in order that their howls might not keep everybody awake, they were anchored with an ice-claw some distance off. This disgusted them. Tom took his punishment solemnly and quietly, but Wolf yelled incessantly, so much so, that Tom got provoked and thrashed him twice into silence.

The ice bondage that gripped and tilted the ship continued, as did De Long's deepening depression: "I cannot help thinking, as I turn over a new leaf and commence a fresh page, that I am wasting stationery in keeping a daily record of so unimportant matter as our daily life." Even sunshine added to disgust, as it indicated, by computations, how far backwards the route had moved. (For George Tyson, on the ice drift, it showed just how dirty and disheveled they had all become.) Job, De Long grumbled, "was never caught in pack ice and drifted S. and W. with W. Winds."

Hoping to see something consoling—especially open water to the southeast—he took out a team of dogs but was run away with twice and had to apply to Alexey for help. A white man, he said, "inspires no fear among these animals." During successive days he repeated the exercise, surveying the ice that lay around the ship. It was still thick—forty feet in some areas, he calculated. The "gloomy, disagreeable" weather, with temperatures hovering around the freezing point, created damp and penetrating cold that seemed worse than what had been experienced during severe winter conditions. There was nothing to look forward to. The monotony "of doing nothing but waiting, waiting, is very trying." And summer—or what was supposed to be summer—was slipping quickly away in the disguise of fog and rain and snow. It was, indeed, a summer that refused to be.

On July 25, the first bearded seal was shot and secured, a valuable addition, at eight feet long, for the dogs. But the commander's sense of disappointment and frustration deepened. He was beginning to call their situation a "mortification." How could he justify such lack of results? "A ship having the North Pole for an objective point must get to the Pole," he said, "otherwise her best efforts are a failure. . . . and we and our narratives together are thrown into the world's dreary wastebasket, and recalled and remembered only to be vilified or ridiculed."

On the first of August, a third dog died, one called The Tease:

> Yesterday he appeared dull and stupid, and swollen. Being given some jalap [a purgative drug] he did not respond to treatment, but, to quote Chipp [Lieutenant Charles Chipp, executive officer], in his account to Danenhower, "calmly passed away breathing his last at three p.m." As we are of an inquiring turn of mind a post-mortem was held, Iversen [Nelse Iversen, coal-heaver] acting as coroner, and it was found that the dog's death was caused by his swallowing a sharp bone, which cut through his intestines.

On August 19, another bear was secured, a small one, that was quickly buried in the ice for future human and canine consumption. The dogs, De Long noted, "are now fed about three times a week from the seal yard." A week later, four bears appeared in one day; one was taken after the dogs surrounded their prey in an open pond in the ice, one dog biting the bear on the nose every time he tried to climb out. The next three, a mother with two cubs, escaped by swimming through open lanes that the dogs would never enter. Again, the mother showed remarkable devotion. All three had been shot and wounded, but she kept pushing the cubs in front of her, covering their retreat, and nosing them into the water before she would leave the ice herself. "Unless dogs can surround a bear and hold him at bay," De Long noted, "he may have half a dozen bullets in him and yet escape."

On August 30, the fourth dog died:

> Poor old Snuffy, having reached such a condition that it would be a mercy to kill him, was shot today. For some days his head had swollen to an awful size, and he had wasted away to a shadow. Lying on the ice, the heat from his body had thawed away a hole, and he was sinking gradually from view. No doubt, as far as his usefulness was concerned, he might have been killed months ago; but I felt that even a dog was entitled to his life as long as he could keep it in these uncharitable regions. However, the poor brute is gone now. His three companions, Prince [the alternate name for Jack], Tom, and Wolf, seemed unable to comprehend his disappearance, for they gathered around his old ice hole in inquiring anxiety. But only for a time. The natural though miserable regard for self soon drew them to other things. What a life this is, when the shooting of a dog so impresses me that I give a dozen lines of my journal to its mention.

On September 1, the ship suddenly broke from its hold and righted itself, tumbling a dog that happened to be on the gangplank onto the ice below.

September 5 marked one year in the ice, but the expedition had moved only 150 miles to the north and west of the point where it had entered.

September 15 brought such heavy snow that the dogs, after searching in vain for protection near the ship, gave up and "lay down in disgust to be snowed in." At first, it was possible to distinguish the mounds where the dogs lay, but then the mounds disappeared and it was only when someone tripped over them, causing a howl, that their presence was known. All fighting was suspended.

September 19, the lack of dog food was noted: "Today we (men and dogs) have eaten our last piece of bear, and we have only about half a dozen seals in the larder as our stock of fresh meat." The problem of how to abandon the ship in an emergency loomed: There seemed to be no good plan.

September 28 brought a partial solution to the continuing problem of the "hoodlum gang" of Jack (Prince), Tom, and Wolf, who had been bullying the pack. Early that morning they had attacked a "valuable" dog, Jim, and almost devoured him before he was rescued by the doctor, who happened to witness the assault. The trio maintained a reign of terror among the pack, attacking any member that strayed or allowed himself to be put to work. Previous punishments had not worked. The three had been anchored and tied up but had always been released because of the annoyance of their howling. Now there was a new plan—to tie large blocks of wood to them. But to catch the dogs was the first—and almost impossible—problem.

Several hours later, at 11 a.m., the free-roaming and marauding trio spotted a bear and gave chase. They caught up with him and distracted him until the other dogs arrived and Dunbar approached with his rifle and killed him with two bullets. The "hoodlums" refused to be caught and harnessed to help carry the carcass back to the ship. But when the bear had been skinned and butchered, the three moved close to get scraps, close enough that they were grabbed and weighted down with blocks of wood hung around their necks. Soon after, however, they were back to chasing Jim, their victim of the morning. The punishment, clearly, was not heavy enough.

The next day another dog died—"one of our effective dogs." De Long could not name him, though, as he said, the men may have christened him. The postmortem once more revealed a bone lodged crosswise in his intestines.

In the meantime, the inflicted trio stayed tied to their blocks of wood. When a bear was sighted and the dogs went in chase, the three sprinted off. Wolf stumbled so much, however, he turned back in disgust, "with a look that said plainly, 'You may catch your own bears hereafter.'" Tom kept on, arriving at the scene in time to have the bear, shot on a hummock, fall on him and on "Alexey's brown dog." Both dogs got clawed in the process. As a reward for Tom, the block of wood was removed, and he rejoined his gang in time to meet and attack Alexey's dogs as they returned from the hunt.

With the beginning of September, the commander instituted the practice of serving out two ounces of rum once a week, on Wednesday night; already, two glasses of sherry were served at dinner on Sunday: "What a country this is, and how monotonous a life we lead, may be inferred from the fact that two ounces of rum every Wednesday are looked forward to as a change and excitement."

But there *was* some excitement. The ice was now beginning to heave, with noises of cracking and grinding, and thoughts were once more on abandoning the ship—250 miles from the Siberian coast and the nearest possible settlement.

During this uncertain time, as the crew waited for conditions to become definitive, the tedium of daily life went on, with small adventures noted large. On November 3, Aneguin shot and secured a large seal, and Smike dragged it back over the two-mile distance to the ship, a notable feat for a single dog.

November 10, Alexey's dogs chased but failed to stop a bear, which escaped through the hummocky ice. Coming home to the ship, they lay down extended on their sides, exhausted.

November 12, another dog was dead by bone: "The thirty-four survivors of the canine family do not seem overcome by grief,—the advent of the steward with dishwater and dinner bones admonishes them of the greater importance of the reality of life." Extending his remarks on dog care, De Long wrote:

> The native instinct among Esquimaux is to let sick or wounded dogs take their own chances of recovery, although no lack of regard and good feeling is apparent. If a bear tears a dog, or if in a fight a long cut is inflicted, the victim licks his sore until healed. Sewing up a wound is not adopted. Anything besides a wound is diagnosed by Alexey thus, "Something wrong inside; bymby, perhaps, die." And though we have physicked and operated on dogs, "bymby" they do die.

Bears continued to add zest to the tedious situation. Sometimes they would be secured, other times not. The sounds of moving ice startled and alarmed. An eclipse of the moon was forgotten and slept through.

The winter solstice claimed another dog: Hard-Working-Jack. (This was not Jack/Prince, the leader, but another dog. At times, names of dogs were repeated, with blurred designation.) The postmortem performed by Aneguin revealed ingestion of "several mutton bones, two pieces of a tin can (cutting entrails, as might be expected), a piece of cloth, and the fag end of a rope."

On Christmas Eve came the second minstrel show augmented by the issue of a double ration of whiskey.

As the new year of 1881 overtook the old, the trapped and leaking ship with its weakened crew had drifted 220 miles northwest of where it was first beset. De Long compared its fate to that of a modern *Flying Dutchman*, never getting anywhere, but always restless and on the move, with thirty-three people "wearing out their hearts and souls like men doomed to imprisonment for life."

By the end of January, another dog had succumbed to bones in the intestines. As for the rest, they were, De Long noted, "lean and thin," a situation he hoped to remedy by fattening bear meat. Through the winter they had been eating seal blubber mixed with condemned oatmeal.

One of them, "our little Russian dog Dan," expelled an eight-foot-long tapeworm and was under the doctor's care.

On February 18, showing that they were still fit, the dogs killed a bear by themselves. As soon as the alarm was given of a sighting, the dogs rushed off, headed by the "hoodlums." Tom and Alexey's dog got the bear by the throat and held her while the rest of the pack charged. It turned out to be a very small bear, looking, De Long noted, "like an overgrown cat," and weighing only 129 pounds—probably one of the two cubs wounded along with their mother on August 26.

A ferocious fight with a sow on March 6 resulted in the death of one dog, Plug Ugly, and the wounding of a number of others. It was in the midst of the battle, dogs flying, when Nindemann shot at the bear; the bullet passed through his target and into the lungs of Plug Ugly, a case of friendly fire. After the struggle, the doctor was busy:

> When injuries came to be examined, we found it a very costly bit of bear. One dog killed, Plug Ugly; Prince with his back and fore shoulder cut, where Bruin had caught him in his mouth and flung him; Tom had a long gash on his rump, which had to be sewn up; and Wolf, the third hoodlum, had a long cut from his rump to his stomach, requiring considerable sewing. Bingo [the name clearly is a mistake, or a reuse of a name, since Bingo, also called Dandy, was the first dog to die, killed in a dogfight, on October 29] was torn in

his side in two places clean through to the intestines, making plenty of stitching necessary. One of Alexey's dogs had a gash in his throat from the claw. Snoozer had his mouth lengthened by a claw on the cheek. Smike was torn in two places, and cuts of less importance were more common. Such a fight we have never had. The bear was seemingly a mother of recent date, for she was plentiful in milk.

On March 17, one of the dogs, Skinny, disappeared. Always thin and more so recently, he was assumed to have wandered away and to have become covered and buried with drifting snow: "He never would have been of any use to drag a sled, but still it is unfortunate that his end should have occurred in this way."

On March 19, the commander noted the dogs on the sick list:

Poor Tom received a severe hurt in the memorable bear fight, for today the doctor got a piece of broken bone out of his back, and it would seem that Bruin must have taken him in his mouth and bitten deep before flinging him to one side. It will be a long time before Tom is on duty again. Wolf is mending slowly, his injury giving him a strong disinclination to sit down, however, but this is favorable to his improvement. The other dogs are also improving. Smike was succeeding, by judicious management, in keeping his wound open, but Wilson [Henry Wilson, seaman] made him a one-legged pantaloon and clapped it on him, and now Smike is so proud of his clothes that he has forgotten all about his injuries.

On April 15, another dog was dead: Dan, who had suffered with the tapeworm. Though De Long stated, "we now mourn his loss," no mention is made of a postmortem examination.

The next day brought excitement that occasioned a long report. The Chinese cook, Ah Sam, and the steward, Charles Tong Sing, who enjoyed flying kites, started off at 2:30 in the afternoon on a walking-hunting exercise routine and had not returned by five. At 7:30, the steward came back alone, greatly excited, to tell in broken English his tale: He and Ah Sam had started out with one dog, had seen bear tracks, and, while following them, saw Prince/Jack and Wolf on a hummock, then they saw the bear. In the chase, Charles Tong Sing fell on some rough ice and a piece broke off and fell on his back, pinning him down. Ah Sam got him up and they both ran three or four miles after the bear and the dogs. Ah Sam's dog came back when called. The cook ordered the steward back to the ship to cook supper while he went on after the bear and the dogs. Not knowing where Ah Sam might be, De Long decided they would wait for his return.

At midnight he did return, with only one dog, and filled out the story. The bear and dogs, he said, would fight every now and then, and the dogs were bleeding. Finally, he gave up and turned back as Prince/Jack and Wolf continued to follow the bear. Now the two best dogs were missing.

No one had taken Prince/Jack and Wolf away from the ship. They had, apparently, scented or seen the bear and gone in chase voluntarily. It was only because Tom was still in the hospital that he had not joined his companions.

The next day three men, accompanied by dogs Smike, Snoozer, and Kasmatka, started off on a search but came back with no success. They had followed the tracks for about ten miles. The bear, it seemed, had come down to a walk with a dog on each side of it—perhaps all three in a temporary truce of exhaustion. There was no telling how far they might continue. As they started back, the men found themselves on moving, grinding ice, and that evening the ship received a sharp jolt.

A week later, Prince/Jack arrived at the ship thin and worn out. There was no sign of Wolf. It was presumed that Wolf was badly injured by the bear and that Prince/Jack stayed with him until he died.

With such moments of excitement interspersed in the boredom, the dreary days stumbled into May. The ice was breaking up around the ship and wild geese and ducks were flying west. On the fifth of May, a bear was spotted and Prince/Jack made for him immediately and seized him by the hind leg. Prince/Jack then shot ahead of him, cutting off his retreat until one of the men came up and brought the bear down with a shot. Though with an empty stomach, the bear weighed 790 pounds, a badly needed addition to the diet of all.

The dogs, De Long said, would if they could complain of the small amount and strange variety of food they had been getting. After the dried fish was gone, they got pressed scraps consisting of horseflesh and other matter. They liked seal and walrus meat, but it had been a year since a walrus was spotted, and there had been so few seals they had been put aside for human consumption. There hadn't been enough bear meat to go around, either; the entrails made just a "hasty lunch." For a long time, he said, the dogs had been on short rations: First, they had been given condemned oatmeal, then condemned cornmeal and suet, then spare cornmeal from the naturalist's stores, with suet added. Now, they were about to be served desiccated potatoes and suet. Aneguin came up with something even more creative: "Pie," he called it, because that is how he had eaten it, but now it was simply a condemned package of dried pumpkin. (Pumpkin now is considered healthful for dogs and in specialty pet shops shelved alongside canned meat.)

On May 16 came the unexpected cry of "Land!"—the first land seen since March 24, 1880, and it was land that was unknown. Finally, De Long's Polar Expedition of 1879 had discovered *something*, no matter how small it was. They watched it with fascination—this *terra incognita*, which they named Jeannette Island.

On May 21, however, came the report of the disappearance of another dog: Lauterbach, named for coal-heaver John Lauterbach and recognizable by a hairless tail, the result of a scalding accident: "He has gone and laid himself away somewhere, for he has been missing several days."

Another island came into sight, one De Long named Henrietta Island. (*Henrietta* was the name of backer James Gordon Bennett's yacht, which he loaned to the federal government during the Civil War and on which he won a transatlantic race in 1866.) Still, in spite of leads opening, it was impossible to move toward the new islands or in any direction.

An enormous flock of ducks, approximately 500, flew low and to the north. The dogs, as a pack, took after them until stopped by open water.

De Long decided to send a party of two officers, four men, and fifteen dogs, along with a sledge, dinghy, and seven days' provisions, to make a landing on Henrietta Island. It was a decision made out of not just curiosity but need:

> We are now beginning to be straitened for dog food; all our condemned meats, fish, and other suitable articles are ended. Having tried the dogs upon everything to their seeming satisfaction, we at last tried them with potatoes (desiccated). But here was the dividing line. They turned up their noses and walked away in disgust, and no matter how great their hunger, they cannot be induced to astonish their stomachs with such an excellent(?) anti-scorbutic. In fine, something else had to be done, and so I ordered one half pound English pemmican, and one half pound corn meal to be served out to every dog every second day from the ship's stores; and in order that no more of such precious food than was absolutely necessary should be expended for dogs, I gave orders that three old and worn-out dogs should be quietly removed from the ship and shot. Of course I regret taking even a dog's life, but where it is a question of sentiment only in putting priceless food into a dog, from which no work can ever be obtained, the sentiment cannot be tolerated.

On May 31, the designated party headed out across the ice to the island. Before long, some of the dogs ran away and returned to the ship. De Long sent them back, following up the sledge partway.

In the meantime, an outbreak of lead poisoning manifested on board, probably the result of badly soldered canned tomatoes, which had been eaten in great quantity. And a bear, coming to the ship and seeing so few dogs—and those dogs giving no sign—easily escaped, a loss of 600 pounds of fresh meat.

On June 5, the discovery party was back from Henrietta Island, with one man disabled by snow blindness. They reported having landed on June 3 and claiming it for the United States. The island, they said, was a desolate rock with only dovekies for game and with inaccessible cliffs and torturous ice between it and the ship. The panicked dogs had had to be dragged through the shore ice to the landing.

Almost as soon as the explorers were back on board, the drifting increased. On June 11, the ice suddenly opened alongside and the ship righted itself. The next day, the ship appeared to be breaking in two. Orders were given to land one half of the pemmican and all the bread, while the dogs and sledges were moved to a position of safety. Later in the day, the ship began to buckle. Orders were now given to remove provisions, clothing, and the ship's books and papers, and to transport the sick to a place of safety. At 6 p.m., the ship was beginning to fill with water. Now everything possible was offloaded to the ice. At 8 p.m., De Long gave the order to abandon ship. Assembling on the floe, the men dragged the supplies and boats—two cutters and a whaleboat—clear of cracks and settled down for the night. At 4 a.m. on June 13, 1881, the *Jeannette* sank.

The focus now was on preparing for travel—south to Siberia, by way of the New Siberian Islands. The goal was the Lena River delta, 700 miles away on the north Siberian coast. The three boats were set on sledges and food was placed in bags. Another five sledges were packed. In the meantime, an organized camp and routine were set up with regular times for meals and watches.

On June 18, the retreat south began—an agonizingly slow process of ferrying goods forward while looping back to collect more, while all the time challenged by jagged and breaking ice, deep snow, fog, open water, heavy loads, breaking runners, and men who were weakened at best, disabled at worst. Because of burning, blinding sunlight, the group traveled by night. Twenty-eight men and twenty-three dogs could barely pull the heaviest sledge weighing 1,600 pounds. As with Kane's retreat, there were the patients—five of them—who required special care; these went on the "medical" sledge, under the doctor's care.

Shortly after, as De Long noted, open water was causing critical problems for the dogs:

I hardly had gone one fourth mile when I came to an ice opening, and in spite of my strongest efforts, the dogs scattered across some lumps, capsized the sled, dragged me in, and sent all my mess gear flying, having accomplished which, and reached the other side themselves, they sat down and howled to their hearts' content.

To get through this gap, it was necessary to fashion haphazard bridges by pushing small floes together, and sometimes to paddle instead of pulling. But worse was to come. "To the southward of us the ice is terribly confused," the commander reported. During the slow process, he commented, "There is no work in the world harder than this sledging." There was crisis after crisis: A sledge went into the water and the dogs had to be cut free; sometimes water on top of the ice would be knee-deep; one of the patients weakened until he could no longer walk and had to be carried constantly in a sledge; fog was followed by burning sun that only made more clear how challenging their course: "The country to the southward of us is terribly wild and broken."

The road across it was also shattered, necessitating the use of ice bridges and boats, sometimes in roundabout directions. De Long was avoiding the officers lest they inquire about position; often the straggling group was moving more northwest than southwest. But on the Fourth of July, they made the unprecedented distance of two and one-quarter miles southwest in eight hours and twenty minutes. It was three years to the day that the *Jeannette*, formerly the *Pandora*, had been christened in Le Havre, France, and showered with such hopeful comments as she headed for San Francisco and final preparations for her journey north.

July 6, the weather turned colder and wetter. The men were all in tents, but the dogs crouched under the boats or whatever else offered shelter. When under way, the dogs were working hard. As the complicated ferrying process continued, teams would go back repeatedly to the day's starting point to pull forward equipment to the new goal: "One mile made, therefore, means seven miles traveled by men, and nine by dog sleds."

July 12, a live butterfly was discovered, a fragile and unexpected emblem of hope. But the next day came the first breach of discipline among the crew when one of the seamen refused the order of one of the officers. De Long had to intervene, make the mutineer stand apart, and then put him off duty.

It was now that the dogs began to show signs of stress, some of them attacked with fits:

First, the dog Jim; his fit took him while in harness, and lasted for some time after he was cut adrift. Not much foaming at the mouth, but long continued shaking, as if suffering from the cold. Next, Foxy had a bad fit. Then Tom had a queer sort of attack; he acted as if dizzy, and spun around for a minute or two before attacking his partner in the harness, Wolf, which he did as if thinking Wolf answerable for it. [Though not reported, Wolf must have returned from his encounter with the bear; this seems to be the same member of the triumvirate of Prince/Jack, Tom, and Wolf.] With Tom it has seemed to stop, for two days have elapsed without any new cases. Foxy now heads the team which the doctor has to draw the dingy, which team consists of seven of our poorest dogs. Ericksen [Hans Halmoi Ericksen, seaman] has seven of our best. Alexey seven good ones. Poor Jack (Joe), with the lame back, has been accidentally left behind at some lead or other, and the remainder are so mean that they are not worth hitching up. [Here, again, De Long shows his own stress, becoming more vague with the naming and description of dogs. This Jack (Joe) is not Jack/Prince, the leader.]

Soon after De Long completed this report, while the men slept, some of the dogs ate the hide parts of two harnesses, causing a particularly frustrating delay.

A seal was successfully taken, its twenty pounds divided equally among the thirty-three men, and the next day, a larger seal; a walrus was also sighted—the first one in many months.

Land came into sight. Not knowing exactly what island it was, De Long decided to head for it, over a punishing ice road.

In De Long's journal, the words given for dogs were fewer and fewer, with less emotion and no humor. De Long was exhausted. On July 20: "Found Foxy dead in the water. He probably had a fit and fell in."

Later that day, a walrus was shot and secured. Because relatively little could be carried in the retreat, the dogs were allowed to gorge themselves, some of them "too fat for comfort." And before long, a bear was bagged.

Less and less was reported as loquaciousness gave way to shorthand. The closer they got to the unknown island, the harder the road to it became. Then, as they were carried alongside the island's steep shore on a floe, it seemed as if it might be impossible to land. Only when their floe fortuitously caught on a cape were they able to succeed.

After everyone had managed to get on the icy slope of the shore, De Long announced that the island was newly discovered land that he was taking possession of in the name of the President of the United States and that he was naming Bennett Island, in honor of his benefactor. Three cheers were given for the acquisition and three cheers for De Long. The date was July 29, 1881. The landing cape he named Cape Emma, in honor of his wife.

Fresh water and abundant murres cooked over driftwood refreshed the ice wanderers, but cold, wet weather set in and a gale delayed departure for the New Siberian Islands. A record was written and filed—the discovery of the island, its claiming, and the state of the party as they prepared to leave: "We have three boats, thirty days' provisions, twenty-three dogs, and sufficient clothing, and are moreover in excellent health."

The record was deposited, and then De Long added a sad addendum:

I, this afternoon, was forced to have shot ten of our poorest dogs, including Tom and Jim. We now have twelve left: Prince [Jack, the leader], Smike, Snoozer, Armstrong, Dick, Pilgarlic, Geyotack, Magalan, Kasmatka, etc. The amount of food these ten dogs eat is not compensated for by the work done, and I must think of human life first. The dogs were all worn out or subject to fits.

August 6, the seafarers crossed two miles of open water while leaving Bennett Island behind; then it was back to the ice. Still, on Sundays, the Articles of War were read, followed by divine service. Still, the dragging, hauling, faltering travel continued while men and dogs weakened.

August 8, a seal was shot and three murres. The starving men cut up a dinghy for firewood and cooked a meal. Supplies were jettisoned—many had already been abandoned on the island—and unnecessary words as well:

Supper at six. Turn to at 7:30. Shoot Prince and Pilgarlic. Lose Smike, Armstrong, Wolf, Dick. Two miles by 9:30. Halt and camp. Coffee giving out. Tea for dinner instead.

The next day, cheered by having made seven miles instead of the usual one or two, De Long became more discursive in writing up his account of the previous day:

Sat down to supper at six p.m. on a hard ice floe, letting our loaded boats ride alongside. It was my desire to keep the twelve dogs we had on leaving Bennett Island, and if we could possibly carry them to bring them with us to the end. But on Sunday, when we were starting, four of them jumped from the boats, and time was too precious to stop and run after them. Today four more, Smike, J. Armstrong, Wolf, and Dick, did the same thing, and though their doleful howling could be heard long after we had stopped for dinner, I could not spare the time to chase them even if the crowded condition of our boats would have permitted their being carried. But as our boats are so heavily loaded that the slightest motion causes the water to wash in through the rowlocks, carrying dogs becomes a risk. Perhaps the most sensible thing would have been to shoot them all, but, with the island so near, I thought if they escaped from us they might get back and perchance live. So that chance for life was given them.

Tonight, however, after carrying four dogs in the first cutter, I came to the conclusion that I was wrong so to lumber up the boat, and much to my regret (and to Ericksen's grief) Prince was one of the two victims led off to execution. Pilgarlic was the other. We now have two of our original forty,—Snoozer and Kasmatka,—and these two I shall keep until it becomes perilous to do so.

The water was more open now, with increasing time spent boating rather than hauling. There was also, at times, heavy snow falling, and increasing young ice. Still, no land or open sea was in sight, and De Long's anxieties were increasing. August 15, a seal was shot, providing food for the two dogs as well as the men, but bread was coming to an end and other supplies as well.

August 20, believing they had come very close to open water, De Long ordered the overhauling of the boats in preparation for ocean sailing. Later that day, land was sighted. De Long was sure it was New Siberia and gave directions to Executive Officer Charles Chipp and Chief Engineer George Melville, who were to command the other two boats: All were to make for the Lena River and a Russian settlement that could feed and shelter them. And then:

> The wind is moderating, and the barometer rising rapidly at six p.m., and I hope for good weather tomorrow, when, with God's blessing, I expect to start on our journey afloat. Kasmatka too clumsy and big,—shot him.

On August 21, ice had solidified around the sailors and held them in place through the following day, De Long's thirty-seventh birthday, and the day after that, and for some days more. Provisions now consisted of tea, beef extract, and pemmican. The lack of tobacco had forced some to try smoking coffee grounds or coffee grounds mixed with tea leaves. De Long, down to his last pipeful of tobacco, was given some as a gift, and then turned to tea leaves, which, he claimed, gave him "considerable comfort."

It was only on August 29 that the prisoners of ice were finally able to break free: The three boats set out with a total of thirty-three men and one dog, Snoozer. On August 30, they landed on what De Long called Faddejew Island, finding themselves on soil—with moss and grass—for the first time in two years. The men camped on the mossy level ground back from the beach, while Snoozer "tore around in glee, chasing lemmings, whose holes were abundant."

But the next day, the three boats left their glorious anchorage and soon were struggling through shoals and heavy seas and winds that separated De Long's cutter from Chipp's cutter and Melville's whaleboat; it was an anxious time until the three were reunited.

September 4, the three boats made another landing, but where, De Long was not sure. A moccasin track was found and fresh axe cuts as well as several ruined huts and artifacts such as a wooden spoon, a wooden fork, and a Russian coin dated 1840. Once more, the three boats got underway but soon were stopped by ice. They turned back to the unknown land with its hopeful signs of habitation. After the ice and the weather cleared, they returned to the sea. A landing on another island—Semenovski—provided a deer and firewood, but provisions were quickly running out and they had no choice but to move on.

September 12 and 13, a gale blew with squalls and a "tremendous" sea. De Long and his thirteen sailors in the first cutter lost sight of Chipp's cutter with its crew of eight and Melville's whaleboat with its crew of eleven. Chipp's cutter and crew would never be seen again, nor would De Long and Melville see one another again.

September 16, De Long and his thirteen men reached the delta of the Lena River but could not land. Eventually, with the cutter grounded, they unloaded and waded ashore with a raft through knee-deep water over a distance of a mile and a half. When, after numerous trips, they had off-loaded most of their cargo, they made a fire and settled down for the night. The boat was abandoned. After a period of drying out, and with rations down to three and one-half days, along with pemmican and tea, De Long ordered the march to begin. All sleeping bags were to be left behind.

It was Monday, September 19, 1881. The party setting out still consisted of fourteen men—and, though not mentioned in the record left in the instrument box at what De Long assumed was the Lena Delta—the dog named Snoozer.

Now the party, a land party, was trudging through ponds with thin ice and mossy swamps. Feet were wet and numb and progress painful and slow.

September 20, the last forty-five-pound can of pemmican was opened and divided into four days' provisions: "Then we are at the end of our provisions, and must eat the dog, unless Providence sends something in our way. When the dog is eaten—?"

One of the men, Ericksen, was giving out. Deer tracks were found but no deer. A snowbird flew around De Long's flagstaff and landed on it, a momentary symbol of hope.

September 21, the straggling group came upon two huts, one appearing fairly new. In the newer hut, De Long found a checkerboard, wooden forks, pieces of pencil, and evidence of the use of tools. After assessing their situation—three days' rations, three lame men, and, by De Long's calculations based on questionable charts, eighty-seven miles to the nearest probable settlement—the commander decided to stop and take possession of the hut. He would send two strong walkers—Nindemann (who had survived the *Polaris* ice-floe drift) and Ambler, the doctor—on a forced march to get help. That night, Alexey returned late from a hunting trip with a hindquarter and news he had secured two deer. Everyone jumped out of bed for a feast, and plans were changed; now, after a rest, all would continue on together toward human habitation and help.

The desperate trek began on the morning of September 24, with the temperature at 27.5°. Ice, along with wet and freezing feet, continued to slow progress. Once more, the patients weakened, especially Ericksen, who now had an ulcer on the sole of his foot.

By September 26, supplies were down to provisions for three meals—plus the dog. Then, the next day, just as De Long was about to have Snoozer killed, a deer! And the next day, another one—a stay of execution.

But the crisis was looming. The deer meat was quickly eaten and the flesh of Ericksen's foot was sloughing away. The men of the *Jeannette* were caught at a fork in the river and had no raft to cross to the west side and continue in the direction De Long had determined they needed to go. The doctor had to operate on Ericksen's feet, removing four toes from the right and one from the left.

By the next morning, four more of Ericksen's toes had to be removed. The temperature was 18°. It was October 1 and there was now ice enough to cross the river. The party successfully got over to the west side and continued south, though bewildered by the frequent narrowing and rambling of the river and much weakened by hunger and cold.

October 3, the last deer meat was eaten: "Our remaining food now consists of four fourteenths pounds pemmican each, and a half-starved dog. May God again incline unto our aid." Ericksen began to talk incessantly in Danish, German, and English.

Snoozer's end came quickly: That night, after De Long and two others had fallen through the ice into the river during a crossing and after a desperate and futile search for shelter:

> And now for supper! Nothing remained but the dog. I therefore ordered him killed and dressed by Iversen, and soon after a kind of stew was made of such parts as could not be carried, of which everybody

except the doctor and myself eagerly partook. To us two it was a nau-seating mess and—but why go on with such a disagreeable subject. I had the remainder weighed, and I am quite sure we had twenty-sev-en pounds. The animal was fat and—as he had been fed on pemmi-can—presumably clean, but—

The cold, wet night proceeded with the three soaked men trying to dry out by a fire and Ericksen now delirious. The last thermometer had broken in one of De Long's many falls on the river ice, but he guessed the temperature to be below zero.

With Ericksen unconscious and lashed to a sled, the party set off for a hut Alexey had found the previous day and, once there, achieved some warmth while a gale roared around them. A first meal, at six that eve-ning, consisted of half a pound of fried dog meat and a cup of tea appor-tioned equally.

There now could be only one such meal a day, with tea leaves used from the day before. By October 6, the third-use tea had half an ounce of alcohol added. Ericksen died. The men had all weakened. Alexey came back from hunting empty-handed: "What in God's name is going to be-come of us,—fourteen pounds dog meat left, and twenty-five miles to a possible settlement?"

There was no burying Ericksen. The ground was frozen and they had nothing with which to dig. The only answer was the river. They sewed him up in the flaps of the tent and covered him with the commander's flag but barely found the strength to carry him to the river, where they placed him in a hole in the ice. At five, a supper of one-half pound dog meat and tea was served to each.

The next day, October 7, brought the last portions of the dog meat and the tea. Now the party, provisioned only with some old tea leaves and two quarts of alcohol, as well as two Remington rifles and 243 rounds of ammunition, prepared to decamp and head for the settlement De Long hoped they could reach in time. Later that day, Alexey shot a ptarmigan; then, as the thirteen men slogged on, there was nothing left but alcohol.

October 9, De Long sent Nindemann and seaman Louis P. Noros ahead for relief. They carried their blankets, one rifle, forty rounds of am-munition, and two ounces of alcohol. The other eleven men followed in their tracks, as best they could. The alcohol was soon gone, leaving only deerskin scraps from clothing.

October 10: "Nothing for supper except a spoonful of glycerine." The men were in a hole in the river's bank with a gale blowing from the southwest.

October 11: There was no game and no wood: "One spoonful glycerine and hot water for food."

October 12: They tried drinking a tea of arctic willow.

October 14: Alexey shot one ptarmigan.

October 15: There was willow tea and two old boots for breakfast; signs of smoke at twilight to the south.

October 17: Meteorologist Jerome J. Collins's fortieth birthday; Alexey died from exhaustion and starvation and was buried in the river ice.

October 21: Heinrich H. Kaack, seaman, and Walter Lee, machinist, died and were carried around the corner, out of sight.

De Long's last entry is Sunday, October 30, 1881: "One hundred and fortieth day [since sinking]. Boyd [George W. Boyd, 2d class fireman] and Görtz [Carl A. Görtz, seaman] died during night. Mr. Collins dying"

Another ice journal had ended, with no punctuation, and a terrible silence fell over the camp.

Nindemann and Noros, meanwhile, traveled 120 miles—much farther than the twenty-five De Long had been hoping for—before finding native people. These took them in reindeer sleds to Ku Mark Surka, the settlement De Long had been aiming for, another thirty-three miles beyond their first encounter. It took days before the two men could make their hosts understand their predicament and urgent mission. At one point, a native person pointed to a dog in the room and asked if the strangers had any dogs. Nindemann explained, as best he could, that they had had forty and "had shot the most of them, and left some of them behind on the ice." The two sailors tried over and over to explain their need. Only after Nindemann broke down in tears of frustration and grief did a woman mention a "commandant." This, apparently, was the official in Bulun, a larger settlement. A man said he would take Nindemann there. Late that evening, a Russian arrived who seemed to know of the *Jeannette*. He took a note that Noros wrote. In the morning, he returned, saying that he was going to Bulun, and that they were to follow shortly.

They reached Bulun on October 29 and were taken to the commandant, who spoke of telegraphing to St. Petersburg. The men prepared a dispatch. The commandant went off with their note, supposedly on this mission, and the two survivors, weak and sick with dysentery, huddled in a hut assigned to them, too miserable to go out. On the evening of November 2, three days after the commandant had left with their dispatch, a man dressed in fur entered their hut. It took some time—and shock—to recognize Melville, captain of the whaleboat.

It was now time for Chief Engineer Melville to tell his story of what happened after the three boats became separated in the gale of September 12—

how he and all his ten men survived (though one went insane and one, Aneguin, the dog-driver and hunter, would die in Siberia during the subsequent searches for De Long's party). He had no news of Chipp and the second cutter.

The following spring, Melville found the bodies of De Long and his men (except the two buried in the ice of the river) and gave them temporary burial. In 1883, the remains were brought back to the United States for interment, with much ceremony and publicity.

De Long's journal was found three or four feet behind his body, as if, with his last energy, he had thrown it to higher ground that it might be spared the flooding waters of the Lena River. This was his bequest—the story of thirty-three desperate men and the forty dogs that served them.

Some of the expedition's dogs, from a sketch by ship's naturalist Raymond L. Newcomb.
De Long, p. 255

Crewmen returning from a bear hunt while the Jeannette was icebound north of Siberia, 1880.
Woodcut engraved by George T. Andrew after a Design by M.J. Burns. De Long, p. 363

19

The Polar Bear

The explorers' tales of encounters with polar bears occur so often they tend to become tedious. They were anything but tedious to those who experienced them, however. Looking back from an age when melting ice endangers these animals' very existence, we find it hard to imagine that these huge marine mammals were ubiquitous in the Arctic and a constant source of danger—as well as life-saving food.

The "lion of the north" was a particularly intelligent and dangerous foe. Charles Francis Hall described what Inuit hunters observed: how polar bears kill walrus by ascending a cliff and throwing rocks down on their heads; and, if the walrus is not instantly killed, the bear rushes down, takes hold of the rock and hammers away at the head until the skull is broken. Hall's friend Ouela said he had seen a bear kill a walrus by using a large piece of ice: "The bear rounds the ice into a ball, and stealthily runs on his hind legs toward his sleeping victim; if the first blow on the head of the walrus fails to kill, he finishes his work by repeated blows on the thick skull." He also told the tale of a polar bear that seized a woman outside her igloo, scalped her and disemboweled her child. An old man inside the igloo fastened a long knife to the end of a pole and braced the lance against the icy floor; when the bear entered the igloo and sprang at his new victim, he landed on the knife, which went directly through his heart.

Patient as well as clever, the bear is astute at killing seals. In the water, the bear drops his body beneath the surface, with only his head sticking out, looking like a piece of ice. While the seal has its head above water, looking about, the bear sinks, swims under it, and grabs it from beneath. On the ice, the bear throws himself down on his side and pulls himself along toward the napping seal. The bear, as he approaches, begins to "talk" to the seal, which continues in its relaxed state until the bear gets close enough to snatch it. If a young seal is in its "igloo," the bear runs and jumps with all his weight upon the dome, breaking it apart and grabbing the young seal inside. He then lets the young one flounder in the water until its alarmed mother surfaces, at which point he nabs both of them.

William Scoresby, Jr. (1789–1857), chronicler of the Arctic and its whale fisheries, wrote, in 1820:

> This formidable animal is, among quadrupeds, the sovereign of the arctic countries. He is powerful and courageous; savage and saga- cious; apparently clumsy, yet not inactive. His senses are extreme- ly acute, especially his sight and smell.... He is found on field-ice, above two hundred miles from the shore. He can swim with the velocity of three miles an hour, and can accomplish some leagues without much inconvenience. He dives to a considerable distance, though not very frequently.

In spite of his sagacity, the bear lives a challenged life. As Isaac I. Hayes said:

> The bears, wandering continually through the night, must needs have a hard struggle to live. During the summer, the seal, which fur- nish their only subsistence, crawl up on the ice, and are there easily caught; but in the winter they only resort to the cracks to breathe, and, in doing so, barely put their noses above the water, so that they are captured with difficulty.

Often, it is reported, they were found with rocks in their stomachs, or nothing. Fridtjof Nansen reported one with a piece of paper in his stomach that read "Lütken and Mohn," a wrapping paper that had been left by his crew somewhere on the ice. After this discovery, crew members dared not leave the ship without being armed.

The bear dog, like his prey, had to be intelligent, cunning, patient, and fast. Such a dog was considered essential in the hunt. Indeed, to kill a bear without the assistance of dogs was considered a remarkable accomplishment.

Hall and Ebierbing managed such a feat while on their way home at the end of the second expedition in 1869 during a stop at Whale Point. And Ebierbing and Hans saved the *Polaris* ice-floe prisoners from starvation by securing a polar bear a week before they encountered a sealer and were rescued.

The best bear dogs made hunting relatively easy for their masters. Boas told the story of Acherelwa, a hunter from Padli, who set his dogs loose to attack a bear: "They kept it at bay, and made it lie down without so much as attempting to defend itself. The dogs began to tear his ears, and soon tore the animal all to pieces."

Whether a noted bear dog or not, any dog would bark ferociously when a bear approached a ship or camp, usually providing enough warning for the men to loose the dogs, grab their guns, and, with the help of the dogs, dispatch the bear. But sometimes there were multiple bears—sows and their cubs—and the battle, with its different fronts, would be long and bloody. Sometimes, too, extreme hunger would drive a bear to what would seem like reckless measures. One night, a young bear climbed up on the *Fram* and took off first one dog to eat, then returned for another, which he ate in part, then came back for a third, which managed to escape, while, in the melee, he bit a crew member on the hip—all before a general alarm could be sounded.

The tales of sows and cubs protecting one another when under attack were prolific and poignant. Mother and young would battle to the end for one another while showing great emotion and tenderness. Rarely is such an encounter reported without commensurate expressions of sympathy and anthropomorphic language.

As Scoresby attested:

> Bears, though they have been known to eat one another, are remarkably affectionate to their young. The female, which has generally two at a birth, defends its young with such zeal, and watches over them with such anxiety, that she sometimes falls a sacrifice to her maternal attachment. A pleasing and very extraordinary instance of sagacity in a mother bear was related to me by a credible and well informed person, who accompanied me in several voyages to the whale-fishery, in the capacity of surgeon. This bear, with two cubs under its protection, was pursued across a field of ice, by a party of armed sailors. At first she seemed to urge the young ones to an increase of speed, by running before them, turning around, and manifesting, by a peculiar action and voice, her anxiety for their progress; but finding their pursuers gaining upon them, she carried, or pushed, or pitched them alternately forward, until she effected their escape. In throwing them before her, the little creatures are said to have placed themselves across her path, to receive the impulse; and, when projected some yards in advance,

they ran on until she overtook them, when they alternately adjusted themselves for a second throw.

Nansen, describing tracks found in the snow the day after a protracted battle with a sow and cub, said of the mother, "One shudders to think of her watching over her poor young one, which must have had his back shot through."

Sometimes whalers, after killing the sow, took cubs back with them to England for zoos and research. Much sought after for exhibit, they could bring a good price. Scoresby, in his journal for June 15, 1812, referred to two cubs he took alive. One he gave to another captain and one he gave to his mentor at Edinburgh University, Professor Jameson, from whom a letter survives asking what food he should give the cub.

Captain John Gravill of the *Diana* also took cubs. In one instance, a cub brought aboard raged to such an extent the crew hoisted up the dead sow to comfort him. The cub then

> laid down beside her and moaned and sobbed most pitiful, and licked the blood from her wounds and tried to lift her head up with its paws. 'Twas most distressing to look at.
>
> Yes, bears is very affectionate animals, I assure you. We took that young bear home and sold him for £12.

Captain Gravill explained how they would "snickle" a cub by throwing a rope around its neck while it was swimming. Once captured, it would be put in a cask with an iron grating on top. They would feed it crang, or whale skin, heave buckets of saltwater over it daily, and hose it off. If the weather allowed, they would hoist up the cub in its cask and drop it overboard or set the cask on end and half fill it with water.

The cub would get to know the person who fed it, Gravill remarked, but it could not be trusted. Once, in Lerwick Harbor, when the inspector came aboard, his dog put his nose through the cage and the bear tore its jaw off. "We had to drown the poor dog," Gravill said.

Such captures were not the sole province of the whale fishery. In 1910, after serving as Robert Peary's captain, Robert Bartlett spearheaded a hunting expedition that brought back an adult polar bear, two cubs, and various other animals. Bartlett captured the six-year-old male, which was taken to the Bronx Zoo, where he lived out his life. In 1928, the U.S. Coast Guard Cutter *Marion* completed a seventy-three-day mission through arctic waters, returning with a polar bear cub the crew had taken in Greenland. Named for her transport, Marion went to live at the National Zoo in Washington, D.C., for the twenty years left of her life.

20

Gypsy, Old Sneak, Ritenbenk, Disco King

The Abandoned

Traveling with Adolphus Washington Greely:
The Lady Franklin Bay Expedition, 1881–1884

U nlike his immediate predecessors, Frederick Schwatka and George Washington De Long, Adolphus Washington Greely (1844–1935) had no formal military education but, during the Civil War, entered the U.S. Army as a volunteer at age seventeen. After the war, Greely remained in the Army as a member of the Signal Corps, laying telegraph lines in the Northwest and the Southwest. A growing interest in meteorology and the importance of weather forecasting coupled with energy and capability marked him as a leader in his field—and Greely wanted to make a name for himself. A trip to England ignited interest in the exploits of Sir John Franklin and, more recently, Sir George Strong Nares, commander of the British North Polar Expedition of 1875–1876.

In March 1881, in spite of much political contention, Congress passed a bill authorizing a scientific expedition to the shores of Lady Franklin Bay on Ellesmere Island. The purpose was to establish one of a series of meteorological stations in observance of the First International Polar Year while also collecting astronomical and polar magnetic data. President Garfield named Greely as commander of the Lady Franklin Bay Expedition. Later,

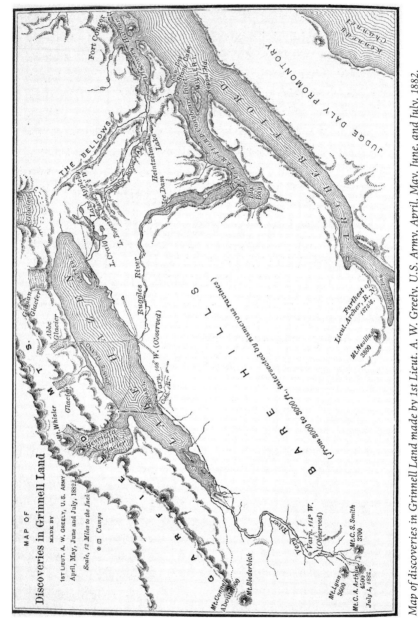

Map of discoveries in Grinnell Land made by 1st Lieut. A. W. Greely, U.S. Army, April, May, June, and July, 1882.
Greely, p. 346; Semi-Rare Book Collection, Alaska and Polar Regions Collections & Archives, Rasmuson Library, University of Alaska Fairbanks

another duty was added to Greely's scientific expedition: to search for the missing *Jeannette*.

Set on the west shore of the channel separating Canada from Greenland in what is now known as Nunavut, the station is located at 82° N, approximately 500 miles south of the North Pole. It was an area that had most recently been visited and well recorded by Nares. It was also the place Isaac I. Hayes dubiously claimed to have attained on May 19, 1861—"the most northern land ever reached."

The Lady Franklin Bay party consisted of twenty-five men, mostly U.S. Army volunteers, but also a contracted medical doctor, Octave Pavy, and two Greenlanders hired as hunters and dog-drivers, Thorlip Frederick Christiansen, who had served Nares, and Jens Edward. Best known of the group is James Booth Lockwood, second in command, who set the expedition's record for the farthest northing. Pavy and one other crew member, Sergeant George Rice, the photographer, had been to Greenland the previous summer; none others but the Greenlanders had any arctic experience. To fill the gap, Greely brought along an arctic library of 1,000 volumes, including the work of Elisha Kent Kane.

The plan was to transport the initial group from St. John's, Newfoundland, by chartered ship, pick up the others on the Greenland coast, then leave the expedition members at their post for two years. A steamer was to visit the station annually, bringing supplies and new recruits.

The *Proteus*, a 467-ton barkentine with armored prow, set sail with the Lady Franklin Bay Expedition from St. John's on July 7, 1881. Back home, President Garfield was slowly dying of an assassin's gunshot wound. On the other side of the polar sea, De Long and his shipwrecked crew and dogs were struggling slowly across the ice toward the Lena River delta, not knowing that Greely was looking for them.

Arriving in Godhavn, Greenland, Greely quickly noticed the importance of dogs—and their care:

> The dog is an important animal in Northern Greenland, and he seems to know his vantage. He looks on every stranger as an enemy, who must be watched and harassed. They are annoying only on their own domain, and are experts in those false attacks which are trying to one's temper and dignity.
>
> It is amusing, when not personally interested, to note how suddenly a snarling, yelling pack, snapping at one's heels, will turn and flee when they near the ground of some other king. He is a rare dog, indeed, who dares travel alone through the entire village of Godhavn. A stick or stone generally quiets a pack, but occasionally,

when very harshly treated, and when long starved they are dangerous to children, and even, though very rarely, to men.

The twelve dogs Greely purchased in Godhavn were, he noted,
"stout, surly animals of apparently incurable viciousness, which, as we
shall see later, completely vanished under the benign influences of kind
treatment and good food." He also purchased a supply of dog food and
took on the dog house and pemmican stashed there by the unsuccessful
Henry W. Howgate expedition of the previous year. Farther up the coast
at Ritenbenk, more dogs (unnumbered) and their food were added. There
was instant dislike between the "old" and the "new" groups, which, according to Greely, led to battles that never diminished.

On August 11, 1881, the *Proteus* entered the destination of Discovery
Harbor, Ellesmere Island (Grinnell Land, Greely called it), to the ac-
companiment of musk oxen, eider ducks, and arctic poppies—"kindly
greetings on Nature's part to our new home," Greely noted. While crew
members were hunting, Greely quickly found a "post-office cairn" left
by a previous visitor, Captain Stephenson of the *Discovery*, one of Nares's
two ships, dated August 11, 1876, exactly five years before. Nearby were
barrels of spoiled pork and beef, along with empty cans and other debris
left by Captain Stephenson. (Nares's lead ship, the *Alert*, wintered farther
to the north.) Signs of the recent expedition—the one that had motivated
Greely—were abundant. On May 13, 1876, Stephenson had honored Charles
Francis Hall by erecting a brass tablet at his grave site across Smith Sound
on the Greenland side. At the time, Stephenson reported all was well at the
site, a willow planted by George Tyson still alive.

Greely named his station Fort Conger, after Senator Omar D. Conger
of Michigan, who had enthusiastically supported the polar expedition.
With supplies unloaded and two disabled soldiers discharged, it was time
to say goodbye to the supply ship and settle in for the winter.

The *Proteus* made a slow ice-choked exit from the harbor on August
19, not able to reach open water until August 26. The *Proteus* and the Lady
Franklin Bay party would never meet again.

Home for the remaining twenty-five men now consisted of a prefab-
ricated wooden house sixty by seventeen feet, double walled, divided into
three rooms and covered on the outside with tar paper—a construction,
it would be found, particularly unsuited to the climate. At the north and
south ends, two lean-tos made of canvas and tar paper were added. During
the second year, a third was attached to the west side.

Greely made no comments regarding arrangements for the dogs, nor
of training and preparation for the sledge trips that were soon to begin. He

enumerated but did not discuss the dogs cited in the sledging trips of that first autumn, nor did he mention the dogs used for hunting musk oxen except in the tally of the game taken.

During September and October, Greely noted, twenty-six musk oxen, ten ducks, a hare, two seals, and a ptarmigan were secured by hunters, "which afforded about six thousand pounds of fresh meat for the party, and nearly an equal amount of offal for our dogs."

In mid-September a large band of wolves, numbering as many as eighteen, appeared near the house. Shrouded in the shape-changing fog, they appeared as large as yearling steers. Unafraid but cautious, they eluded those who went after them. A few days later, another, smaller band also escaped the hunters. September 26, a lone wolf came within a hundred yards of the house and, though shot and bleeding, ran until he fell down dead, substantially bloodless.

Disturbed by the proximity of such a pack and with the dogs terrified at the approach of the wolves, Greely decided to poison the intruders; the task, however, proved far more difficult than he imagined. Wary, the wolves avoided the poisoned meat. Eventually, he succeeded in killing only four wolves as well as a fox, but the rest of the pack disappeared for the season.

Busy as he was with managing his own expedition, Greely was mindful of the *Jeannette*. He had all members of his party on the lookout for signs, while, at the same time, De Long and his men, many weeks without a ship, were dying one by one on the icy banks of the Lena.

By November, the long darkness had settled over Fort Conger, but the sledging parties were still going out to explore, hunt, and prepare caches for future travels—largely to keep the men fit and occupied. Among other items, hundreds of pounds of coal were moved. On one such trip, as Greely mentioned, the hardiness of the "Eskimo" dog was made clear: Gypsy, a favorite, and pregnant, had been kept back but insisted on following the sledge. On the second day out, she gave birth to four puppies, which were left in a snowbank until the return of the party, apparently none the worse for their temporary abandonment.

The story of Gypsy and her puppies pales by comparison, however, with a story told by Albert Hastings Markham of the preceding Nares expedition concerning a dog named Sallie. While out on a sledge journey, Sallie had a fit and was cast off from the team and disappeared. A week later, she showed up, following the team and picking up food left for her, though she would not let herself be caught. After the sledge party returned to their ship, the *Alert*, she vanished. Two months later, she reappeared but was driven off by the other dogs. The next day, she allowed herself to be caught and, after being nursed back to health, became "the strongest and best dog in our whole team."

Now, in autumn, it was a time for puppies, as Greely noted:

> Other than the departure of the sledge parties which left the station in the early days of November, the most important incidents were the births of the two litters of pups, five of which came on the 2d and five on the 3d of the month. My journal of November 4th says: "Two of the last litter and one of the first have died, and another was eaten by one of the pack. This evening the remaining pups of the last litter were for a time abandoned by their mother, who left them to quarrel with the mother of the other litter, which were in the same room with her. During the temporary absence of the mother, we placed one of her pups with the other litter, but it was pushed away by the indignant parent, who declined any addition to her cares. Finally the deserting mother returned to her puppies."

A few days later, another litter was born, and one of the other mothers seized one of the new pups and tried to devour it before being discovered— but too late to save the life of the pup. It was common practice, Greely noted, for the dogs to seize and gobble down young pups, but he and his men never noticed a mother eating one of her own, an assessment neither Kane nor Hall agreed with.

Gypsy ("the brightest and most cunning dog of our teams") exhibited special maternal concerns. When another mother killed her last puppy, she "sorrowed long for her lost litter. For a considerable time after this she improved every opportunity, in the absence of their own mothers, to suckle the young in other litters."

Distemper had thinned the ranks of the teams and Greely was anxious to raise new recruits. The Greenlanders said the young dogs would not survive, and history seemed to indicate it was unlikely that litters born early in the winter would make it. Perhaps there was something else: Nares had written pointedly of his former employee that, "although Frederick [Christiansen] is a valuable man in other ways, he cannot be induced to take sufficient care of the young dogs."

As substitute nurse, Greely chose Private Roderick Schneider, who lavished care and attention on the young dogs and eventually raised fifteen to valuable adulthood. Schneider also broke them to harness and drove them successfully the next summer. Greely was to comment, on a number of occasions, as to how important these young dogs became.

Greely, quoting from his journal, maintained the pack was transformed by kindness:

Our dogs would now never be recognized as the same wolfish, snapping, untamed animals obtained at the Greenland ports. Good care,
plenty of food, and kind treatment had filled out their gaunt frames,
put them in good working condition, and made them as good-
natured, affectionate, and trustful as though they had never been
pounded, half starved, and generally abused from their puppyhood
upward....They were regularly fed, first on alternate days, and then
once daily, and we never found it necessary to maltreat and beat them
to ensure fair behavior at feeding-time. Indeed feeding-time was the
only occasion on which rival dogs would not fight, for long experience had taught them it was a losing game; whichever dog won, both
invariably lost their food through neutral and wiser parties.

On December 18, Greely reported that the six-week-old puppies were
doing well during intensely cold weather:

They rush out from the lean-to into the open air at a temperature
of –40 degrees and –45 degrees, in order to obtain bits from the
slop-bucket, and tonight two or three running into the water as it
was thrown out, and remaining quiet for a minute, were actually
frozen to the spot, and had to be cut out with a hatchet. They appear
none the worse for their misadventure.

Christmas brought the usual arctic entertainments. Schneider, the
dog guardian, provided a female impersonation. Dressed in a local woman's outfit he had purchased en route, he carried in his woman's hood
one of the puppies, who was "nearly frightened to death" by the unaccustomed applause.

During the exceedingly cold weather of January 1882, Greely monitored the dogs closely, expecting to see signs of suffering, but, he noted,
they seemed to suffer no ill effects. The only way they showed they were
cold was by sometimes lifting one foot and then another as though the
ground was burning them. Greely had a tent erected for them, and later
the doctor had some snow huts excavated for them, but they never entered the huts and never sought shelter in the tent except during severe
windstorms. One dog occasionally crept into a closed-up tent where bedding or clothing could be found.

Where the dogs preferred to sleep (as with De Long's) was on freshly
strewn ashes. The most favorite place was the top of the ash barrel.
Often, Greely noticed, a dog would leave the barrel to attack a rival, only
to return, vastly disappointed, to find his place taken. Sometimes a dog
would even jump on top of another already settled on the ash barrel. The
under dog would stay as long as he could bear the weight of the intruder.

Others preferred the part of the coal pile that was free of snow. Unless they had litters, they seldom chose to sleep under cover and, if they did, they were chastised by the pack.

In the clear, cold days of February, before the sun returned, it was difficult to travel without the perspective of light and shadows. All was flat. On one such dark blue day, a dog team, unable to see what lay ahead, ran over a break in a floe and fell eight feet.

But, for the dogs, good vision wasn't always necessary; they could rob cleverly no matter what the degree of light or darkness, and often leave little in the way of clues. It was during those sunless days of February that two dressed hares disappeared. Suspicion rested on two of the dogs, which later accepted their food from the cooks in a nonchalant manner. This was the first thievery of meat of the Lady Franklin Bay Expedition but certainly not the last.

As the sun returned, it was time to start the serious business of spring sledging. Only now, with logistics critical, did Greely give a clear inventory of the dogs:

> It had been my original intention that the greater part of the work of exploration should be done with dogs, of which three full teams had been purchased in Greenland. Of twenty-seven dogs purchased at the Danish ports, only twelve were living at the end of 1881. All the teams had been attacked by disease introduced by the dogs sold to me by the governor of Upernavik, from which sickness the greater part perished. Fortunately there were three private dogs in the expedition, one of which belonged to Dr. Pavy and two had been given to me personally. This enabled me to put into the field two teams of seven dogs each, to which Dr. Pavy added to his own team his private dog. Careful attention had resulted in the saving of nine of the puppies born the previous November, but their use in the field that spring was quite out of the question, though I counted, and properly, on making them useful later in the season. This loss of dogs caused me to modify my original plans, in which I had intended that the supporting sledges, drawn by men, should never be absent from the station for more than a week.

Later, Greely would express his appreciation for Schneider's work, whose "intelligent and zealous efforts" made possible the success of the puppies born at Conger.

One of the first spring sledging parties was sent across Smith Sound to Thank God Harbor and Hall's grave, where all was found in good shape, though the "dreariness and desolation" of the setting was clearly noted, a setting considered much less desirable than that of Fort Conger. Here, too, adding to the somber nature of the place, were the graves of two sailors from the recent Nares expedition who had died of scurvy.

This first exploratory journey, which proceeded to Cape Sumner, following Hall's route, covered 135 miles and, though difficult, resulted in no serious problems. The dogs held up well, Greely reported, except for a nine-month-old youngster that was "somewhat tired" at times.

On March 5, another party was sent to establish a cache at Polaris Boat Camp near Cape Sumner. For this effort, seven dogs pulled a sledge load of 700 pounds. In spite of severe weather, the trip was accomplished in four days.

Two weeks later, Dr. Pavy, Sergeant Rice, and Jens Edward set out with a team of "excellent dogs" to push considerably farther north. On this journey, one of the dogs, Old Sneak, proved (in the style of De Long's "gang of hoodlums") a remarkable ability to avoid work. In harness, he did his job because he knew Jens's keen eye was on him—as well as the possibility of the lash—and at feeding time he was on hand. But he showed no eagerness to work. On one occasion, when the sledge was ready to go, Old Sneak was not to be found—until Jens discovered him in the vacated snow hut awaiting departure of his work mates.

Six weeks later, on May 2, the party made it back to Fort Conger in good health but without having achieved the distance sought.

Greely then led an exploratory party into the interior of Grinnell Land, covering over 250 miles in twelve days with five crew members pulling sledges, unassisted by dogs.

When Lieutenant Lockwood went north in April to explore the northern coast of Greenland, his supporting sledges were hauled by men, but the advance sledge was hauled by a team of eight dogs, averaging sixty-two pounds each in weight; although, as Greely pointed out, one bitch weighed only forty pounds and "never hauled the food she ate." As temperatures fell as low as −48°, the dogs added their share of misery. According to Sergeant David Brainard, who was serving as cook:

> Ritenbenk, the king-dog, ably assisted by Gypsy, the queen, entered the tent while we were sleeping, and carried away the meat already prepared for our evening meal. As no allowance for thieving dogs was made in our scale of provisions, we are compelled to fast until the next meal.

Brainard was left facing the disappointment and anger of his traveling mates who had to accept hard bread as a substitute for the pilfered meat.

Then, violent storms broke out. During a forced stop, with the men distracted, the dogs succeeded in stealing forty pounds of bacon and beef.

At another halt in a storm, while Lieutenant Lockwood was having dinner, some of the dogs found their way to his tent and rested on his sleeping bag, covering it with snow. (There is no mention of sharing sleeping space with the dogs for extra warmth.) Another night, the dogs managed to eat all that was remaining of the bacon—about twenty pounds—and half as much English beef.

Well into the trip, and after many such difficulties, Lockwood read to his party a letter from Greely promising a reward of $900 and upwards to any attaining a new farthest northing. Lockwood offered a fifty-percent bonus, the amount to be distributed according to merit.

The men moved on with new motivation, Lockwood's marches now averaging eleven hours each for a total of twenty-two miles daily. On April 29, the supporting party turned back as Lockwood, Brainard, and Christiansen prepared for the final run, with a load of 783 pounds to be pulled by the eight dogs, or an average of ninety-eight pounds per dog.

The dogs, Brainard noted, "not being accustomed to hauling such heavy weights, sit down as soon as the runners cut through the crust . . . and complacently watch us, with a puzzled expression . . . until we lift the sledge bodily and place it on the firm crust."

The marauding dogs struck again, one night stealing their allowance of pemmican for two and a half days. At Cape Britannia, Lockwood established a cairn, depositing in it his record of the journey, five days' rations, three days' worth of dog food, and various pieces of equipment.

Farther on, at a camp site, the dogs were "running about like ravenous wolves, gnawing at everything, and badly chewed and splintered the thermometer-box before it could be secured." Suddenly, there was the rush of feet and a thump against the tent—and king-dog Ritenbenk had seized a ptarmigan hanging from the ridge pole. In spite of his look of innocence, a few feathers in his bloody mouth revealed him as the thief.

After another march, this one of seventeen miles, the hungry dogs attacked again. While the men were sleeping, they broke the bindings, entered the tent, and stole the provision bag and a hare that had been shot. In their excitement, they made enough noise to wake the men, who regained everything except a quarter of the hare, which Ritenbenk quietly ate while his starved companions watched.

On May 13, Lockwood made his farthest north camp at what he determined to be 83° 23.8′, beating the record set by the Nares expedition and attaining the highest latitude yet reached by a foreign explorer—an enormous coup for the Lady Franklin Bay Expedition and the American effort to reach the Pole.

On the night before turning back to Conger, Lockwood recorded:

As I awoke, a small piece of pemmican (our only remaining dog food) was slowly but surely moving out of the tent. The phenomenon astonished me, and, rubbing my eyes, I looked more carefully, and saw Ritenbenk's head without his body, and found that his teeth, fixed in one corner of the sack, were the motive power. His eyes were fixed steadily on me, but head, eyes, and teeth vanished as I looked. He had burrowed a hole through the snow and had inserted his head just far enough into the tent to lay hold of a corner of the sack. The whole pack are ravenous, and eat anything and everything, which means substantially nothing in this case.

Brainard, in his notes, described another voracious attack, when the dogs nearly upset the tent in their anxiety to get breakfast: "Their wolfish propensities were aroused, and neither blows nor Eskimo imprecations were of avail until food was thrown them." Another time the dogs, "evidently preparing for war," tore open the ammunition bag, bit several shotgun cartridges, and ruined another dozen.

According to Greely, the party of three returned to Fort Conger on June 1, after an absence of sixty days—all in good health except for debilitating snow blindness; two of the three had to be led into Conger. Traveling with the dog sledge and eight dogs in severe cold, Lockwood had made forty-six marches, traveled 928 geographical miles, explored 125 miles of the Greenland coast previously unvisited by foreigners, and had broken the British record for the farthest northing by four miles. The average temperature on the outward portion was below zero. Going out, his average speed was 2.1 miles per hour, and on the way back, 2.3. "This sledge trip," Greely remarked, "must stand as one of the greatest in Arctic history." He also remarked that Lockwood's success would have been even greater if the Greenland dogs had not been susceptible to disease. What he did not say was that Lockwood's success was dependent on the eight dogs that survived the epic journey.

While these explorations were going on, Private Schneider continued to train his team of seven pups. On May 5 he took them on their first long haul: a round-trip of over fifty miles made in twenty hours, each young dog pulling from forty to sixty pounds. The outing was so successful, the youngsters were now considered fit for light field work and were to earn the constant praise of Greely. Their success, Greely had already noted, was due to "the intelligent and zealous efforts of Private Schneider, who, after an experience of several months, drove nearly as well as an Eskimo."

The summer season brought little news of the dogs, except how, at the beginning, their feet were badly cut by sharp ice under surface water, requiring sealskin boots for protection. As the temperature increased, however, it was no time for dogs and sledges but for walking and wagons. Continuing explorations of nearby areas were done by foot, with numerous Inuit artifacts discovered.

Above all, it was a time for hunting. Numerous musk oxen were killed and, at one point, four calves taken alive and maintained at the fort like domestic animals, being fed cornmeal and milk and "almost any food." They became attached to their keepers, Private Francis Long and Private Julius Frederick, and would follow them around, sticking their noses into the men's pockets looking for something to eat. They fared well except for one that had its throat torn open by the dogs. Greely intended to send them home with the visiting vessel expected in 1882—the ship that never came.

With the return of winter—and the grim realization their 1882 supply ship had failed them—Greely had to establish strict control over the remaining provisions. On September 11, the first calf was slaughtered; it dressed out at forty-two pounds.

Like Kane and Hayes before him, Greely needed companionship. A few days after the butchering of the first calf, he decided to keep a pure white fox that Jens had caught. The captive quickly became tame, making a purring sound like a cat when stroked, and "invariably jump[ing] at one's face when it is brought near to him." He was named Reuben. Another, probably older, fox caught soon after Reuben's capture remained wild and "as vicious as when caught, biting us at every opportunity." He was killed on October 13. (Hayes's experience with foxes was similar—one easily tamed, a second one not.)

On October 1, the temperature went below zero for the first time that autumn and the tracks of a bear became evident. Greely sent a party with dog sledge out to hunt for the potential predator. The search was unsuccessful and the bear returned to Conger—the only one known to visit the fort. Because of the danger, Greely required the men to obtain permission for any extended absence.

Early in October, one of the remaining calves died, and Greely sent the surviving two, on dog sledge, to a nearby island, where one died immediately. The last remaining one was led up a ravine, following Long like a dog, but refused to be left, running after him and the sledge back to the fort. Once back at the house, he followed Long everywhere until finally he was carried to his old pen. He died the next day.

In the meantime, Reuben the fox prospered. Early in November, Schneider took him outside the house, where he became much alarmed at the dogs, clearly wanting to be taken back into the house and his confinement in the lean-to (one of three attached to the building).

Early in November, Dr. Pavy's dog died on a sledge trip he took with Brainard—the first death of a dog since the distemper outbreak. The team was exhausted, the journey severe.

On December 11, Lockwood suffered a misfortune by means of a dog. While collecting meteorological records, he left a lantern and the record book by the shelter where temperatures were taken and went to another area to make magnetic observations. While he was gone, a dog bit out and swallowed a third of the record pages.

In another incident, a dog grabbed a dishrag that was mistakenly thrown out with the dishwater and bolted it.

At the same time, Reuben decided to leave the lean-to by digging a hole in the snow wall surrounding the house. He would show his nose to those inside the house but seemed to not want to return. The dogs were digging for him but he seemed to have outgrown his fear of them, even catching a one-month-old puppy by the nose and flinging him away yelping. Early in January 1883, Greely recaptured his pet but did not stroke him, "as I was without gloves and he was much excited over his new imprisonment." At this point, Reuben disappeared from the narrative, only to reappear in the appendix to Greely's work, under the heading *Vulpus lagopus*, the Arctic fox: "He finally escaped in April, selecting a time doubtless when the dogs were asleep."

It was only in November that Greely and his men tasted fox for the first time. Seasoned with "ravenous hunger," it proved delicious.

At the beginning of February, a puppy belonging to a bitch named Millitook was found gasping and nearly dead, his tail frozen solid. He refused meat—a sign of hopelessness—but finally, after his tail was thawed in cold water, he recovered. The men named him General Grant for his persistence.

The spring of 1883 brought renewed efforts for hunting and exploration—as well as fervent hope for a relief ship. An inventory of the dogs proved some were too old for work at a time when provisions were short. A number were shot. In his summation, Greely stated:

> We are now better off for dogs than on our arrival; having twenty which can be depended on for long sledge journeys, and nine others which are fit for short trips. Our dogs have been fed regularly every other day, and, in addition, have been given daily the leavings of the table. The Polaris people, according to the report, fed theirs only twice a week. It is not to be wondered that they were savage and wolfish. Our dogs have not been as well fed as I could desire, as I have no food this winter but pork, beef, and fish (all salt). Their food has always been thoroughly soaked and freshened, and, what I consider an important point, always fed to them in an unfrozen and generally

warm condition. Hard bread has been given to as many as would eat it, which includes the puppies raised here and one or two of the old dogs. Most of the Greenland dogs will not touch bread, even when very hungry. Of the fifteen puppies born in Grinnell Land, which now are fit for work, five were from one bitch and seven from another. There is a great difference in the manner in which the bitches care for their young.

Well treated or not, the dogs were deficient in manners. On one exploratory trip, the dogs broke into a cache and stole and ate their harness and whip, which had to be replaced by leather that fortunately had already been cached in the same place. Greely noted that the only safe place to keep anything in the field was under one's head or body.

On March 27, Lockwood set out with a party totaling five men with two teams of ten "strong" dogs each. His mission was to beat, if possible, his farthest northing. The challenge was daunting. The dogs averaged seventy pounds each in weight and were to haul, at the utmost, 2,100 pounds. Careful experiments and measurements had been made: The dogs, which could start on a long journey pulling one and a half times their weight, could rarely travel more than six miles per hour with a light load, and half that distance with a heavy one.

Lockwood was back on April 12, stopped by open water. He narrowly missed disaster, he reported, when the pack ice suddenly moved away from shore and several of the dogs plunged into the water. Christiansen, lashing the dogs to a gallop, overtook Brainard, who had gone on ahead, to warn him. A small floe, by chance, jammed between the edge of the moving pack ice and the shore ice, enabling men, dogs, and baggage to be pulled up over the edge.

On April 25 Lockwood was off again, this time to explore the interior of Grinnell Land from east to west. He, Brainard, and Christiansen had a team of "our best ten dogs." Steep terrain and deep snow impeded their way.

On May 16, they started homeward only to find worse conditions. There was now nothing left to feed the dogs and they began to weaken. The following day, the dogs had to climb a snowbank with an almost vertical face of sixty feet, pulling up the sledge with everything on it. Settled in camp, Lockwood killed the feeblest dog for food. During the night, its teammates devoured it.

Closer to home, they were able to make use of supplies cached earlier. Reporting on his supper before starting on the last march, Lockwood noted another theft by a dog: "No bread, sugar, or coffee. Rabbit stew, the pieces of meat being stolen by Howler." On the next page, he noted: "Howler, being unwell, was left behind." Later, he underscored the loss: "Howler gave out and was left behind, and has since been found dead." Still later, he repeated the story of the desertion. Clearly, Lockwood carried a sorrowful weight of regret.

On May 26, after traveling 437 miles, the three men reached Fort Conger. Within sight of the house, they abandoned one of the dogs, Disco King, causing Greely to note: "The case of this animal illustrates the spirit of faithfulness to be found in a good Eskimo dog. He worked until his strength was entirely gone, and when released from the harness died of exhaustion, without being able to crawl to the station, which was in sight." Schwatka and Heinrich Klutschak, in accounts of their 1878–1880 expedition, remarked on the same phenomenon of dogs dying in the traces or as soon as freed.

In the meantime, while Lockwood and others explored, preparations for retreat to the south were under way in case the long-awaited relief ship once more failed to show up. Greely had clear orders from the War Department: "If not visited in 1882, Lieutenant Greely will abandon his station not later than September 1, 1883, and will retreat southward by boat, following closely the *east* coast of *Grinnell Land* until the relieving vessel is met or Littleton Island is reached."

One of the first efforts in this regard was to visit Thank God Harbor and bring from there a boat left by Lieutenant Beaumont of the Nares expedition in 1876. The puppy team, driven by Schneider, hauled much of the weight of the boat and supplies south to Cape Baird to await possible evacuation.

In the meantime, a disciplinary problem grew larger: The always independent and obstructionist Dr. Pavy, having declined to renew his contract, insisted he was no longer in service and refused to obey Greely's orders. Greely placed him under arrest but allowed him free movement within a mile of the station. (There were numerous disciplinary problems with other men, as well, most glossed over in Greely's account but evident in the journals of crew members.)

By July 29, all arrangements had been made for the retreat: The station was to be abandoned on August 8 if no ship had shown up by then. The scientific records—fifty pounds of them—were packed in tin boxes and soldered for watertightness. Each man was allowed eight pounds of baggage, each officer sixteen pounds. Diaries, photographic negatives, thermometers, and medical supplies were all carefully packed.

While these preparations were made, the ice continued to hold firm; and, while the ice held, supplies dwindled. On August 4, Lockwood wrote:

> Rit [Ritenbenk] and Askim [Ask him] had a terrible fight this morning. . . . They are rival lovers, Askim got Rit down once. I think it will end by Askim being king and Rit going about with drooping head and tail,

like that debased monarch, Old H [Howler]. I should rather say would end thus under ordinary circumstances, but when we leave here—if in boats, as probable—the dogs will be shot, or perhaps left with a few days' food against the possible event of our return. Of course, in the latter event (barring our return), they would soon starve to death.

A southerly storm stayed the party until August 9—a day not only of departure but of abandonment. Greely wrote:

> Brainard, by my orders, opened several barrels each of seal-blubber, pork, beef and bread, so that the dogs could maintain life for several months. I regretted exceedingly to leave those faithful animals, to whom we were strongly attached, but they could be of no use in our retreat. I could not safely kill them, for in case of our return to Conger, through any contingency, they would be essential to us for hauling in our game and fuel.

And so the dogs were left—with fossils, musical instruments, and other superfluous baggage. The abandoned had become abandoners. Greely gave no description of the desertion—whether the dogs tried to follow the boats or stood howling on the shore as the distance widened between animal and man. But a month later, September 11, he hinted at what the separation had meant: "Dr. Pavy and Sergeant Brainard saw several walruses in the young ice, and thought that they heard a dog bark. It caused a faint hope to rise up in our hearts, but after several shots were fired we concluded they must have been mistaken."

Not knowing that the 1883 supply ship, their old friend the *Proteus*, was sunk and that its consort, the U.S. steamer *Yantic*, had turned back with almost all its stores to Upernavik (not establishing caches as ordered), the retreating party struggled bravely south into the floes, fog, and snow that were only the beginning of their travails.

On September 29, after excruciating battles with moving ice, cold, and wretched conditions, the party landed, intact, on the mainland of Grinnell Land south of Cape Sabine—more than 400 miles' travel by boat and 100 by sledge and boat. Of the long struggle to reach shore, Greely commented: "I can only add that many occasions of great peril came on days so eventful that time and strength failed with which to even allude to them in my diary, and their story can never be fully told."

Sergeant Rice took a difficult and dangerous trip to Cape Sabine, where he found caches from previous expeditions as well as from the *Proteus*, the U.S. Relief Expedition of 1883, which had sunk on July 23 on its way to Fort Conger. Still not knowing the full story, Greely decided to move his men to an encampment near Cape Sabine. Once there, after an enormously exhausting haul, he found the cache left by the *Proteus* to be less than he hoped—far less. A supply of lemons wrapped in newspaper told the story of how the 1882 relief ship, the *Neptune*, had failed in its mission as well.

Disappointment and ravenous hunger set in. At one point, when rotten dog biscuits covered with a green mold were thrown on the ground, the men sprang on them like wild animals. But rations had to be cut, even more drastically, as winter closed in—then cut again, and again. The Lady Franklin Bay Expedition had claimed a cruelly barren place, an arctic desert that would exact a long, slow toll. Lockwood's lengthy journal became an obsessive report on food, or the lack thereof, punctuated by grim medical reports.

The first death came in January 1884. After April, the deaths came rapidly—all by starvation and exposure except one by drowning (Jens Edward) and one by execution for stealing food (Private Charles Henry).

When U.S. Navy Commander Winfield Scott Schley of the rescue ship *Thetis* arrived near midnight on June 22, 1884, seven members of the original twenty-five Lady Franklin Bay Expedition were alive—barely. They included Greely but not Lockwood. One man died on board on the way to Godhavn, after multiple amputations. Schneider, the puppy trainer, who had been eating his boots and "an old pair of pants," had died four days earlier. Of him Greely noted, "Schneider had done good service as clerk, and more especially in raising and training the puppies born at Conger, which contributed materially to the success of our geographical work."

Ironically, one of the officers of the rescue operation was Chief Engineer George Melville, U.S.N., formerly of the *Jeannette*, the ship for which Greely, among his other duties, had been seeking. Melville had successfully led the search for De Long's body found on the bank of the Lena River. Previously, he had been on board the *Tigress* during its commission to search for the missing crew members of the *Polaris*. (Earlier, as a private sealer, the *Tigress* had found and picked up the *Polaris* floe party.)

In another irony, pieces of the *Jeannette* started showing up in Greenland in 1884, encouraging Fridtjof Nansen to move forward with his plan to circle the Pole in an ice-locked ship specially constructed for the purpose. With debris from the shattered *Jeannette*, he now had a map of the arctic currents.

There were few positive outcomes to the Greely expedition, however. As with the *Polaris* and the *Jeannette* but more so, a fog of dissension settled over the Lady Franklin Bay story. Greely blamed Lieutenant E. A. Garlington, commander of the wrecked rescue ship of 1883, *Proteus*, for any number of failures, including keeping a large dog—a Newfoundland—which could not be justified under the circumstances, he claimed. In the meantime, a growing circle of critics blamed Greely for many lapses in leadership that led to not only poor morale and a questionable execution but, they claimed, cannibalism. A *New York Times* story of August 12, 1884, waved the title "Horrors of Cape Sabine," with subheadings shouting "Terrible Story of Greely's Dreary Camp. Brave Men, crazed by starvation and bitter cold, feeding on the dead bodies of their comrades—how Private Charles Henry died—the awful results of an official blunder."

Greely, who later was named Chief Signal Officer of the U.S. Army as well as head of the Weather Service until it was transferred to the Department of Agriculture in 1891, became the first person to enter the Army as a volunteer private and rise to the rank of Major General. This rank, however, was not conferred until 1906. In 1935, on his ninety-first birthday, he was presented with the Congressional Medal of Honor and a citation that made no mention of the Lady Franklin Bay Expedition. The horrors of Cape Sabine had apparently made the enterprise unspeakable.

Fifteen years would pass before any attempt was made to reach Fort Conger again, and nothing more was said of the "faithful" dogs abandoned there.

The tragedies of De Long and Greely had taken a toll on the national consciousness. The American public, as well as Congress, had lost its once enormous appetite for the questionable heroics of arctic exploration and colonization. The people had tired, as of a war fought too long. The Army and Navy withdrew to other frontiers, ceding the quest for the Pole to entrepreneurs. It was now a private battlefield for the rich, the famous, and those who would be famous. Above all, it became a playground for journalists.

Lady Franklin Bay Expedition members Lt. Greely and Jens with dog team on floe in Discovery Harbor, Oct. 1881.
Library of Congress (LOC)# 3c36196u

Greely dog team.
The Peary-MacMillan Arctic Museum (img# 3000.32.1002)

21

The Nameless

Known by Their Number

Traveling, Perhaps to the Pole,
with Frederick A. Cook, 1907–1909

Like Elisha Kent Kane, Isaac I. Hayes, and Frederick Schwatka before him, Frederick Albert Cook (1865–1940) was a physician, but there the similarity ends. More like Charles Francis Hall, he came from an impoverished background, the son of German immigrants (the family name was Koch), who settled in Sullivan County in upstate New York. His father, a physician, died when Cook was five, condemning the family to poverty. Cook worked his way through Columbia University by delivering milk early in the morning but, once graduated, was unable to establish a successful practice. The first year after his marriage, his wife died with their baby in childbirth. Vicissitude followed and clung to him. But adventure called as well, and the buoyant, flexible, and charming doctor-in-search-of-a-job followed—to the lands of ice.

First he served as surgeon on Robert Peary's 1891–1892 expedition to the Arctic (during which time he set Peary's broken leg). He turned down the next opportunity to go north with Peary, in 1893, when the commander denied him the right to publish a report on his studies. Instead, seeking money however he could, he accompanied the son

Route to the pole and return. A triangle of 30,000 square miles cut out of the mysterious unknown.

Frederick A. Cook. *My Attainment of the Pole, Being the Record of the Expedition that First Reached the Boreal Center, 1907–1909, with the Final Summary of the Polar Controversy* of a Yale professor to Greenland on board the schooner *Zeta*. Polar fever had seized him.

During the winter of 1893–1894, he attempted to raise funds for an expedition to Antarctica by lecturing in eastern cities. He enhanced the lectures by exhibiting two children from Labrador whose parents had given him permission to take them to the United States. Billing them as uncivilized "Eskimos," he gathered up a group of other Labrador natives abandoned after the Chicago World's Columbian Exposition and put them on display in Boston and Philadelphia. He then made a deal with John H. Henderson, proprietor of Huber's Dime Museum on Fourteenth Street in New York, to exhibit them for $300 a week. Having set up an "Eskimo camp" on the main stage, he would appear nine times a day to lecture on Eskimo life. The show continued for four weeks. Mr. Henderson recalled:

> In that time one of the Eskimos died. The weather was pretty warm, for it was in May that he appeared with the show, and I noticed that the Eskimos seemed to suffer acutely. Besides the Eskimos there were half a dozen dogs with the exhibition, and these Dr. Cook put through some kind of performance. He said he had brought the dogs from the arctic region, too. The dogs seemed to suffer as much as the Eskimos.

Neighbors remembered that after one of the Peary trips, Cook brought two Eskimo boys home with him who camped out in a tent in his backyard, at 338 West 55th Street, New York. There were also two dogs, reported to have come from the far north as well. Neighbors reminisced seeing Cook walking with a boy on either side of him and the two dogs, on leash, trotting up ahead. One remembered that the Eskimo boys, who spoke only a few words of English, had fun cussing: "We used to stand around to hear them do it."

But the summer of 1894 was hard on the Eskimos and the dogs. One day one of the dogs was overcome by heat while out on the street with the boys, and one of the neighbors ran out and put ice on its head until it revived, but the dog died a few days later.

Cook's lectures, like so much else he attempted, were a financial failure, but he kept finding new ways to visit the polar regions. In 1894, he organized an excursion for tourists and sportsmen, but his inappropriate, unlucky, and ill-fated ship, the iron steamer *Miranda*, was wrecked. (Among many previous accidents, it had even sunk and been raised to carry freight between New York and Central America.)

Next, he signed up as surgeon on the *Belgica*, the Belgian Antarctic Expedition of 1898–1899, befriending for life first mate Roald Amundsen, who would go on to become one of the most accomplished and heralded polar explorers of all times.

In 1901, he sailed on the *Erik*, a relief ship sent to find and assist Peary in his first north polar expedition, and again, Cook provided the commander valuable medical treatment.

Not content with polar adventures, Cook claimed to have summited Mount McKinley in 1906—a claim later thoroughly discredited—and then returned to the Arctic in 1907, ostensibly on a hunting trip with John R. "Gambler Jim" Bradley, though with the hope that, in extending the trip, he could make a run for the Pole. His wish came true. After a successful hunting sojourn at Anoatok (Kane's "wind-loved" refuge north of Etah on the northwestern coast of Greenland), Bradley left for home and Cook stayed on to prepare for his assault. He had brought little with him, but he had the enormous advantage of the goodwill of the people of the Anoatok-Etah area who had already been so helpful to Kane, Hayes, Hall, and Peary. Through the dark arctic winter they worked assiduously to assemble food, clothing, and gear for him.

Cook, who had learned from his predecessors, knew that dogs were a critical need and that he could not succeed without them. Like Verne, however, he never named them. He counted them. Cook constantly expressed his dependence on them by careful itemizing, always keeping track of the number in his party.

It is easier to kill and eat what has no name. For Cook, the number of dogs to be eaten—twenty—was part of the formula he calculated for success. Numbers don't watch you intently, follow your gaze, and jump up to greet you, wagging their tails. They don't howl as you leave them behind on a barren beach and haunt your dreams.

From his first landing on the Greenland coast at Godhavn in 1907, Cook commented on dogs—excited greeters, along with the inhabitants, "jumping about on the rocks, eagerly gazing at our schooner." Farther up the coast, at Karnah, "the place was far from being deserted, for five women, fifteen children and forty-five dogs came out to meet us." Farther yet to the north, at Cape Robertson, "ten men, nine women, thirty-one children and one hundred and six dogs came out to meet us. I count the children and dogs for they are equally important in Eskimo economy. The latter are by far the most important to the average Caucasian in the Arctic." Upon arrival at Anoatok, he found "more than a hundred dogs." As he engaged in hunting trips through the late summer and autumn months, he noted the number of dogs and often their intelligence: "I felt each moment the imminent danger of a frightful death; yet the dogs with their marvelous intuition, twisting this way and that, and sometimes retreating, sensed the open leads ahead and rushed forward safely."

Cook set out for the Pole from Anoatok on February 19, 1908, with his assistant, Rudolph Francke, nine Inuit drivers, eleven sledges, and 103 dogs.

On March 2, the dogs participated in a particularly lively bear hunt in which the trapped bear knocked them down from a high rock. That night, according to Cook, the temperature reached 83° below zero—the lowest temperature noted by any explorer so far.

On March 18, at the edge of the Polar Sea, Cook sent back most of his party. He was now followed by four sledges with forty-four selected dogs with four drivers:

> The dogs pranced; the joyous cries of the natives rose and fell. My heart leaped; my soul sang. I felt my blood throb with each gallop of the leaping dog teams. The sound of their feet pattering on the snow, the sight of their shaggy bodies tossing forward, gave me joy.

Soon after, two more drivers turned back, leaving Cook with his companions Etukishook and Ahwelah and their twenty-six dogs. He was then, in terms of witnesses and credibility, alone; and what he had to say after this point (as well as before) is questionable.

By March 29, Cook commented:

> New leads and recent sheets of new ice combined with deep snow made travel difficult. Persistently onward, pausing at times, we would urge the dogs to the limit. One dog after another went into the stomachs of the hungry survivors. Camps were now swept by storms. The ice opened out under our bodies, shelter was often a mere hole in the snow bank. Each of us carried painful wounds, frost bites; and the ever chronic emptiness of half filled stomachs brought a gastric call for food, impossible to supply. Hard work and strong winds sent unquenched thirst tortures to burning throats, and the gloom of ever clouded skies sent despair to its lowest reaches.

April 11: "Now our dog teams were much reduced in numbers. Because of the cruel law of survival of the fittest, the less useful dogs had gone into the stomachs of their stronger companions."

On April 21, 1908, Cook claimed, he reached the Pole and started on his return trip two days later. There were eleven dogs left from the original twenty-six, and a bond was strengthening with them (or perhaps it was Cook writing for an audience):

> The dogs, though still possessing the savage ferocity of the wolf, had taken us into their community. We now moved among them without

hearing a grunt of discord, and their sympathetic eyes followed until
we were made comfortable on the cheerless snows. If they happened
to be placed near enough, they edged up and encircled us, giving
the benefit of their animal heat.... We had learned to appreciate the
advantage of their beating breasts. The bond of animal fellowship
had drawn tighter and tighter in a long run of successive adventures.
And now there was a stronger reason than ever to appreciate power,
for together we were seeking escape from a world which was never
intended for creatures with pulsing hearts.

June 13, there were ten dogs.

June 14, he commented on the starving state of the dogs: "I regarded
the poor creatures with tenderness and pity. For more than a fortnight
they had not uttered a sound to disturb the frigid silence. When a sled dog
is silent and refuses to fight with his neighbor, his spirit is very low." Soon
after, he wrote:

> In camp, the joy of coming back to earth was chilled by the agoniz-
> ing call of the stomach. The effervescent happiness could not dispel
> the pangs of hunger. A disabled dog which had been unsuccessfully
> nursed for several days was sacrificed on the altar of hard luck, and the
> other dogs were thereupon given a liberal feed, in which we shared.
> To our palates the flesh of the dog was not distasteful, yet the dog had
> been our companion for many months, and at the same time that our
> conscienceless stomachs were calling for more hot, blood-wet meat, a
> shivering sense of guilt came over me. We had killed and were eating
> a living creature which had been faithful to us.

July 7: Finally, summer had come. The three men reached open water
and, in order to continue their homeward trek to Anoatok, had to make
use of their small canvas boat. Here, again, loomed the "Sea of Separation":

> We now had the saddest incident of a long run of trouble.... What
> were we to do with the faithful dog survivors?... We must part. Two
> had already left us to join their wolf progenitors. We gave the others
> the same liberty.... Our sleeping-bags and old winter clothing were
> given as food to the dogs.... With sad eyes, we left the shore. The
> dogs howled like crying children; we still heard them when five miles
> off shore.

Eight dogs abandoned.

After a winter spent living like cavemen—with no dogs and only a
rifle with four cartridges and sticks and stones for protection and hunting—the three men found their way back to Anoatok, crawling into camp

on their hands and knees on April 18, 1909. They had been gone fourteen months and were presumed dead. Now would come the long trek home and the biggest battle of all—that for credibility.

What Cook had to say, particularly about his return trip from the Pole, was extraordinary. The only problem was, there was an equally remarkable lack of proof. The harrowing adventure he described—via Axel Heiberg Island to Anoatok—certainly one of the most dramatic epics of arctic travel—had stripped the three men of almost everything but the rags they wore for clothes. With the possible exception of the *Polaris* ice drift, there is no more heroic story.

But, there were no credible witnesses. Etukishook and Ahwelah were not qualified to take navigational sights or make computations, let alone write accounts of their travels. By his own admission, Cook had given them false information as to where they were, not wanting to increase the fear they exhibited over being far from land. He admitted taking advantage of clouds and mirages (one of a volcano) to fool his companions into thinking they were within sight of land. He was never upfront with them about his search for the "Big Nail," as he and Peary referred to the Pole. (According to arctic historian and linguist Kenn Harper, the term derives from the local phrase "Big Navel," with explorers having turned "navel" to "nail.") If those closest to him did not—and could not—know where they were, it was unlikely anyone else could.

The imaginative doctor might have gotten away with his epic romance but for one surprising fact: His old boss, Robert Peary, was hot on his heels—so hot he was only days away from announcing his attainment of the Pole.

On September 1, 1909, Cook cabled a message from Lerwick, in the Shetland Islands, that he had reached the Pole on April 21, 1908. On September 6, 1909, Robert Peary cabled his message from Indian Harbour, Labrador, that he had reached the Pole on April 6, 1909, almost one year later.

James Gordon Bennett's *New York Herald*, to which Cook sold his account for $3,000, broke the first claimant's narrative, followed by the *New York Times* with Peary's claim, for which it had paid $4,000 in advance to help underwrite the expedition. The media war was on, raging across the column inches of the two papers, with the competitors using whatever means they could to present their cases. (Cook even produced a movie in 1912 to illustrate his claim.)

Cook was hard pressed to provide evidence. He asserted, implausibly, that he had kept a journal by means of microscopic handwriting on the small supply of paper—a prescription pad and two "miniature memoran-dum books"—he had with him. He also maintained that he had left three boxes of records and instruments at Anoatok in the care of visiting hunt-er Harry Whitney, who would travel home with Peary, but that Peary had refused to allow the boxes on board. Explorer Peter Freuchen stated that he and Amundsen suggested trips to Etah to find this material but that Cook opposed them. In later searches, no such boxes were ever found, nor a microscopic journal.

Cook kept promising evidence and reports that never materialized. Reporters hounded him. He tried to disappear. In November 1909, he was said to have become the first patient at the Pine Tree Sanitarium in Wells Depot, Maine. The proprietor, Dr. T. S. Pitt, said the explorer was suffering from a nervous breakdown. Later, Cook hid in Europe. But he could never hide from the persistence of his adversary Peary, who pursued him like a Greenland dog on the trail of a wounded polar bear until finally he was trapped. Infamy was now his identity.

In 1910, when Huber sold his New York museum, the *New York Times* for July 16 blared: "Famous Dime Show in 14th Street Bought Out for a Restaurant/Home of Countless Freaks/Dr. Cook of Polar Notoriety Among Those Who Have Exhibited There/Place Made Its Owner Wealthy."

In 1922, Cook ventured into the Texas oil business. A year later, charged with overstating the value of his company, he was convicted of mail fraud. In 1925, after exhausting his appeals, he entered Leavenworth Prison, where he was incarcerated until 1930. During his imprisonment he served as night warden of the prison hospital, wrote articles for the prison's paper, and taught in the literacy program. Amundsen, remaining a faithful friend, visited him. After being paroled in 1930, and without a medical license, Cook helped out in a friend's ophthalmology practice and lived with his daughters and sister. President Franklin D. Roosevelt par-doned him in 1940, shortly before his death on August 5 of that year. And, it turned out, the oil prospects were more valuable than Cook had stated.

Perhaps Cook, a romantic who seemed strangely remiss about plans and record keeping and who was given to florid prose, was consciously following in the fictional footsteps of Jules Verne's Captain Hatteras. One commentator, Randall J. Osczevski, maintains the ties were close and that Cook's route closely followed that of Hatteras (which followed that of Kane). In the Sullivan County (New York) Museum's display of Cook material, Osczevski found a copy of *The English at the North Pole*, which may have been Cook's.

Whether inspired by Verne or not, whether true or not, Cook's tale depends upon dogs. He had no Duke, only common, nameless Greenland dogs, but when he had to leave them, he knew he was leaving friends who deserved better than abandonment.

Ice shelter at campsite with dog team and sledges somewhere in the Arctic during Cook's expedition to the North Pole.
LOC # 3c03156u

Dogs pulling sled, Cook polar expedition, 1891–1910.
LOC # 3a01313

New-York Tribune.

SUNDAY, SEPTEMBER 26, 1909.

PART II.

EIGHT PAGES.

PHOTOGRAPH OF THE NORTH POLE MADE BY DR. FREDERICK A. COOK, AS HE ASSERTS.

It shows his two Esquimau companions standing beside the Stars and Stripes, raised April 21, 1908, upon the spot which has been vainly sought by explorers for centuries.

(Copyright, 1909, by The New York Herald Company.)

DR. COOK.

ESQUIMAU GIRL, WITH MAIDEN'S TOPKNOT.

A MUSK OX.   HELPING A DOG TEAM THROUGH DEEP SNOW.   A POLAR BEAR.

22

Heart-hungers

Years later, when writing *Return from the Pole* (1930–1935), Frederick A. Cook remembered his dogs during their final, desperate days together:

We still had eleven faithful sled dogs, all like ourselves in a deplorable state of semi-starvation. These were the survivors of a pack of twenty-six. The others had been eaten. We loved these thin, ragged-looking warriors of better days. Though the offspring of but half-tamed wolves, these animals had been to us thus far life-savers. Each dog was to one of us a personal friend.

With the hindsight of all those years (or was it political correctness and a desire to please readers?), the dogs had become more important and the bond deeper. The abandonment of the remaining ones had struck deep:

But figure the tragedy as we would, the parting was that at the graveyard of loved ones. We stepped into the boat and pulled east. We heard their parting howls for an hour, and in our dreams for months and years. And how lonely life was to us in the months of famine,

cold, and darkness to follow! We had yet to learn that heart-hungers
for dog companions can open the door to the doom of suicide.

The dirge of abandonment is a powerful motif running through
nineteenth-century arctic history: For whalers and the crews of discovery ships, abandonment of home and family—sometimes for years. For
some, like Robert Peary and his assistant Matthew Henson, who both
fathered half-Inuit children but did not acknowledge them, abandonment
of responsibility. And, for those like Peary who exploited the Inuit people, abandonment of principles of fairness. For Frederick Schwatka and
Adolphus Washington Greely, abandonment by their own supply vessels.
For Elisha Kent Kane, abandonment by his secessionists, and for Charles
Francis Hall, abandonment by his unfaithful *Polaris* crew. For the John
Franklin party, abandonment by local people who did not have enough
to share with them. For the indigenous people, abandonment of the aged
and dying and sometimes newborn girls or malformed children. For everyone driven to starvation, abandonment of compassion and charity. For
those driven to pilfering or to cannibalism, abandonment of humanitar-
ian instincts.

The "doleful howling" of George Washington De Long's dogs left near
the desolate shore of Bennett Island and the "parting howls" of Cook's left
on the ice are the sound and physical manifestation of desertion. Echoing
down through the ages, they cannot be silenced.

If, as was said in Newfoundland, "the sea is made of mothers' tears,"
surely the wind blowing over the Polar Sea was made of the howling of deserted dogs. In no account is there mention, later, of attempts to find them.

How long these dogs (and Greely's abandoned at Fort Conger) lived
and how they died can be only speculation. That they suffered emotionally
as well as physically cannot be doubted.

As animal behaviorist John Bradshaw points out, domesticated dogs
are powerfully attached to their people and have a strong need for a
"human attachment figure." "Most dogs seem to become more distressed
when they are separated from their owners than when they are separated
from other dogs," he states. For dogs abandoned by their owners and living
in a rehoming center, the need for attachment is acute:

> Research has shown that just a few minutes of friendly attention from
> one person on two consecutive days is enough to make some of these
> unowned dogs desperate to stay with that person; when left on their
> own, these dogs will howl, scratch at the door that the person has left
> through, or jump up at the window to try to see where he has gone.

When the "Withdrawing Party" pulled away from the *Advance*, Kane's dogs ran after them. As Sonntag explained in his journal:

> The dogs had followed us; and, as all exertions to drive them back were in vain, McGary ordered Hans to shoot at them. A dog was so severely hit in the neck that it was unable to keep up with the others, who still continued to follow our track.

For at least a day they continued to follow the runaways. How much longer, Sonntag did not tell us—nor did he say whether they howled with distress.

It might be said that the dogs followed out of hunger or the hope for food; but there must be something else. Why did Cook's and De Long's dogs howl as they watched their people pull away? (There is every reason to believe that Greely's dogs howled also as they were deserted, but Greely, the soldier-scientist, would not tell us.)

Why would "those faithful animals, to whom we were strongly attached," as Greely said—those dogs that were so harshly used and quickly dismissed—cry upon separation from their people?

"Love," says Bradshaw, is what biologists call "attachment." By whatever name, it is the force that creates the bond between dog and human. In the young wolf, Bradshaw states, strong attachment to its parents is vital for its protection and its education: "In short, there's a sound *biological* reason for supposing that dogs *actually* love us rather than just appearing to do so." The dogs left behind on the other side of the unswimmable water were *attached* to the men who left them.

Chemistry plays a vital part. Dogs experience a surge of oxytocin during friendly interactions with people, Bradshaw points out. Oxytocin, a hormone (popularly known as the "feel good" hormone), encourages mammalian mothers to lactate and bond with their young and fosters a sense of warmth, closeness, trust, and affection, while reducing fear. Research indicates that oxytocin levels rise in both people and pets when they interact with one another, both species benefitting. Increasingly, oxytocin research reveals the validity of animal-assisted therapies. People and animals, for whatever profound and inexplicable reason, are meant to touch, bond, and attach. It is easier, once a person has bonded with an animal, to bond with another human being. Perhaps the most important service pets provide is to help people connect with one another. Perhaps the real work of the sledge dogs was to keep their people together, bound with an invisible harness of comfort and mutual assistance. Together, people driving dogs could do what individuals could not do alone.

With time, circumstances and consciousness change.

A century after De Long's, Greely's, and Cook's dogs were left, a different story of abandonment was told: In 1957, a Japanese expedition to Antarctica had to temporarily leave their fifteen sledge dogs because of weather conditions. They expected to return to them in a few days but could not make it back until the following year. Two dogs survived— brothers and lead dogs Taro and Jiro—while seven died in their chains, with six unaccounted for. The story, made popular by a 1983 Japanese movie, *Nankyoku Monogatari*, was updated in a fictionalized Disney film in 2006: *Eight Below*, filmed in Greenland (dogs are no longer allowed in Antarctica). Production involved fourteen "Hollywood" dogs as well as indigenous dogs. Officials of the American Humane Association's Film and TV Unit and representatives of the Greenlandic Sledding Association oversaw production, making sure that no harm came to the dogs and that no interaction occurred between members of the two groups. In order to maintain purity of the ancient breed, no other dogs are allowed in the northern part of the country. Greenland's shoreline has become a protective barrier.

There were different ways of abandoning dogs at the water's edge. When Fridtjof Nansen and his companion Hjalmar Johansen reached open water and had to part with their lead dogs, the last two dogs, they shot them, instead of stabbing them as they had all the others: "we sacrificed a cartridge on each of them," wrote Nansen. Nansen shot Johansen's dog, a male Samoyed whose name was Suggen. Johansen shot Nansen's male Samoyed named Kaifas. Nansen wrote, "We were sorry to part with them; we had become very fond of these two survivors. Faithful and enduring, they had followed us the whole journey through; and now that better times had come, they must say farewell to life."

"Bitter self-reproach" was Nansen's share; but the kayaks—their escape—could not carry both men and dogs.

23

Nalegaksoah

King of the Team

Serving Robert E. Peary in His
Claim to the Pole, 1908–1909

Robert E. Peary (1856–1920), who had established an early and solid friendship with Frederick A. Cook, was the first American explorer to reach Fort Conger after Adolphus Washington Greely's departure. His visit came fifteen years later, in 1899, during one of his early attempts at the Pole. He could never forget the place because he lost seven toes to frostbite and amputation there. While recovering, he carved in a wall Seneca's words, *"Inveniam viam aut faciam"* ("I shall find a way or make one"). And so he did, hobbling across years of ice toward his obsessive goal.

Upon arrival at Fort Conger, Peary declared that Greely's three-room, tar paper–covered house was "grotesque in its utter unfitness and unsuitableness for polar winter quarters." He and his crew disassembled the building and constructed three small huts out of the wood: what would become the base for his later efforts to reach the Pole. The deteriorating remains of these constructions are now within the protection of Quttinirpaaq National Park, Nunavut, Canada, and are classified as Federal Heritage Buildings.

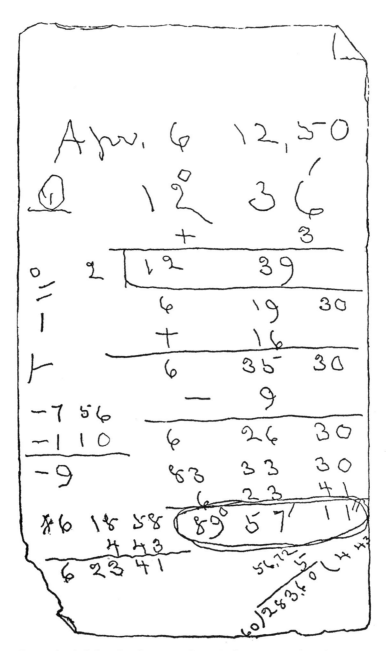

Facsimile, slightly reduced in size, of Peary's observations of April 6, 1909.
Peary, p. 362

What Peary also found at Fort Conger was supplies left from Greely's expedition: canned vegetables, potatoes, hominy, rhubarb, pemmican, tea, and coffee. Many were in good condition, so much so that members of Peary's party ate them with relish. If the deserted dogs could have opened them, these items might have fed them, but we will never know. No one was looking for canine bones or clues to a secret loss. No one knew—or sought to know—that a colony of dogs had disappeared.

Peary, a U.S. Navy civil engineer, had started his arctic career in Greenland, which he first visited during a summer trip in 1886. His initial Greenland expedition followed five years later, in 1891–1892, followed by another in 1893–1895, and two summer voyages there in 1896 and 1897. By then, he was intent on the geographic North Pole and would strive unrelentingly until he achieved it. His first north polar expedition, 1898–1902, was followed by a second in 1905–1906, and finally the one for which he claimed success, 1908–1909.

From the beginning, Peary recognized the importance of dogs and made extensive use of them. The plan for his final voyage was based on three principles: choice of the "American Route" up Smith Sound, following in the route of Kane, Hayes, Hall, and Greely; selection of a winter base accessible to the Polar Sea; and use of local dogs and sledges, along with their Whale Sound Inuit drivers.

"Man and the Eskimo dog," Peary stated, "are the only two machines capable of such adjustment as to meet the wide demands and contingencies of Arctic travel. Airships, motor cars, trained polar bears, etc., are all premature, except as a means of attracting public attention." Much more so than Cook, Peary factored into his equation a certain number of dogs *to be* eaten, not just as a reserve in case they were needed. It was a large number.

Peary had planned carefully for his final voyage. His brand-new ship, the 184-foot steamer *Roosevelt*, was designed to ride above and smash through ice. His captain, Robert A. Bartlett, one of the most accomplished ice navigators of his day, had piloted the expedition of 1905–1906. Once again, Peary had with him his African American assistant, Matthew Henson, who had accompanied him on every trip but the first, and whom he considered to be a better dog-driver than almost anyone else. As it set out for the Arctic, the expedition consisted of twenty-two men. Also on board were 16,000 pounds of flour, 1,000 pounds of coffee, 1,000 pounds of tobacco, and 3,000 pounds of dried fish.

Accompanying the commander were his "Eskimo" dogs from previous expeditions, which he kept on an island near his home in Casco Bay, Maine. One of these was named North Star. (He does not name any others.) During a luncheon stop at Sagamore Hill, Oyster Bay, New York, President Theodore Roosevelt came aboard with his family and was introduced to the dogs.

The *Roosevelt*, flying the pennant of the New York Yacht Club, steamed out of North Sydney, Cape Breton, Nova Scotia, on July 17, 1908. Two days later, it made a stop along the Labrador coast at the Cape St. Charles whaling station to purchase a whale, taken just the day before, as food for the dogs. At Hawks Harbor, they met their supply steamer and took on another twenty-five tons of whale meat.

While steaming north up the west coast of Greenland, they made a stop at Cape York, marking the northern end of Melville Bay. Here, Peary reconnected with the Inuit people he had come to know on previous trips. In his account of the expedition he asked, "of what use are Eskimos to the world?" then answered:

> They are too far removed to be of value for commercial enterprises and, furthermore, they lack ambition. They have no literature nor, properly speaking, any art. They value life only as does a fox, or a bear, purely by instinct. But let us not forget that these people, trustworthy and hardy, will yet prove their value to mankind. With their help, the world shall discover the Pole.

Of these people, Peary said, he was to select the "pick and flower of the hunters of the whole tribe, extending from Cape York to Etah." They were his "debtors," he said, for having saved them and their families from starvation over and over; for eighteen years he had been making them "useful for my purposes." They were, he said, happy to go with him, for being with him meant security and freedom from want. His gifts to them, he claimed, were equal to those of a millionaire "descending upon an American country town and offering every man there a brownstone mansion and an unlimited bank account." They were, he said, like children and should be treated as such, needing a management that blended gentleness and firmness and always made good on promises.

Peary selected some of his men at Cape York, where he had arrived at seven in the morning, telling them to be aboard with their families and dogs by evening. The women, he said, were essential for their sewing skills; the dogs for their pulling force.

The dogs, he said, were "sturdy, magnificent animals." And, most importantly, "there is no dog in the world that can work so long in the lowest temperatures on practically nothing to eat." Though thought by some scientists to be descended from the wolf, he maintained, they are "as affectionate and obedient to their masters as our own dogs at home." They could eat meat only, he said; he had made the experiment. For water, they eat snow. They are not housed, he said, but are kept tied by the igloo or tent. Sometimes a special pet or a bitch with a litter will be taken inside for a short time, but puppies a month old could withstand severe weather.

When the *Roosevelt* steamed out of Cape York with the Inuit families, there was also the addition of about 100 dogs bartered from the local people. Two days later at North Star Bay, they took on several more families and yet more dogs. Peary and Henson, then separating themselves from the *Roosevelt* and transferring to their smaller supply ship, the *Erik*, traveled along the coast to find yet more local people and dogs. The *Roosevelt*, meanwhile, went on to Etah, the village so important to Kane, Hayes, and the shipwrecked *Polaris* crew after their separation from the ice-floe party. By the time Peary and Henson rejoined the *Roosevelt*, there was now a total of 246 dogs! Some of the families, however, were only seeking transportation up the coast and were not part of the expedition.

On August 11, with both the *Roosevelt* and the *Erik* at Etah, the dogs were unloaded onto an island while the *Roosevelt* was washed down and its cargo re-stowed for its journey into the ice. Fifty tons of coal was cached at Etah for the party's return the following year, with two men left in charge. Other passengers and crew members got on and got off. More Inuit men came aboard, including Ootah and Egingwah, who were to be part of Peary's final push to the Pole along with Ooqueah and Seegloo, who got on at North Star Bay and Cape York, respectively. After the final choosing and sorting out, the *Roosevelt* now held forty-nine Inuit people—twenty-two men, seventeen women, and ten children—along with twenty white men, and the 246 dogs. Also on board were seventy tons of whale meat and the meat and blubber of nearly fifty walruses.

On August 18, the companion ships parted and the *Roosevelt* headed north alone into snow, rain, wind, and heavy seas—soon to meet the ice. The dogs that had been housed on the main deck stood with "dejected heads and dripping tails" and fought only at feeding times, when courage returned to them.

The dogs got their first chance to go to work on September 1, hunting musk oxen and caribou. The *Roosevelt* was tightly held by the ice just south of Cape Sheridan on the north coast of Ellesmere Island. Cape Sheridan was the chosen anchorage for the winter (or, if possible, a point twenty-five miles to the northwest), as it had been during Peary's previous expedition.

Four hunters started off with a sledge and a team of eight dogs but had to turn back because of lack of snow. The crew was anxious to get the dogs to work, not only for the purposes of hunting but also to relieve the ship of "stench and disorder." The problems caused by the dogs, Peary noted, were more than compensated for by the gain: "it must not be forgotten that without the dogs we could not have reached the Pole."

On September 5, a lead widened to the north and Peary ordered "every pound of steam and full speed." As the *Roosevelt* worked its way north and rounded Cape Rawson, Cape Sheridan came into view, but Peary again gave orders to steam ahead. After achieving two miles, the ship reached an impassable barrier of ice and turned back to Cape Sheridan to settle in for the winter. That gain of two miles was small but significant: It gave Peary the farthest north that any vessel had reached under its own steam, 82° 30'. (Although Fridtjof Nansen's *Fram* had reached farther north, Peary claimed that it had merely drifted there, stern first, "a plaything of the ice.")

The dogs were the first item unloaded. Having made the ship "a noisy and ill-smelling inferno for the last eighteen days," they were dropped over the rail onto the ice, where they ran and barked with obvious delight. Then, the decks were washed and the serious task of unloading began. First came the twenty-three sledges that had been built during the northward journey, but only after the ship was prepared for the winter did preparation for their use begin. The dogs were tied, "in teams of five or six, to stakes driven into the shore or holes cut in the ice. They made a fine picture," Peary said, "and their barking could be heard at all hours."

Heavy work lay ahead. Thousands of pounds of supplies needed to be moved ninety miles north and west to Cape Columbia, the northernmost point of land on the shores of the frozen Arctic Ocean and base camp for the springtime push to the Pole. Teams—with dogs numbering from eight to twelve—would move back and forth over a broken trail as they hauled goods to the northernmost point.

Peary had put careful thought into the design and construction of both sledges and harnesses. He had created a sledge considerably longer than the "Eskimo" type. For harnesses, which hitched the dogs fanwise to the sledge, he exchanged sealskin—always a temptation to hungry dogs—for a braided linen cord.

But there was no technology to change the temperament of the dogs. Peary stated that a person might well "believe with the Eskimos that demons take possession of these animals. Sometimes they seem to be quite crazy." Their ability to snarl their traces had been commented on liberally by all previous dog-dependent explorers. What Peary experienced was no different, except in the size of the problem: Never before had a foreigner set forth with so many dogs and had so many opportunities for frustration with them and their gear. The men new to the Arctic had to learn what it was to lose their dogs as they were trying to untangle the traces and then to have to walk back to camp to collect them, only to hear the derisive laughter of the Inuit drivers. Humiliation was but one chapter in the textbook of driving.

Broken in or not, on September 16, 1908, the first party moved out to establish the trail north. It consisted of three Caucasian crew members, thirteen Inuit drivers, sixteen sledges, and about 200 dogs.

There was, at the same time, plenty of opportunity to hunt, and it wasn't long into a search for musk oxen that Peary and his group came upon a polar bear. The three Inuit drivers threw everything they could off the sledges and flew after their prey with abandon, not daunted by deep snow. The first hunter to get close to the bear loosed his dogs. When the dogs caught up with it, the bear kept going, not turning around and fighting as is the usual case. The devil most certainly was in that bear, the hunters said, and Peary had to agree when he was unable to fell it with a shot. Suffering with the stumps of his feet (frostbitten in 1899 at Fort Conger), Peary gave over the hunt to the three men, who managed to bag the bear. And before long there was a successful musk oxen hunt, with the dogs, as usual, holding the herd in their defensive circular position that was so vulnerable to rifles.

The hunting season gave way to the uninterrupted darkness of winter, that aspect of arctic life so consistently recorded with dread. Rigorous schedules, carefully planned menus, prescribed exercise, and entertainments could do little to dispel the inevitable depression and the madness it could cause. Peary described a limited view of *piblokto*: An afflicted person, "usually a woman," he noted, would begin to scream, tear off her clothing, and, after walking up and down the decks, jump off the ship and run on the ice until she froze to death, unless forcibly brought back to the ship. An attack inside would usually end in a "fit of weeping."

The dogs, Peary said, suffered from the same malady. He thought *piblokto* different from hydrophobia, or rabies, and noted that dogs so afflicted were usually shot and often eaten by their keepers.

By November, a number of the dogs had died. With the others in poor condition and no abundance of food for them, Peary was concerned; but this is why, he said, "It is always necessary to take up twice as many dogs as will be needed, in order to provide for probable accidents." On November 8, 193 dogs remained. The whale meat, Peary explained, seemed to be lacking in nutrition. Four dogs in the worst condition were killed, and two days later, five more. When pork was fed to the pack, another seven died. The health of the dogs was perplexing, Peary remarked:

> The creatures will endure the severest hardships; they will travel and draw heavy loads on practically nothing to eat; they will live for days exposed to the wildest arctic blizzard; and then, sometimes in good weather, after an ordinary meal of apparently the best food, they will lie down and die.

By the next inventory on November 25, there were 160 left, but fortunately for the expedition, it turned out that there was more frozen walrus meat on board than had been thought, assuring a greater allowance for the dogs. Peary claimed it was a critical discovery for the success of the expedition:

> Dogs, and plenty of them, were vitally necessary to the success of the expedition. Had an epidemic deprived us of these animals, we might just as well have remained comfortably at home in the United States. All the money, brains and labor would have been utterly thrown away, so far as concerned the quest of the North Pole.

Teams continued to go out from the ship to find what game they could. They were also continuing to move supplies from one cache to another north up the coast in preparation for the spring assault on the Pole. Out of four field parties in December, only one found game, and that consisted of five hares. The number of dogs had to be reduced. Fourteen of those in the poorest condition were killed and fed to the others.

Christmas was celebrated on board with special meals and entertainment. There was musk ox meat, plum pudding, sponge cake with chocolate, wrestling contests, a graphophone concert, and presents to all from Mrs. Peary. (Josephine Peary had accompanied her husband on the expeditions of 1891–1892 and 1893–1895, and during the second, gave birth to their daughter.)

On December 29, a party under Ross Marvin ("next to Captain Bartlett, the most valuable man in the party") headed east across the ice of Robeson Channel for the Greenland coast. It included nine Inuit drivers and fifty-four dogs. They were to make tidal observations and to hunt. Another hunting party set out the next day, the two parties covering a radius of about ninety miles in all directions from the ship. In the meantime, the women were busy sewing fur garments for the spring campaign.

On January 11, 1909, the second group returned, having secured no game but hares, of which they were able to round up and kill by hand eighty-three. Marvin's group returned the next month.

"Astrup and my dogs."
Special Collections, University of Maryland, Baltimore County (UMBC)# P78-118-052

"Royal banquet of my dogs."
(Special Collections, UMBC# P78-118-061)

February brought faint light, the last moon of winter, and Peary's admonitions to his Inuit helpers, who remembered the dangers of the last attempt. He told them of his plans and promised that each man who went with him to the farthest point would be rewarded with a boat, tent, Winchester repeater, shotgun, ammunition, box of tobacco, pipes, cartridges, knives, hatchets, and other goods. Only one of his assistants, he claimed, would admit any fears.

Then, after all the planning and all the work, the time had come.

Starting in mid-February, teams moved out to haul supplies north from cache to cache ninety miles up to Cape Columbia, the jumping-off point for the final push to the Pole. Beyond the cape stretched more than 400 jagged, ever moving, icy miles to the elusive destination.

February 22, Washington's birthday, 1909, Peary set out from the *Roosevelt*: "the final chance to realize the one dream of my life." It was not, as he explained, a "dash," but, rather, a "drive," an orderly effort long planned to the last minute detail. Every possible accident and problem had been taken into consideration. One good sledge could be made out of two broken ones, and "the gradual depletion of the dogs was involved in my calculations." He had allowed for the loss of sixty percent of the dogs.

Peary, who was leaving the ship one day earlier than he had on his previous attempt three years before, had with him two Inuit drivers, two sledges, and sixteen dogs. Light snow was falling and the temperature was 31° below zero. Ahead of him were six advance parties with seven crew members, nineteen Inuit assistants, twenty-eight sledges, and 140 dogs. He had planned to have twenty teams of seven dogs each for the sea ice, but at Cape Columbia "throat distemper" broke out and killed six dogs in one team. Two Inuit drivers became disabled as well.

In his short account of the expedition, *A Negro Explorer at the North Pole*, Henson provided a telling view of Peary on February 26, with the temperature at 57° below zero:

> With a "Whoop halloo," three Komaticks [sledges] were racing and tearing down the gradient of the land to our camp, and all of us were out to see the finish. Kudlooktoo and Arkeo an even distance apart; and, heads up, tails up, a full five sledge-lengths ahead, with snowdust spinning free, the dog-team of the ever victorious Peary in the lead. The caravan came to a halt with a grandstand finish that it would have done you good to witness.
>
> The Commander didn't want to stop. He immediately commenced to shout and issue orders, and, by the time he had calmed down, both Captain Bartlett and George Borup had loaded up and

pushed forward on to the ice of the Arctic Ocean, bound for the tro-
phy of over four hundred years of effort. The Peary discipline is the
iron hand ungloved. From now on we must be indifferent to comfort,
and like poor little Joe, in *Bleak House* we must always be moving on.

From the first step out onto the ice, on March 1, the road to the North
Pole was a challenge, as Henson revealed:

We were still in the heavy rubble-ice and had to continuously hew
our way with pickaxes to make a path for the sledges. While we were
at work making a pathway, the dogs would curl up and lie down with
their noses in their tails, and we would have to come back and start
them, which was always the signal for a fight or two.

Rough going was only a prelude to the real trouble that soon appeared:
open water, a lead about a quarter of a mile wide, which had appeared since
the advance party went through the day before. There was one consolation: Peary had now exceeded the 1876 British record of Albert Hastings
Markham—at 83° 20' N. And, by the next morning, the lead had closed.
Soon after, open water again held back the party; for some hours they
could not pick up the trail of the group ahead, and, when they did, it was
difficult to follow. As they proceeded, they encountered yet another break,
one much larger than the previous lead: a "malevolent Styx."

The water, widening, glared at them for five days. Increasingly wor-
ried, Peary made contingency plans: After the oil and alcohol were gone,
he could burn the sledges to fuel the cookers; after that, with no heat
source, he and his men would suck ice for water and take their pemmican
and raw dog without tea.

Some of the Inuit men began to lose their nerve and feigned sickness.
Two of them returned to the ship.

On the seventh day, the lead had frozen over sufficiently that Peary decided to cross, even though his supply party had not caught up with him.
During the course of that day, March 11, he crossed seven leads filmed over
with young ice. He also reached the 84th parallel.

On March 13, the temperature reached 53° below zero; 59° below
zero the preceding night. The dogs, as they hauled, were "enveloped in
the white cloud of their own breath." The happy news came that the supply party was within two days of catching up. Henson was sent ahead with
Inuit helpers to "pioneer the road" for the next five marches.

During this period, Henson wrote:

Traveling was slow, and the dogs became demons; at one time, sullen
and stubborn; then wildly excited and savage; and in our handling

of them I fear we became fiendlike ourselves. Frequently we would have to lift them bodily from the pit of snow, and snow-filled fissures they had fallen into, and I am now sorry to say that we did not do it gently. The dogs, feeling the additional strain, refused to make the slightest effort when spoken to or touched with the whip, and to break them of this stubbornness, and to prevent further trouble, I took the leader or king dog of one team and, in the presence of the rest of the pack, I clubbed him severely. The dogs realized what was required of them, and that I would exact it of them in spite of what they would do, and they became submissive and pulled willingly.

A different kind of beating occurred later when one of Henson's dogs fell through thin ice and, though rescued, was thoroughly soaked. The dog shook himself off but, when his coat froze, Henson gave him a "thorough beating" in order to loosen up the ice particles. In a short time, however, the frozen dog showed symptoms of "the dread *piblokto*," and was shot. "One of the Esquimo boys did the killing," Henson noted.

On March 15, after sorting out supplies and parties, Peary's group consisted of sixteen men, twelve sledges, and 100 dogs. Soon after starting out, one sledge and its team were almost lost when the dogs fell into open water. George Borup, the man in charge, grabbed hold of the sledge, keeping it from following the dogs, while also grabbing their traces and pulling them out: a miraculous feat at 50° below zero.

Henson recorded another near disaster that occasioned a rare comment of affection toward the dogs. It was March 19, and the teams were running over young ice that undulated beneath them when one of the sledges broke through. The driver was able to pull out the sledge and the dogs. With gentle urging and encouragement the shaking dogs succeeded in crossing the thinly iced lead, to wait on solid ice for the rest of the party to catch up:

> My team had reached there before me and, with human intelligence, the dogs had dragged the sledge to a place of safety and were sitting on their haunches, with ears cocked forward, watching us in our precarious predicament. They seemed to rejoice at our deliverance, and as I went among them and untangled their traces I could not forbear giving each one an affectionate pat on the head.

In spite of all the challenges of weather, ice, and constant danger, Peary continued to plan methodically: "At the end of each five-march section I should send back the poorest dogs, the least effective Eskimos, and the worst damaged sledges."

Borup, renowned as a great athlete, now turned back with his support party, while Henson and Bartlett went ahead. Peary now had with him Marvin, four Inuit drivers, five sledges, and forty dogs.

They passed the Norwegian record set by Fridtjof Nansen in 1895 at 86° 13' 6" N, then the Italian record achieved by Umberto Cagni of the Abruzzi party in 1900 at 86° 38'.

With their mission completed, Marvin and his party then turned back. Peary would never see him again.

By the time Peary's group reached the 87th parallel, they experienced perpetual daylight—and also intense danger. Camped one night near Bartlett, Peary was awakened by one of Bartlett's men shouting: A lead had opened between the two encampments, with water lapping close to Peary's igloo and within one foot of a dog team; at the same time, another team came close to being crushed by a pressure ridge.

Both parties were now adrift on small and separate pieces of ice. Peary quickly got his men and dogs onto a larger floe. Luckily, Bartlett's ice raft drifted up against Peary's floe and the two parties joined. Four new igloos had to be constructed, but Peary's consolation was that he had passed his record of three years before.

After two anxious days, the lead closed with roars, groans, and what sounded like the shot of rifles. Peary, Henson, and Bartlett continued on together, mostly over young ice. The fragile surface of one lake buckled under them for a distance of seven miles as they rushed across as fast as they could.

Bartlett now pushed on ahead. His mission was to reach the 88th parallel, then turn back to solid ground with two Inuit drivers, one sledge, and eighteen dogs. While Bartlett was walking the five or six miles north to his goal (which he failed to reach), Peary culled the best dogs from Bartlett's remaining teams, replacing them with dogs from Peary's own teams in worse condition:

> The dogs were on the whole in very good condition, far better than
> on any of my previous expeditions. I had been throwing the brunt of
> the dragging on the poorest dogs, those that I judged were going to
> fail, so as to keep the best dogs fresh for the final spurt.

In similar fashion, he sought to keep the main party fresh by working the supporting parties as hard as possible. It was the same with the Inuit drivers: "If any accident occurred to those men whom I had originally chosen, I planned to fill their places with the next best ones who were all willing to go."

Though short of his goal (and surely deserving of sharing victory with Peary), Bartlett followed orders and turned south, back to the ship. The main party now consisted of Peary and his drivers, Egingwah and Seegloo, and Henson and his drivers, Ootah and Ooqueah, five sledges and forty dogs, "the pick of 140 with which we had left the ship." By Peary's calculations, they were 133 nautical miles from the Pole.

This was also the point beyond which no credible witnesses were allowed—no one, as in the case of Cook, who could make or interpret navigational computations. There was also no threat to Peary of any other white man getting to the Pole with him or ahead of him. What follows, in Peary's narrative, was conjecture, raising thoughts of Captain Hatteras.

Henson and Ootah had been with Peary when he had reached his farthest north three years before. Henson, Peary pointed out, was useful to him within limits: "If Henson had been sent back with one of the supporting parties from a distance far out on the ice, and if he had encountered conditions similar to those which we had to face on the return journey in 1906, he and his party would never have reached land."

As to the dogs, Peary was pleased:

> most of them were powerful males, as hard as iron, in good condition, but without an ounce of superfluous fat; and, by reason of the care which I had taken of them up to this point, they were all in good spirits, like the men....My food and fuel supplies were ample for forty days, and by the gradual utilization of the dogs themselves for reserve food, might be made to last for fifty days if it came to a pinch.

The dogs were already being eaten. On April 1, a day of rest spent repairing sledges, the Inuit drivers, Peary reported:

> stopped from time to time to eat some of the boiled dog which the surplus numbers in Bartlett's returning team had enabled them to have. They had killed one of the poorest dogs and boiled it, using the splinters of an extra broken sledge for fuel under their cooker. It was a change for them from the pemmican diet. It was fresh meat, it was hot, and they seemed thoroughly to enjoy it. But though I remembered many times when from sheer starvation I had been glad to eat dog meat raw, I did not feel inclined to join in the feast of my dusky friends.

Henson, too, wrote that he refused to eat dog, even when he was craving fat. Eating dog, he said, is the last resort—and raw dog is "flavorless and very tough." The killing of a dog, he commented, is:

such a horrible matter that I will not describe it, and it is permitted only when all other exigencies have been exhausted. An Esquimo does not permit one drop of blood to escape.

On April 2, a clear day, Peary started out, in front, leaving the others to break camp. Before long, he maintained, the whole group was over the 88th parallel: the first visitors to that elusive spot. Toward the end of an exhilarating march, they once more came upon ice that was beginning to open up. The dogs had to be encouraged across widening cracks, always an ordeal that required patience and cunning. One of the methods was to have someone go ahead of the dogs, shaking his hand low as though it contained food—a bribe.

Two days later, almost at the 89th parallel, Peary put the poorest dogs in one team and began "to eliminate and feed them to the others, as it became necessary." And, at the next camp, he had another dog killed. It was six weeks since they had left the *Roosevelt*.

Early on the morning of April 6, good weather and smooth going cheered the group on. Some of the dogs—there were thirty-eight now—even tossed their heads and barked as if caught up in the high spirits of the men. Stopping at noon, Peary made his first observation at the polar camp. The reading, he reckoned, was 89° 57' N. After a few hours of sleep, he and his drivers and a double team of dogs hauling a light sledge pushed on—by his calculations (which have been much argued)—to the Pole, and beyond. Since there was no one with him who could corroborate or challenge his readings, his claim will always remain that—his claim.

According to his narrative, after thirty hours in the vicinity of the Pole, planting flags, taking photographs, and securing records—even writing a postcard to Mrs. Peary—it was time to head home. At 4 p.m. on April 7, the six men and thirty-eight dogs turned their faces south to solid land and the *Roosevelt*. Now came the ultimate forced march—one that had to beat the return of the moon and coming ravages of the spring tides.

Peary was attempting to double the speed of the northward push by cutting back radically on sleep. With every double march, he doubled the rations for the dogs. "I was able to do this," he said, "on account of the reserve supply of food which I had in my dogs themselves, in the event of our being seriously delayed by open leads."

On April 10, after a strenuous run that tired the dogs and with concerns about problems likely the next day with young ice, Peary had three more dogs killed. As he put it: "At this spot certain eliminations which we were compelled to make among the dogs left us a total of thirty-five."

Eskimo sledge-traveller and dogs.
Special Collections, UMBC# P78-118-112

Peary on board the steamer Roosevelt *with some of his sled dogs, at about the time of his expedition to the North Pole, in 1909. Photo appears to have been taken on the* Roosevelt's *after deck, looking forward on the starboard side.*
Robert E. Peary, Naval Historical Foundation

In spite of his concern, good weather and relatively smooth conditions prevailed, with no impassable leads. Only several days later did the ice begin to heave and break up under them, but they were never long delayed. They pressed on, as fast as they could, continuing to make double marches whenever they could and keeping to the main trail. They made up more time by using the igloos constructed on the way north.

But, as they drew within sight of land, the dogs became exhausted—"utterly lifeless"—with three "played out entirely" and killed. The remaining dogs were fed extra rations and given a longer rest period.

On April 19, another dog was killed, leaving thirty, Peary stated. (Either he did not account for another dog killed, or his figures were off; according to his previous statements, there should have been thirty-one dogs.)

As if charmed, the southward rush continued smoothly. Although they encountered leads, the homeward-bound men either found a way around or over them, never having to wait for more than two hours.

Eventually, they came to the area of the "Big Lead," which had been almost disastrous for Peary in his previous try at reaching the Pole in 1906, but this time the ice favored them. The Big Lead was frozen over. Bartlett, traveling ahead of them, here had lost the main trail and struck out on a new one, which the retreating party now followed. Once more, the dogs were exhausted, seeming "utterly without energy or spirit."

On the last day before reaching land, there was one troublesome lead. In trying to cross it, one of the teams went into the water but without calamity. Eventually, Peary's group managed to pick up Bartlett's trail again and they were soon in sight of the glaciers that fringed the shore.

At six in the morning on April 23, they reached Cape Columbia and Peary wrote in his diary: "My life work is accomplished....I have got the North Pole out of my system after twenty-three years of effort, hard work, disappointments, hardships, privations, more or less suffering, and some risks."

Peary claimed that the return trip had taken sixteen marches; the round-trip fifty-three days and forty-three marches. Calculations indicate an impossible speed, one that could have been achieved only by the likes of Captain Hatteras.

At Cape Columbia, the alleged victors slept for two days. The dogs revived: "They were different animals now, and the better ones among them stepped out with tightly curled tails and uplifted heads, their iron legs treading the snow with piston-like regularity and their black muzzles every now and then sniffing the welcome scent of the land."

The party reached the *Roosevelt* two days later—April 27, 1909—in two marches of forty-five miles each. As soon as he arrived, Peary learned from Bartlett that Marvin had drowned at the "Big Lead," forty-five miles north of Cape Columbia. (Fifteen years later, one of Marvin's drivers would confess to having murdered him during an argument and slipping his body under the ice.)

And then, a stunning blow: Peary learned that Cook claimed to have beaten him to the Pole by almost a year.

On July 18, the *Roosevelt* pulled away from its winter hold and headed south, into the moving ice. On August 8, it passed Cape Sabine, site of Greely's sufferings; on August 17, reached Etah, the village of such generosity; and on August 26, left Cape York, home of Hans Hendrik, Seegloo, and 100 of Peary's dogs.

Peary said nothing more of the dogs, thirty or thirty-one of which apparently made it back from the Pole to the ship, to join others that had returned earlier with the support parties, along with a number of litters. After Peary's return to the ship, the dogs went on with their work—retrieving supplies from caches and hauling in musk oxen meat and skins. But no specific mention is made of them or their fate.

At the end of his account, Henson gave one last view. The *Roosevelt* stopped, on its way south, to pick up some Inuit families and their teams and transport them down the coast. When the first visiting dog boarded, an enormous fight broke out, "the grandest dog fight I have ever witnessed," reported Henson. After fifteen minutes of general battle, the two "king" dogs went at one another. No effort was made to separate them since it was assumed the two dogs would have to establish rank sooner or later. When the fight finally ended, Peary's king dog, Nalegaksoah, or "King of the Team," was dominant. King Nalegaksoah then "went stamping up and down before the pack and received the homage due him; the new dogs, whining and fawning and cringingly submissive, bowed down before him."

There was nothing cringing about Peary.

On September 6, from Indian Harbour, Canada, Peary sent his first dispatch to the *New York Times*, and also one to Mrs. Peary: "Have made good at last. I have the Pole. Am well. Love." April 6, 1909, was the date, he announced, that he had taken the prize—almost a year after the date Cook claimed—nor would Peary ever relinquish the prize.

Before he reached his landing in Nova Scotia on September 21, Peary had begun to plan his campaign against Cook. Calling upon his wealthy and influential friends, especially officers of the Peary Arctic Club, Peary launched a vindictive campaign—reminiscent of that waged by Lady Jane Franklin against John Rae, but far more mean-spirited and obsessive. It was a campaign run largely through the newspapers, with the *Times* supporting Peary and the *Herald* supporting Cook (until James Gordon Bennett lost faith in his most recent scoop). It was also like a political campaign: Neither side would give up, no matter what the facts (or lack of facts).

Peary's claim to victory, scrutinized by experts employing modern technology, has disintegrated over time.

In 1988, the National Geographic Society—original backer of the expedition—published findings by arctic explorer Wally Herbert indicating that Peary had fallen short. In 1990, after further studies, the National Geographic concluded that he had been no more than five miles away from the Pole—and maintained the case is closed.

The case, of course, will never be closed, any more than the Franklin case will be closed. It rests upon the shifting ice and currents of the North Pole and the questionable integrity of two driven men who started out as friends and ended as bitter enemies.

The argument, which continues to fester, traces to character. Dr. Cook lied about his efforts to make the first ascent of Mount McKinley, but then Peary was known for his insensitive, ruthless, and overbearing nature, expending Inuit helpers and dogs to serve his purpose. Greely, angered that Peary had taken apart his Fort Conger house, was among those who took a strong dislike to the commander and his imperious manner—and who refused to accept his claim of winning the Pole. (Greely had no faith in Cook, either.)

While campaigning against Cook's claim, Peary cut off communications with Henson and began relentless lobbying to be recognized by Congress. He never did gain quite the commendation he sought but did succeed in getting promoted to rear admiral with a pension of $6,000 a year.

To this day, acrimony infects the debate and there is no definitive way, at this late date, to ascertain the truth. What can be known is this: While the two men made efforts that could be interpreted as desperate or heroic to fulfill their dreams, a large number of dogs suffered and died to assist them, only to be forgotten along the way.

King (possibly the king-dog Nalegaksoah) and a number of other Greenland dogs returned with Peary to his summer home on Eagle Island, Casco Bay, Maine. Offshore, on nearby Flag Island, the explorer maintained a home for sledge dogs where he could support them in a nondomesticated manner. Sometimes at night when the moon was full and the dogs howled, to quiet them he would pick up a huge megaphone he kept in his house and swear at them in Inuktitut. According to a report in the *New York Times*, at least one of the dogs he brought back from his last expedition, Ipukchu, the "frisky, curly tailed Eskimo dog," got to romp with his young children outside the house on Eagle Island.

In February 1910, Peary exhibited five of his dogs at the twenty-sixth New England Kennel Club Show in Boston—the exhibit "that attracted the greatest attention."

King, who was reported to have been exhibited at a show in Portland, Maine, as well, died on March 29. "The canine," according to the *New York Times*, "was the last survivor of the animals that Peary selected to take him on the final successful dash to the pole. The dog was also with Peary when the explorer reached 'furthest north' three years ago."

The sad truth is, it is hard to know who truly was Nalegaksoah, a generic name Peary gave to the "king" or leader of the team. Writing of his experience with Peary's 1891–1892 expedition, Eivind Astrup commented:

> During this work [climbing steep ice inclines] Nalegaksuak [an alternate spelling], our best dog, and king of the whole team, strained a sinew of his leg, and became unfit for work. We let him walk behind the sledge for a day, when he disappeared: the poor animal probably became so exhausted that he could not keep up with us. We also lost an excellent telescope in a fissure, and only escaped losing another of our dogs by a hair's breadth.

By May 14, 1910, twelve of fourteen dogs on Flag Island were reported to have died of "some form of distemper." Peary's days of exploration were over.

Peary expedition: four teams.
Peary, Naval Historical Foundation

Peary expedition: close-up of team. Note booties on middle dog.
Peary, Naval Historical Foundation

Peary expedition: sledge with sail.
Peary, Naval Historical Foundation

Peary expedition: front view of team.
Peary, Naval Historical Foundation

Engingwah holding dog, with Eskimo woman sewing.
Donald Baxter MacMillan. The Peary-MacMillan Arctic Museum (img# 3000.1.105)

Dog resting on ropes on S.S. Roosevelt.
The Peary-MacMillan Arctic Museum (img# 2010.2.389b)

Peary sledge aboard the S.S. Roosevelt.
The Peary-MacMillan Arctic Museum and Arctic Studies Center, Bowdoin College, Brunswick, Maine (img# 2010.2.387a)

Eskimos and dogs on S.S. Roosevelt.
Donald Baxter MacMillan. The Peary-MacMillan Arctic Museum (img# 3000.32.1809)

Dogs in action, each on his trace.
Donald Baxter MacMillan. The Peary-MacMillan Arctic Museum (img# 3000.32.536.2)

24

Commemoration

King is remembered in two ways. In 2007, the Navy launched USNS *Robert E. Peary*, a dry cargo/ammunition ship (and the fourth naval ship named for Peary), with the ship's coat of arms featuring Peary's lead dog, Nalegaksoah. Its motto declares "King of the Team," the name in English. The crest shows him pulling a sledge with a driver across a gold demi-disc that represents the "land of the midnight sun."

Between 1960 and 1984 the Robert E. Peary High School of Rockville, Maryland, graduated close to 5,000 students. Its mascot was "King," a series of dogs that represented the famous lead dog, just as "Nalegaksoah" might have been a series of dogs. King II and King III are buried on the school grounds, which now house a private school. A Class of 1976 student remarked, "I'd say our biggest memory and tradition was King, the dog. Even today if someone was to mention the Huskies, it still brings back the whole Peary thing."

A vague and nameless remembrance came in 1959, when the U.S. Postal Service produced a four-cent stamp commemorating fifty years of arctic exploration. The top half shows a team pulling a sledge and driver;

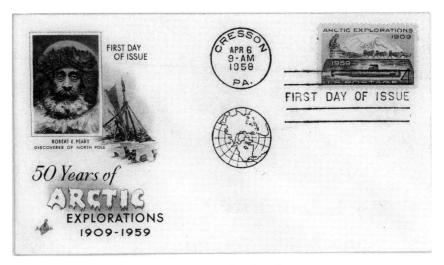

"50 Years of Arctic Explorations, 1909–1959": first day of issue stamp.
U.S. Post Office

the bottom half the USS *Nautilus*, the nuclear-powered submarine that became the first vessel to complete a submerged transit to the North Pole. In 1986, the U.S. Post Office issued a set of four twenty-two-cent stamps commemorating arctic explorers. One shows Henson and Peary in the foreground, with a dog team pulling a sledge in the background.

But commemoration for the valiant dogs that served American explorers of the Arctic ends there, with a naval motto, a decommissioned high school named for a generic lead dog, and two postal stamps.

More progress has been made in Antarctica, where recently eleven names of Roald Amundsen's sledge dogs and Robert Falcon Scott's ponies have been established on navigation waypoints. Thanks to the work of U.S. Air Force Colonel Ronald J. Smith, who used to fly the route, Helge, Mylius, Uroa, Per, Frithjof, and Lasse—some of Amundsen's Greenland dogs—and Jimmy Pigg, Snippets, Bones, Jehu, and Nobby—some of Scott's Manchurian and Siberian ponies that took part in the epic race to the South Pole in 1911–1912—are now on the map (with some names modified to fit the format of waypoints). The bodies of Taro and Jiro, the dogs that survived a year of abandonment in Antarctica, are stuffed and on display in Japanese museums. But there is no such recognition for the animal heroes of the Arctic.

Military working dogs have served in many capacities and have been acknowledged through the years.

Sallie, one of the most famous Civil War dogs, served with the 11th Pennsylvania Volunteer Infantry Regiment during almost the entire war. She was killed in battle and buried under enemy fire at the Battle of Hatcher's Run, Virginia. A well-known heroine of the war, she is commemorated with a bronze sculpture on the front of the 11th Pennsylvania Monument on the Gettysburg battlefield.

Sergeant Stubby, the most decorated military working dog of World War I, served with the 102nd Infantry, 26th (Yankee) Division in the trenches in France for eighteen months, participating in four offensives and seventeen battles. Among other accomplishments, he was solely responsible for capturing a German spy in the Argonne. He was honored with a brick in the Walk of Honor at the United States World War I monument in Kansas City in 2006.

Mascots in all branches of the military abound as well as dogs in service. The Coast Guard boasts Sinbad, a mixed breed that served on board the cutter *Campbell* for eleven years. Other Coast Guard mascots include not only many other dogs but also cats, horses, and even a Vietnamese pot-bellied pig. During the Civil War, the 104th Ohio Volunteer Infantry (the "Barking Dog Regiment") boasted at least three dogs, two squirrels, and two raccoons, while the 2nd Rhode Island Volunteers claimed a lamb, and the 8th Wisconsin an eagle.

An outstanding canine companion and mascot was Igloo, the Smooth Fox Terrier that accompanied Admiral Richard Byrd to both poles. He is buried in the Pine Ridge Cemetery for Small Animals in Dedham, Massachusetts, with an iceberg-shaped tombstone bearing an inscription that reads "Igloo—He Was More Than a Friend."

Since World War II, thousands of military working dogs have been trained and employed for the Army, Air Force, Navy, Marine Corps, and Coast Guard. During World War II, hundreds of sledge dogs served in search-and-rescue operations, some air-dropped (including some without parachutes).

The U.S. military now employs approximately 3,000 dogs, a number that has been growing steadily as canine skills such as bomb-sniffing, weapon detection, and tracking are increasingly needed. Sometimes military working dogs receive military honors. In 2009, for instance, the Navy awarded a Silver Star to Remco, a dog that gave his life charging an insurgent in Afghanistan. Sometimes a military working dog receives a flash of fame, such as Cairo, the Belgian Malinois that assisted the Navy SEALs on their May 1, 2011, raid into the Pakistani complex of Osama bin Laden. Some high-profile cases have involved lengthy procedures for reuniting a working dog with its former handler or the family of a handler killed in action. But, for the most part, military dogs are not known outside their working environment, while inside their working environment they are classified simply as "equipment."

Retirement too often has meant euthanasia. These dogs were not allowed to be adopted by civilians until 2000 when President Clinton signed a law allowing their adoption. Although permitted, adoption can be expensive. Once claimed, a dog is no longer considered military property and cannot fly on military planes; if adopted from an overseas site, it must be brought back to the United States on a commercial flight at the expense of the adopter. Legislation has been proposed that would classify military working dogs as "canine members of the armed forces," and, in retirement, "canine vets," enabling them to be brought home to the United States on military planes. This goal has not been achieved.

Meanwhile, a campaign continues to create a national military working dogs memorial in Washington, D.C., to honor the many dogs that have served bravely and faithfully as scouts, trackers, messengers, and sentries, guarding installations, seeking out mines and explosive materials, and performing search-and-rescue operations, as well as comforting the frightened and wounded. One such monument, funded solely by donations, has been accomplished—the U.S. Military Working Dog Teams National Monument dedicated in 2013 at Lackland Air Force Base in San Antonio, Texas, where all military dogs are trained.

Precedents for memorials can be found across the country. The Hartsdale (New York) Pet Cemetery established the first such one in 1922 to commemorate the 7,000 military canines that served in World War I. In recent years, war dogs memorials have been created elsewhere in New York, and in New Jersey, Missouri, Alabama, Montana, Florida, Utah, Pennsylvania, Texas, Ohio, Illinois, California, Michigan, New Hampshire, Guam, Australia, England, Scotland, and Norway, among other places. Some of these are dedicated to a particular group, such as Guam's to the dogs that served in the Pacific theater in World War II, and the Flemington, New Jersey, memorial dedicated to Vietnam canines and their handlers. The Fort Benton, Montana, War Dogs Memorial states: "In Memory of the Over 4,000 U.S. Military Working Dogs That Served in the Vietnam War/When the War Was Over These Dogs Were Left Behind in Vietnam, Thailand, Laos and Cambodia." (Most were euthanized or abandoned, with only 200 making it home.) Some monuments are dedicated to individual dogs, such as Smoky in Cleveland, Ohio, and Nemo at Lackland Air Force Base. Some are dedicated to search-and-rescue dogs, some to service dogs. And many

memorials across the country honor police dogs and their human partners. The Vietnam Dog Handlers Association has commissioned a monument for the National Mall in Washington, leading the way, perhaps, for a
unified national monument for all military working dogs.

Rightfully, much honor has been paid to the service dogs of September
11th, with growing recognition of the importance of such dogs in protecting national interests and rescuing disaster victims. The National Disaster
Search Dog Foundation is building the country's first national training
center for search-and-rescue dogs.

On all fronts, interest in the history of dogs has grown. Extensive
research, for instance, has recently revealed how many dogs traveled on
the fatal maiden voyage of the *Titanic*: twelve confirmed, with three surviving—two Pomeranians and one Pekinese—while one human victim's
body was found entwined with that of her Great Dane. (A cat with kittens
is said to have disembarked in Southampton, sensing danger.) An exhibit
at Widener University during the centennial year of the ship's sinking fea-
tured, in part, the dogs on board.

But no mention is made of nineteenth-century expeditions to the North
Pole in spite of their political and historic importance. Many of the dogs
engaged in arctic exploration, though not officially designated as military,
served in a quasi-military fashion. Elisha Kent Kane, a Navy doctor, traveled
under orders from the U.S. Navy. Charles Francis Hall's *Polaris* expedition
had congressional support while Hall himself was designated by President
Grant to be in command and to report to the Secretary of the Navy and the
Secretary of the Interior. George Washington De Long, a Navy officer, was,
like Kane, traveling with orders from the Secretary of the Navy. Adolphus
Washington Greely, a member of the Army Signal Corps, was traveling
under congressional authorization. Robert E. Peary, though financed by
private sources, was an officer on leave from the Navy—and argued his
way to a rear-admiralship partly on the basis of his arctic accomplishments.
Frederick Schwatka was granted a leave of absence from the Army by
President Rutherford B. Hayes.

It could be argued that all American efforts to reach the Pole through
the time of Peary were in the national interest and that the dogs that served
that interest deserve official recognition: They were doing the nation's bid-
ding. Without them, no American flags would have reached the top of the
world. But, as with the working dogs of Vietnam, few were returned to
their original owners.

Balto, the Alaska dog that raced serum to Nome during the diphtheria
epidemic of 1925, is honored with a bronze statue atop a rock in Central

Park, New York, his stuffed body on display at the Cleveland Museum of Natural History. Togo, leader of another team in the "Great Race of Mercy," covered the most distance but is less well known. A life-size sculpture of a running sledge dog in another New York City park, Seward Park, now memorializes his accomplishment. Seaman, the Newfoundland dog that traveled with Lewis and Clark, is commemorated with a large statue on the waterfront of St. Helen's, Oregon. Zephyr, John James Audubon's dog, stands beside the artist in a statue in Audubon, Iowa. The famous Skye Terrier, Greyfriars Bobby, who spent fourteen years guarding the grave of his master, is remembered with a statue and a tombstone in his Edinburgh churchyard. Hachikō, the Akita that spent years waiting at a Tokyo train station for his dead master, is honored by a bronze statue. There was even a statue (which would have pleased Henry Bergh) in a London park between 1906 and 1910 honoring the 233 animals used in vivisection experiments by University College. In 2004, the New Zealand Antarctic Society placed a life-size bronze statue of Mrs. Chippy, the cat, on the Wellington grave of Henry "Chippy" McNeish, the *Endurance* carpenter who brought him aboard and never forgave Ernest Shackleton for having him shot when the ship was abandoned.

But nowhere is there a statue of a sledge dog aimed at the North Pole, straining against her harness, a whip cracking over her back, a driver calling "Huk! Huk! Huk!" into a crystal wind.

Notes

Chapter 1: Jules Verne

References to the monster are from *Frankenstein; or, the Modern Prometheus*, by Mary Shelley (1818; reprint, with an introduction and notes by Maurice Hindle, London: Penguin Books, 1992).

For the story of Captain Hatteras and his dog Duke, see *The English at the North Pole*, by Jules Verne (n.d.; reprint, digitized for Microsoft Corporation by the Internet Archive in 2007 from the University of Toronto).

The story of Captain Hatteras continues with *The Desert of Ice; or, The Further Adventures of Captain Hatteras*, by Jules Verne (1874; reprint, Wildside Press, n.d.).

It is significant to note that *Forward* is the name of Captain Hatteras's ship, clearly inspired by Kane's *Advance*. Later, Norwegian explorer Fridtjof Nansen was to name his famous ship *Fram*, which translates as "Forward."

Fictionalized activity was no different at the South Pole. In 1883, Edgar Allan Poe published his gothic—and only—novel, *The Narrative of Arthur Gordon Pym of Nantucket*, the story of a young man traveling with his dog Tiger to Antarctica and a warm open sea surrounding the South Pole. Referencing contemporary accounts and the hollow earth theory, the novel reflects some of the scientific knowledge and suppositions of the times. In spite of its literary shortcomings, it influenced both Herman Melville and Jules Verne.

Chapter 2: Sir John Franklin

During the second half of the nineteenth century, the search for the expedition of Sir John Franklin, lost in his attempt to find the Northwest Passage, served as the catalyst for much of the exploration of the Arctic. Ships changed names and commanders. Often a searching ship became the searched—and the lost. Of the numerous accounts of this busy period crisscrossed with tales of heroism, egoism, and tragedy, one modern work stands out: Pierre Berton's *The Arctic Grail: The Quest for the Northwest Passage and the North Pole, 1818–1909* (New York: Lyons, 2001). Franklin's accounts of earlier voyages provide useful context: *Narrative of a Journey to the Shores of the Polar Sea in the Years 1819, 20, 21 and 22* (London: John Murray, 1823) and *Narrative of a Second Expedition to the Shores of the Polar Sea in the Years 1825, 1826 and 1827* (London: John Murray, 1828). A significant account of the period is Sir Francis Leopold McClintock's *The Voyage of the Fox in the Arctic Seas: A Narrative of the Discovery of the Fate of Sir John Franklin and His Companions* (Philadelphia: J. T. Lloyd, 1860). McClintock, who found the only Franklin document, was one of the few British explorers of the era to learn and master sledge-driving.

Although Franklin and his peers did not use dogs, dogs played an important role during the search for his lost expedition. See "The Use of Dog Sledges during the British Search for the Missing Franklin Expedition in the North American Arctic Islands, 1848–59," by William Barr (*Arctic*, Vol. 62, No. 3, September 2009, 257–272).

Chapter 3: What Was the Greenland Dog?

For the history of this ancient breed, see "Willow Smoke and Dogs' Tails: Hunter-Gatherer Settlement Systems and Archaeological Site Formation," by Lewis R. Binford (*American Antiquity*, Vol. 45, No. 1, January 1980, 4–20).

See also "Paleoeskimo Dogs of the Eastern Arctic," by Darcy F. Morey and Kim Aaris-Sorensen (*Arctic*, Vol. 55, No. 1, March 2002, 44–56).

A thorough description and assessment of the breed is given by Eivind Astrup in *With Peary Near the Pole* (1898; reprint, Google Books), 157–173. For his comments on affection and obedience, see 159–160.

For remarks by Desmond Morris, see *The Animal Contract*, by Desmond Morris (New York: Warner Books, 1991).

See also Wikipedia, "The Greenland Dog."

Chapter 4: *Sledge* or *Sled*?

Detailed descriptions and illustrations of dogs, harnesses, sledges, and their equipment and use are found in *The Central Eskimo*, by Franz Boas (1888; reprint, Toronto: Coles, 1974), 529–538.

For illustrations and descriptions of a harness and whip from Cumberland Sound, see *The Eskimo of Baffin Land and Hudson Bay*, by Franz Boas (*Bulletin of the American Museum of Natural History*, Vol. 15, Part 1, 1901), 39–40; and for a whip from Hudson Bay, see ibid., 89–90.

For descriptions of Hall's "Cincinnati" sledge, see *Life with the Esquimaux: The Narrative of Captain Charles Francis Hall, of the Whaling Barque* George Henry, *from the 29th of May, 1860, to the 13th of September, 1862*, by Charles Francis Hall (London: Sampson Low, Son, & Marston, 1864, 2 vols.), vol. 2, 352.

For the description of a sledge Hall used in his second expedition, see *Narrative of the Second Arctic Expedition Made by Charles F. Hall: His Voyage to Repulse Bay, Sledge Journeys to the Straits of Fury and Hecla and to King William's Land, and Residence among the Eskimos during the Years 1864–69*, edited by J. E. Nourse, U.S.N. (Washington, D.C.: Government Printing Office, 1879), 85–86.

For Hayes's description of the fan hitch, see *An Arctic Boat Journey in the Autumn of 1854*, by Isaac I. Hayes, M.D. (Boston: Houghton Mifflin, 1896), 219.

Kane's description of the whip is found in *Arctic Explorations: The Second Grinnell Expedition in Search of Sir John Franklin, 1853, '54 '55*, by Elisha Kent Kane (Philadelphia: Childs & Peterson, 1856, 2 vols.), vol. 1, 124.

For a vignette of Kane practicing with a whip, see *The Biography of Elisha Kent Kane*, by William Elder (Philadelphia: Childs & Peterson, 1858), 259–260.

For another view of the whip, see also *The Open Polar Sea: A Narrative of a Voyage of Discovery Towards the North Pole in the Schooner "United States,"* by I. Hayes (New York: Hurd & Houghton, 1867), 103–104.

Nansen's vignette of his disastrous driving experience is found in *Farthest North: Being the Record of a Voyage of Exploration of the Ship "Fram" 1893–96 and of a Fifteen Months' Sleigh Journey by Dr. Nansen and Lieut. Johansen*, by Dr. Fridtjof Nansen (1898, 2 vols.; reprint, Google Books), vol. 1, 289–290.

For comments on British use and design of sledges and harnesses, see Barr, 2009.

Chapter 5: Toodla and Whitey

The primary source is Kane's account of his second arctic voyage (Kane, 1856). Quotations are from this source unless otherwise noted.

Isaac Hayes's description of Toodla is found in Hayes's account of his adventure with the "Withdrawing Party," or mutineers: *An Arctic Boat Journey in the Autumn of 1854* (1896), 214–215.

For Hayes's description of the harness, see Hayes, 1896, 219–220.

William C. Godfrey, a constant thorn in the side of Kane, wrote his account as well: *Godfrey's Narrative of the Last Grinnell Arctic Exploring Expedition in Search of Sir John Franklin, 1853–54–55: With a Biography of Dr. Elisha Kent Kane, from the Cradle to the Grave* (Philadelphia: J. T. Lloyd, 1857).

Hans Christian, usually known as Hans Hendrik, traveled with Kane, Hayes, and Hall on the *Polaris* expedition, as well as with George Strong Nares on his British North Polar Expedition of 1875–1876. See *Hans the Eskimo: His Story of Arctic Adventure with Kane, Hayes, and Hall*, by Edwin Gile Rich (Boston: Houghton Mifflin, 1934).

Kane's relationship with spiritualist Maggie Fox was closely followed by contemporary newspapers and received much public attention. Fox's account is found in *The Love-Life of Dr. Kane; Containing the Correspondence, and a History of the Acquaintance, Engagement, and Secret Marriage between Elisha K. Kane and Margaret Fox* (New York: Carleton, 1866). See also *The Unhappy Medium*, by Earl W. Fornell (Austin: University of Texas Press, 1964). See, too, the *New York Times*, the *New York Herald*, the *Boston Herald*, and other major papers for the period.

Contemporaneous accounts include *The Life of Dr. Elisha Kent Kane and of Other Distinguished American Explorers*, by Samuel M. Smucker (Philadelphia: J. W. Bradley, 1858), and the Kane family-approved and censored biography by William Elder, 1858.

For a description of Toodla-mik and Kane practicing with a whip, see Elder, 1858, 259–260.

A significant modern biography is *Doctor Kane of the Arctic Seas*, by George W. Corner (Philadelphia: Temple University Press, 1972).

For Petersen's account of the death of Christian Ohlsen, see his diary contained within *Dr. Kane's Voyage to the Polar Lands*, by Oscar M. Villarejo (Philadelphia: University of Pennsylvania Press, 1965), 152.

For information on the panoramas and public appearances of Kane and Hall, see *Arctic Spectacles: The Frozen North in Visual Culture, 1818–1875*, by Russell A. Potter (Seattle: University of Washington Press, 2007). Potter states, "The history of exhibitions of 'Eskimo' and 'Husky' dogs would make a chapter in itself—clearly there were more such dogs out there than Kane's team could account for, even if *every* dog in it had survived" (127).

For the final written report on Toodla, see "Dr. Kane's Boat—The *Faith*," by William Hoyt Coleman (*Robert Merry's Museum*, January 1859, 24).

Chapter 6: Henry Bergh

For further information, see publications by the American Society for the Prevention of Cruelty to Animals (ASPCA), especially http://www.aspca.org/about-us/history.aspx (March 12, 2012).

See also the *New York Times*, 1866–1888.

For dogfighting, see the *New York Times*, February 24, 1867. See also Edward Van Emery, "The Sins of New York as 'Exposed' by the Police Gazette" (the *Richard K. Fox Gazette*, 1876, Part 2, Chapter 6).

Cook, alone among the American explorers, stated that dogfighting was an annual sporting event among the Inuit:

> Just prior to the falling of darkness…the Eskimos engaged in their annual sporting event. It is a curious sight, indeed, to behold a number of excited, laughing Eskimos gathering about two champion dogs which are to fight. Although the zest of betting is unknown, the natives regard dog fights with much the same eager excitement as a certain sort of sporting man does a cock encounter.…A dog which maintains his fighting supremacy becomes a king dog, and when beaten becomes a first lieutenant to the king (*My Attainment of the Pole*, by Frederick A. Cook [New York: Mitchell Kennerley, 1913], 92).

The story of Sedna, Inuit goddess of the sea and its animals, is found in various forms from Baffin Island to Hudson Bay. See Boas, 1888, 583–588.

For Bergh's lecture on vivisection, see the *New York Times*, January 4, 1881.

For remarks by Hall on cruelty, see Nourse, 1879, 183–185. For his description of a sail being used to assist dogs, see Nourse, 1879, 94.

For McClintock's remarks on treatment of dogs, see McClintock, 1860, 244.

Remarks by Eivind Astrup are found in Astrup, 1898, 161–162.

For Hall's last written instructions, see *Narrative of the North Polar Expedition, U.S. Ship* Polaris, *Captain Charles Francis Hall Commanding*, edited by C. H. Davis, U.S.N. (Washington, D.C.: Government Printing Office, 1876), 143.

For articles on dogcatchers of the period, see the *New York Times*, August 11, 1882; July 10, 1885; August 2, 1887; August 11, 1893; August 18, 1910.

Chapter 7: Oosisoak and Arkadik

All quotations, unless otherwise noted, are from Hayes, 1867.

See, too, Hayes, 1896, and Hayes's *The Land of Desolation: Being a Personal Narrative of Observation and Adventure in Greenland* (New York: Harper & Brothers, 1872).

For comment on Hayes's success, see *Harper's Weekly*, October 26, 1861.

Chapter 8: Disease and Diet

I am indebted to Janiene Licciardi, D.V.M., for her interest, support, and advice, particularly in regard to the role of salt poisoning as the likely culprit in many cases of illness and death reported among the sledge dogs, as well as for her insight and information regarding the nutritional needs of northern working dogs.

For Petersen's comments, see Villarejo, 1965, 146.

For McClintock's statements about dogs eating birds, see McClintock, 1860, 70, 72.

For Sonntag's remarks, see Villarejo, 1965, 140.

For Barr's reference to de Bray, see Barr, 2009, 263.

For comments on pemmican, see Hall, 1864, vol. 2, 58; Cook, 1913, 135; "May Use Whale Meat in the Army Ration: Peary Advises Pemmican Made from It and Goethals Is Considering the Suggestion" (*New York Times*, March 4, 1918); *Secrets of Polar Travel*, by Robert E. Peary (New York: Century, 1917), 77–83.

For Nansen's remarks on Kane's feeding of the dogs, see Nansen, 1898, vol. 1, 353.

For Schwatka's comments on frequency of feeding and starvation of his dogs, see *The Long Arctic Search: The Narrative of Lieutenant Frederick Schwatka, U.S.A., 1878–1880, Seeking the Records of the Lost Franklin Expedition*, edited by Edourd A. Stackpole (Mystic, Conn.: The Marine Historical Association, Inc., 1965), 103–105.

For Mauch's quote, see Davis, 1876, 328.

For McClintock's story of the muzzled bitch and her "*amiable* sisterhood," see McClintock, 1860, 168.

For Nansen's story of the dogs Job and Suggen, see Nansen, 1898, vol. 1, 271.

The comments by Margaret Penny are from *This Distant and Unsurveyed Country: A Woman's Winter at Baffin Island, 1857–58*, by W. Gillies Ross (Montreal: McGill-Queen's University Press, 1997), 115 and 122.

For Ninnis's report, see *Parliamentary Paper*, C. 2176, 1878.

Ninnis had a son, Belgrave Edward Sutton Ninnis, who accompanied the Australasian Antarctic Expedition of 1911–1914 as a dog handler. He died in 1912 when the sledge he was walking beside broke through the snow of a crevasse.

Chapter 9: Dogs and Driver: The Essential Team

The principal source is Hayes, 1896.

The Hayes incident of the runaway dogs is found in Hayes, 1896, 287–295.

For Kane's account, see Kane, 1856, vol. 1, 438–443.

Explicit information on dogs, sledges, harnesses, and training and driving dogs is found in Boas, 1888, 529–538.

For Greely's comments on drivers, see *Three Years of Arctic Service: An Account of the Lady Franklin Bay Expedition of 1881–84, and the Attainment of the Farthest North*, by A(dolphus) W(ashington) Greely (New York: Charles Scribner's Sons, 1886, 2 vols.), vol. 1, 196–212, 244–246.

For Peary's comments on Henson, see *The North Pole: Its Discovery in 1909 Under the Auspices of the Peary Arctic Club*, by Robert E. Peary (1910; reprint, Mineola, N.Y.: Dover, 1986), 20, 272–273.

Chapter 10: Seeking Companionship: When Dogs Were Not Available

Duke is found in *The English at the North Pole* (n.d.) and *Desert of Ice* (1874), by Jules Verne.

Hall's letter to Grinnell on what he discovered during his search for Franklin relics—with the hint of a dog in the Franklin party—appeared in numerous newspapers around the world. See, for instance, *Connecticut Courant*, October 9, 1869, and *The Mercury* (Hobart, Tasmania), January 19, 1870.

The information on Nellie is from *The Great Frozen Sea: A Personal Narrative of the Voyage of the* Alert *during the Arctic Expedition 1875–6,* by Albert Hastings Markham (London: Kegan Paul, Trench, Trübner, 1894), 78, 188–189.

For Godfrey's comments, see Godfrey, 1857, 116–117.

For Greely's foxes, see Greely, 1886, vol. 2, 3–7, 367.

Information on the domestication of dogs and foxes is found in *Dog Sense: How the New Science of Dog Behavior Can Make You a Better Friend to Your Pet,* by John Bradshaw (New York: Basic Books, 2011), 53–56.

See also "Taming the Wild," by Evan Ratliff (*National Geographic*, Vol. 219, No. 3, March 2011), 40–59.

See, too, *Animals Make Us Human,* by Temple Grandin (Boston: Mariner Books, 2010), 24–29.

For Greely's comments on the owlets, see Greely, 1886, vol. 2, 3.

William M. Davis put together pigs, cats, game hens, and a mischievous monkey as pets on a whaling voyage in a book based on his experiences as a whaler: *Nimrod of the Sea; or, The American Whaleman* (New York: Harper & Brothers, 1874), Chapters 5, 23, 31. By the end of the voyage, he said, all the pets were "consumed."

For the story of the animals aboard the *Diana,* see *From the Deep of the Sea: The Diary of Charles Edward Smith, Surgeon of the Whale-ship* Diana, *of Hull,* by Charles Edward Smith (Annapolis, Md.: The Naval Institute Press, 1977), 157, 172, 175, 193, 218, 268, 270.

Cook discusses the blue rats in Cook, 1913, 413–415.

For McClintock's cat, Puss, see McClintock, 1860, 90, 113.

For the *Polaris* pets, see Davis, 1876.

Tyson's comments on the seal he tried to adopt are from *Arctic Experiences: Containing Captain George E. Tyson's Wonderful Drift on the Ice-Floe, a History of the* Polaris *Expedition, the Cruise of the* Tigress, *and Rescue of the* Polaris *Survivors,* edited by E. Vale Blake (New York: Harper & Brothers, 1874), 89–90.

Joseph Faulkner's account of the escaped seal is found in *Eighteen Months on a Greenland Whaler,* by Joseph P. Faulkner (New York: Published for the Author, 1878), 296–297.

Charles Edward Smith's memories of the seals taken to England are found in Smith, 1977, 175.

For information on Maggie Fox, her relationship with Kane, and the story of *Undine,* see Fox, 1866.

For stories, legends, and music regarding seals, see *The People of the Sea: A Journey in Search of the Seal Legend,* by David Thomson (Washington, D.C.: Counterpoint, 2002). Also of interest is the film *The Secret of Roan Inish* (1994).

For information on the views of the Polar Inuit, see Hall, 1864. See also Nourse, 1879.

Chapter 11: Barbekark

All quotations, unless otherwise noted, are from Hall, 1864, the only book written by Hall, whose subsequent work was edited and published by others after his death—others who, no matter how dedicated to their responsibilities, could not help but exercise bias in what they chose and how they chose to present it. The 1864 work is significant not only because of its detail and sincerity but also because of its ethnographic focus. Working with Tookoolito, his interpreter, Hall was able to gain much information on the culture and beliefs of the Inuit people as well as historical information regarding both Franklin and sixteenth-century explorer Martin Frobisher. By so doing, he established the veracity and importance of oral history. Twenty years later, anthropologist Franz Boas, writing in *The Central Eskimo* (1888), acknowledged Hall's pioneering ethnography. For stories similar to those Hall recorded, see Boas, 1901.

Critical to an understanding of Hall is the definitive biography by Chauncey C. Loomis, *Weird and Tragic Shores: The Story of Charles Francis Hall, Explorer* (Lincoln: University of Nebraska Press, 1991). In 1968, Loomis led an expedition of his own to the grave of Hall on the northwestern coast of Greenland to exhume his body and oversee an autopsy, which revealed that Hall had died of arsenic poisoning. Whether by self-medication or murder cannot be told, but, given the contentious nature of the crew, murder is likely the cause.

Chapter 12: Dogs as Showmen

For information on panoramas and exhibitions, see Potter, 2007.

See also New York newspapers for the period. An advertisement for Hall's presentation at Barnum's American Museum can be found in the *New York Times*, November 20, 1862.

For background on P. T. Barnum and his views on hucksters and hoaxes, see *Humbugs of the World*, by P. T. Barnum (New York: G. W. Carleton, 1865).

Chapter 13: Wolf, Smarty, Bear, Shoemaker, Tiger

For information on the voyage of the *Polaris*, see Davis, 1876.

Because of Davis's "failing health," final revisions and proofing for the last seven chapters were completed by J. E. Nourse, editor of the previous book: *Narrative of the Second Arctic Expedition Made by Charles Francis Hall* (Nourse, 1879).

See also *Report to the President of the United States of the Action of the Navy Department in the Matter of the Disaster to the United States Exploring Expedition toward the North Pole; Accompanied by a Report of the Examination of the Rescued Party, etc.*, by the U.S. Navy (Washington, D.C.: Government Printing Office, 1873).

See also Loomis, 1991.

Chapter 14: Tommy the Cat and the Lemmings

See Davis, 1876. See also U.S. Navy, 1873, and Loomis, 1991.

Chapter 15: Bear, Spike, and the Nameless Prisoners

The story of the ice-floe party is told in Blake, 1874. It is also told by Davis, 1876, and U.S. Navy, 1873.

Chapter 16: Toekelegeto, Ublubliaq, Miqijuk

The primary source is Schwatka, 1965.

Second-in-command William H. Gilder wrote a longer, more detailed account: *Schwatka's Search: Sledging in the Arctic in Quest of the Franklin Records* (n.d.: reprint, Charleston, S.C.: BiblioBazaar, 2006).

Heinrich Klutschak, naturalist, recorded his impressions in *Overland to Starvation Cove: With the Inuit in Search of Franklin, 1878–80*, translated and edited by William Barr (Toronto: University of Toronto Press, 1987).

Like Kane and Hayes, Schwatka was a doctor, as was Frederick Cook, who followed. Other ship's doctors of the period who wrote of their experiences include the following:

Charles Edward Smith, surgeon of the whaler *Diana* of Hull, took over command after his captain died and then managed to get his crippled ship and decimated crew home after six months beset in ice. Years later, his son edited Smith's diary to tell his father's harrowing story in *From the Deep of the Sea* (1977).

Sir Robert Goodsir, whose brother Harry, also a doctor, disappeared with the Franklin Expedition, told his story in *An Arctic Voyage to Baffin's Bay and Lancaster Sound in Search of Friends with Sir John Franklin*, by Robert A. Goodsir (1850; reprint, Plaistow and Sutton Coldfield, U.K.: Arctic Press, 1996).

Alexander McDonald, assistant surgeon serving on the HMS *Terror*, one of the two Franklin ships, wrote *A Narrative of Some Passages in the History of Eenoolooapik, a Young Eskimo, Who Was Brought to Britain in 1839, in the Ship* Neptune *of Aberdeen* (Edinburgh: Fraser, 1841). Eenoolooapik, a Baffin Island cartographer highly regarded by the whalers, was an older brother of Tookoolito, Hall's interpreter.

The most famous example is Sir Arthur Conan Doyle, who served as ship's doctor on the whaler *Hope* on a trip to the Arctic in 1880 while he was a medical student at the University of Edinburgh, and again later on the SS *Mayumba* during a voyage to the west coast of Africa. For extensive, detailed information on his experiences aboard the *Hope*, see *Dangerous Work: Diary of an Arctic Adventure*, by Arthur Conan Doyle, edited by Jon Lellenberg and Daniel Stashower (Chicago: University of Chicago Press, 2012). For further arctic writings of the master detective storyteller, see *The Captain of the Pole-Star and Other Tales*, by Arthur Conan Doyle.

Doctors might have tended to be good observers and writers but they were not immune to the pressures of the arctic winter. In *This Distant and Unsurveyed Country* (1997), W. Gillies Ross gives the story of Dr. Robertson of the *Alibi*, who went mad in the winter of 1856–1857 in Cumberland Sound. In July, he committed suicide by leaping overboard in the midst of a gale.

Chapter 17: The Importance of Naming

For explanation of the importance of naming dogs in regard to sledge-driving, see Boas, 1888, 537.

For information on Sedna, the Inuit deity, and her relationship with dogs, see Boas, 1888, 583–588.

For Inuit views on dogs, see Hall, 1864, and Nourse, 1879. Also see Boas, 1901.

For the naming of dogs, see Markham, 1894, 78, 245.

For W. Gillies Ross's comments, see Ross, 1997, xl–xli.

For a history of the naming of people in Nunavut, see "What's in a Name?" by Ann Meekitjuk Hanson (*Nunavut '99*, electronic resource, http://www.nunavut.com/nunavut99/english/name.html).

Chapter 18: Kasmatka, Snoozer, Bingo, Snuffy, Tom, Jack, Wolf

As with Hall, De Long did not live to tell his story. When his body was found on the banks of the Lena River, his "ice journal" was discovered behind his head, where apparently he had thrown it to protect it from high water. His widow, Emma De Long, edited his notes and oversaw publication of *The Voyage of the* Jeannette. *The Ship and Ice Journals of George W. De Long, Lieutenant-Commander U.S.N., and Commander of the Polar Expedition of 1879–1881* (Boston: Houghton, Mifflin, 1887). All quotations are from De Long, unless otherwise noted.

Davis, in *Narrative of the North Polar Expedition* (1876), recounted the role of Lieutenant De Long as commander of the *Little Juniata* in search of the crew of the *Polaris*.

Chapter 19: The Polar Bear

For Hall's description of bears killing walrus, see Hall, 1864, vol. 2, 328–330; for killing seals, see Hall, 1864, vol. 2, 325–329.

Scoresby's comments are found in *An Account of the Arctic Regions, with a History and Description of the Northern Whale-Fishery*, by William Scoresby (1820; reprint, with an introduction by Professor Sir Alister Hardy, Newton Abbot, Devon, U.K.: David & Charles Reprints, 1969, 2 vols.), vol. 1, 517–526.

Hayes's comments are found in Hayes, 1867, 239–240.

Nansen's account of the wrapping paper discovered in the bear's stomach is found in Nansen, 1898, vol. 1, 262.

The story Boas told of Acherelwa is found in Boas, 1901, 263. Boas also related a number of bear stories and myths indicating the power with which polar bears were imbued.

Scoresby's comments on the affection of sows for their cubs are found in Scoresby, 1820, vol. 1, 520–521.

For Nansen's comments on the sow watching over her wounded cub, see Nansen, 1898, vol. 1, 284–285.

For Captain Gravill's account of the taking of cubs, see Smith, 1977, 22–25.

Chapter 20: Gypsy, Old Sneak, Ritenbenk, Disco King

The principal source is Greely, 1886.

See also Leonard F. Guttridge, *Ghosts of Cape Sabine: The Harrowing True Story of the Greely Expedition* (New York: Berkley, 2000).

The International Polar Year (IPY), now a continuing tradition, is held every fifty years. The Fourth IPY was celebrated 2007–2008. Organized through the International Council for Science and the World Meteorological Organization, it involved thousands of scientists from over sixty nations pursuing physical, biological, and social research subjects.

The story of Sallie is found in Markham, 1894, 190–191.

Chapter 21: The Nameless

The principal source is Cook, 1913. See also *Return from the Pole*, by Frederick Albert Cook (1951; reprint, Pittsburgh: Polar, 2009).

For comments by John H. Henderson and Cook's neighbors, see the *New York Times*, September 10, 1909.

For the "Big Navel/Nail" comment, see "Liars and Gentlemen," by Kenn Harper (*Polar Priorities: The Annual Journal of the Frederick A. Cook Society*, December 2008, Vol. 28), 45.

It is significant that Cook claimed that among the mirages he saw while approaching the Pole were those of volcanoes, eliciting thoughts of Captain Hatteras. On March 21, 1908, he reported:

> [H]uge mirages wove a web of marvelous delusional pictures about the horizon. Peaks of snow were transformed into volcanoes, belching smoke; out of the pearly mist rose marvelous cities with fairy-like castles; in the color-shot clouds waved golden and rose and crimson pennants from pinnacles and domes of mosaic-colored splendor. Huge creatures, misshapen and grotesque, writhed along the horizon and performed amusing antics.

> Beginning now, and rarely absent, these spectral denizens of the North accompanied us during the entire journey.…

> Every look was rewarded by a new prospect. From belching volcanoes to smoking cities of modern bustle, the mirages gave a succession of striking scenes which filled me with awed and marveling delight (Cook, 1913, 212–213).

For comments by Osczevski, see "Frederick Cook and the Forgotten Pole," by Randall J. Osczevski (*Arctic*, Vol. 56, No. 2, June 2003, 207–217).

For the Pine Tree Sanitarium, see "Wells Sanitarium was the Pitts," by Sharon Cummins (*York County Coast Star*, October 18, 2007).

Chapter 22: Heart-hungers

For Cook's comments on love for dogs, see Cook, 1951, 75, 181–182.

For Bradshaw's comments on love and attachment, see Bradshaw, 2011, 144–147.

For Sonntag's comments, see Villarejo, 1965, 89.

For information on the film *Eight Below* (2006), see the American Humane Association's Film and TV Unit website: http://www.americanhumanefilmtv.org/eight-below.

Chapter 23: Nalegaksoah

Peary wrote extensively of his numerous polar expeditions. His wife, Josephine Diebitsch Peary, who shared two expeditions with him (plus another unexpected winter trapped in arctic ice), wrote *My Arctic Journal: A Year among Ice-Fields and Eskimos with an Account of the Great White Journey across Greenland by Robert E. Peary* (New York: Contemporary Publishing, 1893) and *The Snow Baby; a True Story with True Pictures* (New York: Frederick A. Stokes, 1901).

All Peary citations, unless otherwise noted, are from Peary, 1910.

Henson quotations are from *A Negro Explorer at the North Pole*, by Matthew A. Henson (1912; reprint, New York: Cooper Square, 2001).

For another view of Peary, see *Give Me My Father's Body: The Life of Minik, the New York Eskimo*, by Kenn Harper (South Royalton, Vt.: Steerforth, 2000).

A number of articles on Peary's return and his claim to the pole can be found in the *New York Times*, 1909–1910. See also the *New York Tribune*.

For Peary on Fort Conger, see Peary, 1917, 153.

For more on Fort Conger, see "Fort Conger: Old Tales of Futility and Desperation," by Jane George (*Nunatsiaq News*, August 4, 2000).

For a study of *piblokto* (arctic hysteria), see "'Pibloktoq' (Arctic Hysteria): A Construction of European-Inuit Relations?" by Lyle Dick (*Arctic Anthropology*, Vol. 32, No. 2, 1995, 1–42).

Reminiscent of *piblokto* is the description Cook gives of an annual commemoration of the dead as winter closes in:

> Over the bluish, snow-covered land, formed by the indentures and hollows, stretched dark-purplish shapes—Titan shadows, sepulchral and ominous, some with shrouded heads, others with spectral arms threateningly upraised. Nebulous and gruesome shreds of blue-fog like wraiths shifted over the sea. Out of the sombre, heavy air began to issue a sound as of many women sobbing. From the indistinct distance came moaning, crooning voices. Sometimes hysterical wails of anguish rent the air, and now and then frantic choruses shrieked some heart-aching despair. My impression was that I was in a land of the sorrowful dead, some mid-strata of the spirit world, where, in this gray-green twilight, formless things in the distance moved to and fro (Cook, 1913, 94).

Cook's movie, *The Truth about the North Pole*, was produced in 1912.

The article on Peary's dog, Ipukchu, is found in the *New York Times*, September 26, 1909. The article on Peary's dogs at the Boston dog show is found in the *New York Times*, February 23, 1910.

For the death of Peary's dogs, see the *New York Times*, March 30, 1910, and May 15, 1910.

For Astrup's comments on Nalegaksoah, see Astrup, 1898, 206–207.

Chapter 24: Commemoration

For information on the naming of the Antarctica waypoints, see the *New York Times*, September 28, 2010, and the editorial that ran two days later, "Polar Ponies and Ice Dogs," which states that the naming is

> apt and lovely. Neither explorer would have succeeded without the aid of their animals. Amundsen, who reached the pole before Scott, relied soley on dogs. Scott chose small, stout Manchurian and Siberian ponies.

For photos of the ponies, see the website of the Scott Polar Research Institute.

For information on Civil War military dogs, see *Loyal Hearts: Histories of American Civil War Canines*, by Michael Zucchero (Lynchburg, Va.: Schroeder, 2010).

Bibliography

Books

Astrup, Eivind. *With Peary Near the Pole* (London: C. Arthur Pearson, 1898).

Barnum, P. T. *Humbugs of the World* (New York: G. W. Carleton, 1865).

Beattie, Owen, and John Geiger. *Frozen in Time: Unlocking the Secrets of the Franklin Expedition* (Vancouver: Greystone Books, 1998).

Berton, Pierre. *The Arctic Grail: The Quest for the Northwest Passage and the North Pole, 1818–1909* (New York: Lyons, 2001).

Blake, E. Vale, ed. *Arctic Experiences: Containing Captain George E. Tyson's Wonderful Drift on the Ice-Floe, a History of the* Polaris *Expedition, the Cruise of the* Tigress, *and Rescue of the* Polaris *Survivors* (New York: Harper & Brothers, 1874).

Boas, Franz. *The Central Eskimo* (1888; reprint, Toronto: Coles, 1974).

———. *The Eskimo of Baffin Land and Hudson Bay: From Notes Collected by George Comer, James S. Mutch, and E. J. Peck. Bulletin of the American Museum of Natural History*, Vol. 15, Part 1 (New York: Museum of Natural History, 1901).

Bradshaw, John. *Dog Sense: How the New Science of Dog Behavior Can Make You a Better Friend to Your Pet* (New York: Basic Books, 2011).

Cook, Frederick A. *My Attainment of the Pole: Being the Record of the Expedition That First Reached the Boreal Center, 1907–1909 with the Final Summary of the Polar Controversy* (1913; reprint, Google Books, 2011).

———. *Return from the Pole* (1951; reprint, Pittsburgh: Polar, 2009).

Corner, George W. *Doctor Kane of the Arctic Seas* (Philadelphia: Temple University Press, 1972).

Crouse, Nellis M. *The Search for the North Pole* (New York: Richard R. Smith, 1947).

Davis, C. H., ed. *Narrative of the North Polar Expedition, U.S. Ship* Polaris, *Captain Charles Francis Hall Commanding* (Washington, D.C.: Government Printing Office, 1876).

Davis, William M. *Nimrod of the Sea; or, the American Whaleman* (New York: Harper & Brothers, 1874).

De Long, Emma J. Wotten, ed. *The Voyage of the* Jeannette. *The Ship and Ice Journals of George W. De Long, Lieutenant-Commander U.S.N., and Commander of the Polar Expedition of 1879–1881* (Boston: Houghton, Mifflin, 1887).

Elder, William. *The Biography of Elisha Kent Kane* (Philadelphia: Childs & Peterson, 1858).

Faulkner, Joseph P. *Eighteen Months on a Greenland Whaler* (New York: Published for the Author, 1878).

Fornell, Earl Wesley. *The Unhappy Medium: Spiritualism and the Life of Margaret Fox* (Austin: University of Texas Press, 1964).

Fox, Margaret. *The Love-Life of Dr. Kane; Containing the Correspondence, and a History of the Acquaintance, Engagement, and Secret Marriage between Elisha K.

Kane and Margaret Fox, with Facsimiles of Letters, and Her Portrait (New York: Carleton, 1866).

Gilder, William H. *Schwatka's Search: Sledging in the Arctic in Quest of the Franklin Records* (n.d.; reprint, Charleston, S.C.: BiblioBazaar, 2006).

Godfrey, William C. *Godfrey's Narrative of the Last Grinnell Arctic Exploring Expedition, in Search of Sir John Franklin, 1853–4–5. With a Biography of Dr. Elisha K. Kane, from the Cradle to the Grave* (1857; reprint, Google Books, 2011).

Goodsir, Robert Anstruther. *An Arctic Voyage to Baffin's Bay and Lancaster Sound in Search of Friends with Sir John Franklin* (1850; reprint, Plaistow & Sutton Coldfield, U.K.: Arctic Press, 1996).

Grandin, Temple. *Animals Make Us Human: Creating the Best Life for Animals* (Boston: Mariner Books, 2010).

Greely, Adolphus Washington. *Three Years of Arctic Service: An Account of the Lady Franklin Bay Expedition of 1881–84, and the Attainment of the Farthest North.* 2 vols. (Vol. 1, 1886; reprint, Google Books, 2011; Vol. 2, 1886; reprint, Ann Arbor: University of Michigan Library, n.d.).

Guttridge, Leonard F. *Ghosts of Cape Sabine: The Harrowing True Story of the Greely Expedition* (New York: Berkley, 2000).

Hall, Charles Francis. *Life with the Esquimaux: The Narrative of Captain Charles Francis Hall, of the Whaling Barque* George Henry, *from the 29th of May, 1860, to the 13th of September, 1862....* 2 vols. (London: Sampson Low, Son, & Marston, 1864).

Hayes, I(saac) I(srael). *An Arctic Boat Journey in the Autumn of 1854* (Boston: Houghton Mifflin, 1896).

————. *The Land of Desolation: Being a Personal Narrative of Observation and Adventure in Greenland* (New York: Harper & Brothers, 1872).

————. *The Open Polar Sea: A Narrative of a Voyage of Discovery Towards the North Pole in the Schooner* United States (1867; reprint, Sabin Americana, n.d.).

Henderson, Bruce. *Fatal North: Adventure and Survival Aboard USS* Polaris, *the First U.S. Expedition to the North Pole* (New York: New American Library, 2001).

Henson, Matthew A. *A Negro Explorer at the North Pole* (1912; reprint, New York: Cooper Square, 2001).

Kane, Elisha Kent. *Arctic Explorations: The Second Grinnell Expedition in Search of Sir John Franklin, 1853, '54 '55.* 2 vols. (Philadelphia: Childs & Peterson, 1856).

————. *The U.S. Grinnell Expedition in Search of Sir John Franklin: A Personal Narrative* (New York: Harper, 1853).

Klutschak, Heinrich. *Overland to Starvation Cove: With the Inuit in Search of Franklin 1878–1880.* Translated and edited by William Barr (Toronto: University of Toronto Press, 1987).

Loomis, Chauncey C. *Weird and Tragic Shores: The Story of Charles Francis Hall, Explorer* (1971; reprint, Lincoln, Neb.: Bison Book, 1991).

Markham, Sir Albert Hastings. *The Great Frozen Sea: A Personal Narrative of the Voyage of the* Alert *during the Arctic Expedition 1875–6* (1894; reprint, Google Books, 2011).

McClintock, Sir Francis Leopold. *The Voyage of the* Fox *in the Arctic Seas: A Narrative of the Discovery of the Fate of Sir John Franklin and His Companions* (1860; reprint, Google Books, 2011).

Mirsky, Jeannette. *Elisha Kent Kane and the Seafaring Frontier* (Boston: Little, Brown, 1954).

Morris, Desmond. *The Animal Contract: An Impassioned and Rational Guide to Sharing the Planet and Saving Our Common World* (1990; reprint, New York: Warner Books, 1991).

Nansen, Fridtjof. *Farthest North: Being the Record of a Voyage of Exploration of the Ship "Fram" 1893–96 and of a Fifteen Months' Sleigh Journey by Dr. Nansen and Lieut. Johansen.* 2 vols. (1898; reprint, Vol. 1, Google Books, 2012; Vol. 2, Fairford, Gloucestershire, U.K.: Echo Library, 2012).

Nickerson, Sheila. *Midnight to the North: The Untold Story of the Inuit Woman Who Saved the* Polaris *Expedition* (New York: Jeremy P. Tarcher/Putnam, 2002).

Nourse, J. E., ed. *Narrative of the Second Arctic Expedition Made by Charles F. Hall: His Voyage to Repulse Bay, Sledge Journeys to the Straits of Fury and Hecla and to King William's Land, and Residence among the Eskimos during the Years 1864–69* (Washington, D.C.: Government Printing Office, 1879).

Parry, Richard. *Trial by Ice: The True Story of Murder and Survival on the 1871* Polaris *Expedition* (New York: Ballantine Books, 2001).

Peary, Josephine Diebitsch. *My Arctic Journal: A Year among Ice-Fields and Eskimos with an Account of the Great White Journey across Greenland by Robert E. Peary* (New York: Contemporary, 1893).

Peary, Robert E. *The North Pole: Its Discovery in 1909 under the Auspices of the Peary Arctic Club* (1910; reprint, Mineola, N.Y.: Dover, 1986).

Potter, Russell A. *Arctic Spectacles: The Frozen North in Visual Culture, 1818–1875* (Seattle: University of Washington Press, 2007).

Rich, Edwin Gile. *Hans the Eskimo: His Story of Arctic Adventure with Kane, Hayes, and Hall* (Boston: Houghton Mifflin, 1934).

Robinson, Michael F. *The Coldest Crucible: Arctic Exploration and American Culture* (Chicago: University of Chicago Press, 2006).

Ross, W. Gillies. *This Distant and Unsurveyed Country: A Woman's Winter at Baffin Island, 1857–58* (Montreal: McGill-Queen's University Press, 1997).

Sargent, Epes, and William H. Cunnington. *The Wonders of the Arctic World: A History of All the Researches and Discoveries in the Frozen Regions of the North, from the Earliest Times . . . Together with a Complete and Reliable History of the* Polaris *Expedition* (Philadelphia: John E. Potter, 1873).

Sawin, Mark M. *Raising Kane: Elisha Kent Kane and the Culture of Fame in Antebellum America* (Philadelphia: American Philosophical Society, 2008).

Schwatka, Frederick. *The Long Arctic Search: The Narrative of Lieutenant Frederick Schwatka, U.S.A., 1878–1880, Seeking the Records of the Lost Franklin Expedition.* Edited by Edouard A. Stackpole (Mystic, Conn.: Marine Historical Association, 1965).

Scoresby, William, Jr. *An Account of the Arctic Regions, with a History and Description of the Northern Whale-fishery.* 2 vols. (1820; reprint, with an introduction by Professor Sir Alister Hardy, Newton Abbot, Devon, U.K.: David & Charles Reprints, 1969).

Shelley, Mary. *Frankenstein; or, the Modern Prometheus* (1818; reprint, with an introduction and notes by Maurice Hindle, London: Penguin Books, 1992).

Smith, Charles Edward. *From the Deep of the Sea: The Diary of Charles Edward Smith, Surgeon of the Whale-ship* Diana, *of Hull* (Annapolis, Md.: Naval Institute Press, 1977).

Smucker, Samuel M. *The Life of Dr. Elisha Kent Kane, and of Other Distinguished American Explorers: Containing Narratives of Their Researches and Adventures in Remote and Interesting Portions of the Globe* (1858; reprint, Scituate, Mass.: Digital Scanning, 2000).

Thomson, David. *The People of the Sea: A Journey in Search of the Seal Legend* (Washington, D.C.: Counterpoint, 2002).

U.S. Navy. *Report to the President of the United States of the Action of the Navy Department in the Matter of the Disaster to the United States Exploring Expedition toward the North Pole; Accompanied by a Report of the Examination of the Rescued Party, etc.* (Washington, D.C.: Government Printing Office, 1873).

Verne, Jules. *The Desert of Ice; or, the Further Adventures of Captain Hatteras* (1874; reprint, Wildside Press, n.d.).

———. *The English at the North Pole.* (n.d.; reprint, Microsoft Corporation, Internet Archive, 2007).

Villarejo, Oscar M. *Dr. Kane's Voyage to the Polar Lands* (Philadelphia: University of Pennsylvania Press, 1965).

Zucchero, Michael. *Loyal Hearts: Histories of American Civil War Canines* (Lynchburg, Va.: Schroeder, 2010).

Articles

Barr, William. "The Use of Dog Sledges during the British Search for the Missing Franklin Expedition in the North American Arctic Islands, 1848–59." *Arctic*, Vol. 62, No. 3, September 2009, 257–272.

Binford, Lewis R. "Willow Smoke and Dogs' Tails: Hunter-Gatherer Settlement Systems and Archaeological Site Formation." *American Antiquity*, Vol. 45, No. 1, January 1980, 4–20.

Coleman, William Hoyt. "Dr. Kane's Boat—The *Faith.*" *Robert Merry's Museum*, January 1859, 24.

Cummins, Sharon. "Wells Sanitarium Was the Pitts." *York County Coast Star*, October 18, 2007.

Dick, Lyle. "'Pibloktoq' (Arctic Hysteria): A Construction of European-Inuit Relations?" *Arctic Anthropology*, Vol. 32, No. 2, 1995, 1–42.

George, Jane. "Fort Conger: Old Tales of Futility and Desperation." *Nunatsiaq News*, August 4, 2000.

Hanson, Ann Meekitjuk. "What's in a Name?" *Nunavut '99*, electronic resource, http://www.nunavut.com/nunavut99/english/name.html.

Harper, Kenn. "Liars and Gentlemen." *Polar Priorities: The Annual Journal of the Frederick A. Cook Society*, Vol. 28, December 2008, 41–51.

Morey, Darcy F., and Kim Aaris-Sorensen. "Paleoeskimo Dogs of the Eastern Arctic." *Arctic*, Vol. 55, No. 1, March 2002, 44–56.

Ninnis, Fleet Surgeon Belgrave, M.D. "Results Derived from the Arctic Expedition, 1875–76. Part II. Medical Report on the Eskimo Dog Disease." *Parliamentary Paper*, C. 2176, 1878.

Osczevski, Randall J. "Frederick Cook and the Forgotten Pole." *Arctic*, Vol. 56, No. 2, June 2003, 207–217.

Ratliff, Evan. "Taming the Wild." *National Geographic*, Vol. 219, No. 3, March 2011, 34–59.

Van Emery, Edward. "The Sins of New York as 'Exposed' by the Police Gazette." *The Richard K. Fox Gazette*, 1876, Part 2, Chapter 6.

Archives

Charles Francis Hall Collection, National Museum of American History, Smithsonian Institution, Washington, D.C.

The Elisha Kent Kane Collection, American Philosophical Society Library, Philadelphia.

[Elisha Kent] Kane Collection, Brigham Young University Library, Provo, Utah.

George E. Tyson Collection, National Archives and Records Administration, College Park, Md.

Naval Historical Foundation, Washington, D.C.

The *New York Times* Article Archive

Index

Italicized locators with an *"f"* indicate figures.